# Contents

Preface                                                            vii

**1  Data Abstraction**                                             1
  1.1   Introduction . . . . . . . . . . . . . . . . . . . . . . . .   1
  1.2   Procedural Abstraction . . . . . . . . . . . . . . . .   2
  1.3   Type and Object . . . . . . . . . . . . . . . . . . .   4
  1.4   Object and Type . . . . . . . . . . . . . . . . . . .   9
  1.5   Interaction between Objects . . . . . . . . . . . . .   10
  1.6   Data Abstraction . . . . . . . . . . . . . . . . . . .   14
  1.7   Mapping Data Abstraction into C++ . . . . . . . . .   15
  1.8   Change of Implementation . . . . . . . . . . . . . .   18
  1.9   Specification and Correctness . . . . . . . . . . . .   24
  1.10  List Type . . . . . . . . . . . . . . . . . . . . . .   30
  1.11  Initialization and Clean-Up . . . . . . . . . . . . .   33
  1.12  List Iterators and Friend Functions . . . . . . . . .   37
  1.13  Layering and Dummy Proofing . . . . . . . . . . . .   42
  1.14  Summary . . . . . . . . . . . . . . . . . . . . . .   47

**2  Inheritance**                                                 53
  2.1   Introduction . . . . . . . . . . . . . . . . . . . . .   53
  2.2   Behavioral Inheritance . . . . . . . . . . . . . . . .   54
  2.3   Inheritance of Implementation . . . . . . . . . . . .   57
  2.4   Substitution Principle . . . . . . . . . . . . . . . .   59
  2.5   No Override to `setsalary()` . . . . . . . . . . . . .   63
  2.6   Hidden Bonus . . . . . . . . . . . . . . . . . . . .   64
  2.7   `bonus` Data Member in Derived Class `Manager` . . . .   65
  2.8   Explicit Giving of Bonus . . . . . . . . . . . . . . .   66
  2.9   Behavioral Inheritance Guidelines . . . . . . . . . . .   67

2.10   Denver Syndrome . . . . . . . . . . . . . . . . . . . . .   70
2.11   Private Class Derivation . . . . . . . . . . . . . . . .   75
2.12   Protected Visibility and Class Derivation . . . . . . .   79
2.13   Summary . . . . . . . . . . . . . . . . . . . . . . . .   84

**3   Dynamic Binding**                                              **87**
3.1   What Is Dynamic Binding? . . . . . . . . . . . . . .   87
3.2   Why Should You Care? . . . . . . . . . . . . . . . .   91
3.3   Unions and Switch Case . . . . . . . . . . . . . . . .   92
3.4   Solution with Pointers to Functions . . . . . . . . . .   96
3.5   Solution to Problem in C++ . . . . . . . . . . . . .   100
3.6   Abstract Base Types and Pure Virtual Member Functions   106
3.7   Summary . . . . . . . . . . . . . . . . . . . . . . . .   107

**4   Parametry**                                                   **111**
4.1   Introduction . . . . . . . . . . . . . . . . . . . . . .   111
4.2   Type System . . . . . . . . . . . . . . . . . . . . . .   112
      4.2.1   Justification . . . . . . . . . . . . . . . . . .   112
      4.2.2   Built-In Types . . . . . . . . . . . . . . . . .   113
      4.2.3   Product . . . . . . . . . . . . . . . . . . . . .   115
      4.2.4   Array . . . . . . . . . . . . . . . . . . . . . .   116
      4.2.5   Pointer . . . . . . . . . . . . . . . . . . . . .   117
      4.2.6   Union . . . . . . . . . . . . . . . . . . . . . .   118
      4.2.7   Function<T,S> . . . . . . . . . . . . . . . . .   118
      4.2.8   Type System of C++ . . . . . . . . . . . . . .   119
      4.2.9   Type System of Fortran . . . . . . . . . . . .   120
      4.2.10  Built-In versus User-Defined Parameterized Types   120
4.3   Stack<T> . . . . . . . . . . . . . . . . . . . . . . .   121
4.4   Table<Key,Value> . . . . . . . . . . . . . . . . . .   122
4.5   Container Types . . . . . . . . . . . . . . . . . . . .   125
4.6   Parameterized Functions: Sorting . . . . . . . . . . .   127
4.7   Faking of Parameterized Types . . . . . . . . . . . .   128
      4.7.1   Macros . . . . . . . . . . . . . . . . . . . . .   129
      4.7.2   Template File . . . . . . . . . . . . . . . . . .   133
      4.7.3   Inheritance . . . . . . . . . . . . . . . . . . .   135

**5   Type as Object**                                              **141**
5.1   Introduction . . . . . . . . . . . . . . . . . . . . . .   141
5.2   MegaBuzz Corporation . . . . . . . . . . . . . . . .   144

5.3 Static Class Members . . . . . . . . . . . . . . . . . . 146
5.4 Faking of Type as Object in C++ 1.2 . . . . . . . . 148
5.5 Modular Programming . . . . . . . . . . . . . . . . . 149

**6 Pointers to Member Functions** **155**
6.1 Introduction . . . . . . . . . . . . . . . . . . . . . . 155
6.2 Class Frog . . . . . . . . . . . . . . . . . . . . . . . 156
6.3 Pointer to Data Member . . . . . . . . . . . . . . . . 157
6.4 Pointer to Member Function . . . . . . . . . . . . . . 157
6.5 Compare C Syntax for Pointer to (External) Function 158
6.6 Mapcar . . . . . . . . . . . . . . . . . . . . . . . . . 159
6.7 Pond . . . . . . . . . . . . . . . . . . . . . . . . . . 159
6.8 Polymorphism . . . . . . . . . . . . . . . . . . . . . 161

**7 Design** **167**
7.1 Introduction . . . . . . . . . . . . . . . . . . . . . . 167
7.2 Requirements . . . . . . . . . . . . . . . . . . . . . . 169
7.3 Interaction Model . . . . . . . . . . . . . . . . . . . 171
7.4 External Design Spec: Type Manual Page . . . . . . 172
7.5 Internal Design Spec . . . . . . . . . . . . . . . . . . 175
7.6 Design Process . . . . . . . . . . . . . . . . . . . . . 176
      7.6.1 Initial Decomposition . . . . . . . . . . . . . 178
      7.6.2 Abstraction . . . . . . . . . . . . . . . . . . . 179
      7.6.3 Type Relationships . . . . . . . . . . . . . . . 186
      7.6.4 Type Decomposition . . . . . . . . . . . . . . 196
      7.6.5 Stopping Condition . . . . . . . . . . . . . . 197
7.7 Performance . . . . . . . . . . . . . . . . . . . . . . 198

**8 Case Study: Graphics Editor** **205**
8.1 Introduction . . . . . . . . . . . . . . . . . . . . . . 205
8.2 Graphics Editor Requirements . . . . . . . . . . . . 206
8.3 Shape Type . . . . . . . . . . . . . . . . . . . . . . . 207
8.4 Picture Type . . . . . . . . . . . . . . . . . . . . . . 208
8.5 Editor Type . . . . . . . . . . . . . . . . . . . . . . . 212
8.6 Interaction Model . . . . . . . . . . . . . . . . . . . 215
8.7 Public Interface of Parameterized Set<T> . . . . . . 217
8.8 Type Decomposition . . . . . . . . . . . . . . . . . . 218
8.9 Summary . . . . . . . . . . . . . . . . . . . . . . . . 219

**9 Text Editor: Requirements** **223**

   9.1 Introduction . . . . . . . . . . . . . . . . . . . . . . 223

   9.2 Design Framework . . . . . . . . . . . . . . . . . . . 224

   9.3 Requirements: Description of Editor . . . . . . . . . . 224

   9.4 Initial Decomposition . . . . . . . . . . . . . . . . . 226

   9.5 File: Abstraction Step . . . . . . . . . . . . . . . . . 228

   9.6 File: Implementation . . . . . . . . . . . . . . . . . . 232

   9.7 Summary . . . . . . . . . . . . . . . . . . . . . . . 233

**10 Buffers, Sloops, and Yachts** **237**

   10.1 Introduction . . . . . . . . . . . . . . . . . . . . . . 237

   10.2 Buffer—High-Level Design and Public Interface . . . 238

   10.3 Buffer—Type Relationships . . . . . . . . . . . . . . 240

   10.4 Yacht<T>—Parametric Type . . . . . . . . . . . . . 241

   10.5 Sloop<T>—Abstraction Step . . . . . . . . . . . . . 242

   10.6 Preconditions and Exception Handling . . . . . . . . 243

   10.7 Sloop<T>—Implementation . . . . . . . . . . . . . . 245

   10.8 Yacht<T>—Implementation . . . . . . . . . . . . . 248

   10.9 Buffer—Implementation . . . . . . . . . . . . . . . . 250

   10.10 Summary . . . . . . . . . . . . . . . . . . . . . . . 251

**11 Extension of Text Editor** **255**

   11.1 Introduction . . . . . . . . . . . . . . . . . . . . . . 255

   11.2 Editor—High-Level Architecture . . . . . . . . . . . 255

   11.3 Parser . . . . . . . . . . . . . . . . . . . . . . . . . 257

   11.4 Simple Main Program . . . . . . . . . . . . . . . . . 260

   11.5 Editor Commands—First Phase . . . . . . . . . . . . 263

   11.6 Editor Commands—Second Phase . . . . . . . . . . 264

   11.7 Class Register . . . . . . . . . . . . . . . . . . . . . 265

   11.8 Editor Implementation . . . . . . . . . . . . . . . . . 267

   11.9 Meditation on Further Decomposition . . . . . . . . 269

   11.10 Register Implementation . . . . . . . . . . . . . . . 270

   11.11 Iregister Implementation . . . . . . . . . . . . . . . 271

   11.12 Summary . . . . . . . . . . . . . . . . . . . . . . . 275

   11.13 class Editor—Implementation . . . . . . . . . . . . 275

**A Data Abstraction and Hierarchy** **281**

**Index** **299**

# Preface

## Purposes

This book has several purposes. The primary purpose is to teach C++ programmers object-oriented programming and design. Object-oriented programming is a model of programming based on certain distinct ideas: object, type, implementation hiding, parameterization, inheritance, and others. Object-oriented design is a way of using these ideas to structure and to construct systems—whose virtues are more apparent the larger the system. There is a perception that C++ is an object-oriented programming language. Not exactly. C++ supports a number of programming styles, including procedural (after all, C is essentially a subset of C++), abstract data type, and object-oriented. Just using C++ does not make one an object-oriented programmer. So the book is organized around fundamental object-oriented concepts and attempts to *map* them into C++ syntax, accompanied by lots of examples.

This book is not an introduction to the C++ programming language, nor is it a reference manual on the language. There are a number of excellent books that take care of these needs (complete references in the bibliography) and that should be used as companions when reading this book.

This book may prove useful as an introduction to object-oriented programming and design for non-C++ programmers. How? Object-oriented programming and design are, by and large, language independent. Consequently, the book presents central object-oriented concepts in a way free of language concerns, and then does the mapping to C++. One could map the concepts to any language: assembler, C, Eiffel, Smalltalk. For object-oriented languages (Smalltalk, Eiffel,C++ ...) the mapping into language syntax is simple, almost one to one. For C, it is more work, and for assembler more work still. One wants to program in a language that matches one's programming paradigm. Thus, non-C++ programmers can ignore the C++ code or chose to regard it as pseudo code.

Another purpose of the book is to begin to bridge the gap between object-oriented programming/design and the world of formal methods and formal specification. Formal methods (read Mathematics) are something many programmers are skittish about, yet good programmers do reason—dare one say prove theorems—about their programs, albeit in an intuitive fashion. It is almost as if they don't want to know that what they are doing has mathematical foundation.

Much of the interest in object-oriented programming and design comes from the growing industrial perception that it is a better way of structuring and building complex systems than other methodologies, because it lends itself to the reuse of both software and brain cycles, which improves the quality and reduces the cost of software development. A preeminent aspect of software quality is correctness: The software performs as advertised. Indeed, if a system implementation is not correct, it just doesn't matter how fast it runs or how little memory it consumes. The issue of correctness is ticklish on several counts. First, what is meant by "as advertised"? That is, how is the behavior of a system specified—independent of implementation concerns? Second, how do we know—indeed, how can we guarantee—that a particular implementation (there may be none, one, or many) is correct with respect to the advertising?

Human language specification of system behavior is problematic, because human language is ambiguous, which makes for fine poetry but woefully imprecise description of system behavior. Two programmers can look at the same English-language specification and come up with implementations whose behaviors are quite different. The problem is compounded as the size and complexity of the system grow.

One is ineluctably driven to specifying system behavior in unambiguous mathematical terms. Fortunately there exist a number of formal specification languages. This book touches on one of them, algebraic specification. There is a large and growing literature of formalism in programming, much of which is applicable to object-oriented programming. Indeed there are those in the object-oriented community who are developing formalisms specifically for object-oriented programming. If

Object-Oriented Programming

is good,

Object-Oriented Programming + Formal Methods

is much better.

Let's summarize the benefits of formal methods in object-oriented programming:

- Unambiguous description of system behavior. A person who knows the specification language can understand a specification written by someone else. The understanding of the reader and the understanding of the writer are the same.

- Unassailable criterion against which to judge the correctness of a particular implementation.

- There exist techniques for semiautomatically deriving correct implementation from formal specification.

Even if one does not completely buy into the formal approach to programming, an appreciation of it will leaven, influencing one's programming style for the better. The book attempts to introduce formalism in a balanced way, while at the same maintaining its primary focus, imparting to the reader a solid intuitive feel for object-oriented programming and design.

The purposes of this book follow:

- To teach object-oriented programming and design to C++ programmers

- To introduce object-oriented programming and design to non-C++ programmers

- To begin to bridge the gap between formal methods and object-oriented programming

## Topics

The book is organized into four sections:

**Chapters 1-7:** Concepts of object-oriented programming and their mapping into C++.

**Chapter 8:** Object-oriented design. Derivation and presentation of a design framework.

**Chapters 9-12:** Case studies in object-oriented design.

**Appendix A:** We reproduce in full Barbara Liskov's keynote address to the 1987 OOPSLA conference, "Data Abstraction and Hierarchy." This paper is one of the first to define behavioral inheritance and to distinguish between it and the inheritance of implementation (e.g., C++ class derivation).

The first section addresses the following concepts:

- Object and type

- Implementation hiding

- Abstraction and specification

- Inheritance (of behavior and implementation)

- Parameterized types

- Type as objects

- Pointers to member functions

The table on the following page summarizes the mapping of various concepts to C++ syntax.

| Concept | C++ Syntax |
|---|---|
| Type and object | `class`, `variable` |
| Public interface | `public` member functions |
| Data hiding | `private` data members |
| Object state—no change | `const` member functions |
| Initialization and clean-up | Constructors and destructor |
| Persistence | *No support* |
| Parametric types and functions | C++ 3.0 |
| Single inheritance | `class` derivation (C++ 1.2) |
| Multiple inheritance | `class` derivation (C++ 2.0) |
| Mix-ins | `class` derivation (C++ 2.0) |
| Dynamic binding | `virtual` functions |
| Abstract base type | pure `virtual` functions |
| Type as object | `static class data` (C++ 1.2) |
| | `static class functions` (C++ 2.0) |

The book does not cover object persistence, exception handling, and object-oriented data bases.

## Acknowledgments

I thank my wife, Lucille Guth Bar-David, for her emotional support during the five long years that it took to write the book. I want to thank my editors at Prentice Hall for their encouragement and practical support: John Waite, for having the confidence to sign a contract with me, Joan Magrabi, for encouraging me to stick to a schedule and being a great cheering squad, and Greg Doench, for helping me to see my reviewers as a resource for improving the book but not the final word.

I thank Barbara Liskov for several things: Object-oriented design is essentially abstract data type design and inheritance. By and large, I learned abstract data type design from her book, *Abstraction and Specification in Program Development.* Second, I thank her for pointing out to the object-oriented world that there is a difference between the inheritance of implementation and the inheritance of behavior.

I thank friends and colleagues at AT&T Bell Laboratories: Joe Arfin for case study suggestions; Bob Murray for acting as a sounding board while I struggled with object-oriented design concepts; Stan Lippman for persistently asking the question, "what's an object, really?"; and Bjarne Stroustrup for encouraging me to write a book on object-oriented design as opposed to yet another book on the C++ programming language.

I thank my academic colleagues: Tom Wheeler of Fort Monmouth and Monmouth College for his tremendous intuitive insight into computer science, in particular for his insights into the relationship between behavioral inheritance and data refinement; Serafino Amoroso, Software Engineering at Monmouth College, for nurturing my attempts to apply formal methods to object-oriented programming; and Naftali Minsky of Rutgers University for always insisting that formal definitions make intuitive sense.

I thank the members of the Blue Sky Society, where we sat around eating bagels and other goodies and schmoozed about object-oriented programming, operating systems, and formal methods: David Bern, Ben Reytblat, and David Wonnacott. I especially want to thank John Isner, who kept on insisting about the importance of formal programming methods, until it finally caught.

I thank Semaphore Training and its president, Clive Lee. During the period of my employment with Semaphore (June 1988 to April 1989), I was given time, among my other duties, to work on the book. I also want to thank Clive for encouraging me to write, specifically articles on C++ related issues for the *C Users Journal*.

And I thank God that I'm done!

Any errors of commission or omission are, of course, my own, and I would be grateful for readers to bring them to my attention.

# Chapter 1

# Data Abstraction

## 1.1  Introduction

The purpose of this chapter is to lay a foundation for object-oriented design by carefully defining and discussing the fundamental terms.

- Procedure

- Type

- Object

- Public interface

- System, program

- Data hiding

- Data abstraction

- Initialization and clean-up

- Layering

Terminology has yet to become standardized in the object-oriented community, although some attempts are being made to do so. The most glaring example of the confusion that results from a lack of standard terminology is the distinction (or lack of it) between object and type. There are many who say object when they mean type, and say instance when they mean object of a particular type. This results in incredibly confused conversations when partisans of the two views meet at conferences!

To decrease confusion and ambiguity, within this book I am going to take a "scorched earth" approach, building an object-oriented model from the ground up, based on careful definitions of fundamental terms. Formal (mathematical) definitions will be given when available. However, I recognize the need to provide at the same time intuitively appealing but fuzzier definitions as well.

The general style of the chapter is to provide for each concept a definition, an example that illustrates the concept, the consequences (advantages and disadvantages) of the concept, and possibly an alternative definition if one exists. Object-oriented concepts are, by and large, language independent. In this book, the concepts are illustrated with examples written in the C++ programming language.

## 1.2   Procedural Abstraction

Although the benefits of functions and procedures have been known for decades, I want to review procedural abstraction to set the tone for the subsequent sections of the chapter. There is another reason. An opinion prevalent in the programming community is that one has to throw away completely the procedural mind-set when one does object-oriented programming. This is not so. When one does a strictly object-oriented design, all functionality is encapsulated as operations in the public interface of one type of object or another. These operations (member functions in C++) are, after all, named procedures that hide their implementation. So, we can apply most of our hard-earned intuition about functions to the public interface of types. Furthermore, C++ does not compel programmers to program in the object model. It simply supports doing so, while at the same time providing full support for procedural-style programming.

Ordinary functions in C++ hide their implementations. The only thing that users of a function can do with it is to supply arguments, invoke it, and inspect the return value (if any). Thus, the only thing about a function that a user can "see" is its return value and possible side effect. The only objects that the body of a function has access to are its arguments, its local variables, and global variables (which will be dealt with in a later section).

A subtlety. If an argument to a function has reference semantics, then the function can modify the state of that argument in the caller's context. This state of affairs can cause unforeseen side affects in callers not conversant with the function's specification. In [BERN], my colleague David Bern and I wrote how to provide reference semantics without pointers using the ampersand (&) in the functional prototype. For example,

```
void swap( double &x, double &y)
{
    double t = x;
    x = y;
    y = t;
}
```

the preceding swap function can get the following piece of code into trouble:

```
...
double a = 1.0, b = -1.0;
swap( a, b);
b = sqrt( a);
...
```

Can you tell what the problem is? In contrast, if all the arguments to a function have value semantics, at worst, the function modifies a local copy of the value of its arguments. Using references and not pointers in C++, there is no way of telling whether or not a function is modifying variables in its caller, short of looking at the manual page. Thus we see that reference semantics may provide an undesirable coupling between a function and its caller, which can only be resolved by a careful reading of the manual page.

The classical example of procedural abstraction is a sort function

```
void sort( int *v, int dim);
```

which, given a vector **v** of integers of dimension **dim**, sorts **v** in place into ascending order. There are many algorithms (i.e., implementations) that will provide the specified result (a sorted vector), among them bubble sort and quicksort [KP]. The very name of the function hides its implementation and insulates its users from the details of the selected algorithm. Indeed, all the user has to know is the name of the function and its manual page specification. Liskov [LSK] calls this procedural abstraction and points out that procedural abstraction is the earliest example of parameterization. As stated earlier, the benefit is twofold: abstraction and reuse.

- Abstraction: It is easier to reason about a program built of functions with well-defined manual page specifications, than to reason directly about the implementations of those functions. Functions are a tool which help us manage the complexity of programs, precisely by hiding the (implementational) complexity.

- Reuse: Programs using the above sort function need only be re-compiled if the sort algorithm is changed. Generally, no other code in the program need be touched.

## 1.3   Type and Object

Most schools of object-oriented programming agree that (rough definition) an object is an entity possessing a state that can vary over its lifetime. Thus, objects can be used to model entities in the real world or in the world of ideas [MEY]. Further, it is possible for other entities (objects) to query or modify (some aspect of) the state of the object—during its lifetime—by sending it a message. The public interface of an object is the set of messages to which it responds. Finally, there is no direct access to the state of an object from the outside. The only way other entities can affect an object is by sending it a message. Thus an object *encapsulates* (glues together) both state (data) and operations (code) on the state.

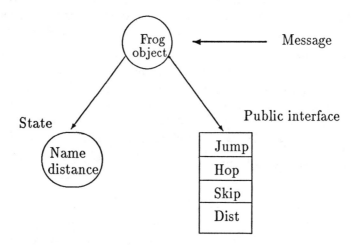

Note the generality and power of this definition. For example, in the context of a graphics editor, both the human user and the graphical objects managed by the editor are *all* objects. The editor (object) merely acts as the human user's agent in understanding (parsing) his or her wishes from the keyboard or from a mouse, and in turn sends messages to graphical objects and window objects to get the task done.

Further, implicit in this definition is an interaction model. Namely, a program or system is a collection of objects that gets the work done by sending each other messages. This interaction model certainly describes C++ programs and (member) function bodies, which are all examples of sequential processing.

The interaction model also encompasses asynchronous and concurrent processing—meaning, the objects in the system could be talking to each other (sending messages) simultaneously, with no particular preordained order. A popular example is the client-server model common in computer networking. A client process on one machine may send messages (service requests) to a server process on another machine requesting that a file be shipped over the network back to the client. An example from the UNIX©operating system [BACH] is two or more processes communicating with each other using IPC (interprocess communication) facilities, such as pipes or message queues.

A third example is any device driver, for concreteness a disk driver. Here the objects are the host computer and the hardware device. They communicate via interrupts. Although the precise details vary from machine to machine, the disk (actually its controller) sends a message to the host by sending a hardware interrupt. The host computer interprets the interrupt as a small integer index into a table (the interrupt table) of function addresses. The disk interrupt corresponds to the disk device driver's interrupt handling function, which acts as the disk controller's agent on the host central processing unit. Typically the host temporarily suspends its activity and services the interrupt by invoking the corresponding handler function. On return from the handler function, the host may resume its activity or go on to do something else.

The schools disagree on the relationship between the concepts of type and object. In that the two concepts are usually defined together, much depends on the *order* in which the definitions occur. As it is useful to look at a thing from several perspectives, we will present two definitions of type and object. In the following pair of definitions, the concept of type is defined first, following Cleaveland [CLEAVE].

*Definition:*   A type is a set of values together with a set of operations on those values. We refer to the set of operations as the public interface of the type.

The problem with the above definition of type is that it describes the syntax of the public interface but not the semantics. Various formal specification schemes [CHJ] remedy this lack by defining a (algebraically specified) type to be a triple $(T, Op, Eq)$ consisting of a value set $T$, a set of operations $Op$, and a set of equations $Eq$ that establish relationships between the operations (i.e., axioms that the type satisfies). More on type as a triple further on in the chapter.

*Example:*   From C++, the built-in type int together with the elementary operations is

$$+, \ -, \ *, \ /, \ \% \ \dots$$

*Example:*   Here is a user defined type: FILE as supported by the C++ standard runtime library with the public interface

```
fopen, fclose, getc, putc, fseek, ftell, ...
```

The functions listed above support the notion of FILE as a sequence of bytes with no other structure. FILE is an excellent example of how to construct a (abstract data) type in procedural languages such as C. Namely, a data structure together with a set of procedures that access and modify the value in the structure. (FILE's data structure is found in the standard header file stdio.h) together with a collection of external functions (e.g., getc). The argument list of each function must contain a pointer to a FILE structure. For this is the only way in C that a function can modify the state (value) of a structure, because C strictly practices call by value (see [KR]).

*Definition:* An object is a container of values from a single type. The state of an object is its current value. An object is called an instance of its type.

To *instantiate* an object means to create it. In terms of programming languages, instantiation means creating or allocating the storage to contain the object's value. This is not the whole truth, because it is sometimes necessary to store a representation of the public interface along with the value. The amount of additional storage required varies widely according to language and according to the desired language feature, and is the subject of considerable optimization. In current implementations of C++, the additional amount varies from zero bytes to a pointer word per base class, for objects of derived type.

In programming languages, the simplest way to instantiate an object is to declare a named variable of some type. That is, a named variable is an object. For example, the C++ declarations

```
int x = 6;
FILE *fp = fopen( "/etc/passwd", "r" );
```

both instantiate (create) objects. In the first, x names an object of type int. In the second, fp points to a FILE object whose storage is managed by fopen and fclose. With regard to pointer variables like fp, it should be noted that there are two objects: the pointer variable and the object that the pointer points to. *Caution:* instantiating a pointer variable does not necessarily instantiate any objects for the pointer to point to. In C and C++, that is a separate matter.

The distinction C++ makes between "ordinary" variables and pointer variables is meaningless in most object-oriented languages (e.g., Smalltalk, Eiffel, CLOS lisp) because these languages do not possess an explicit pointer type. Indeed, these languages consider pointer a low-level programming construct that has no place in an object-oriented language. In Eiffel, for example, all named variables are effectively pointers that refer to objects stored elsewhere. Thus, in Eiffel, assignment has reference semantics; that is, after the assignment both variables refer to (alias) the same object. In contrast, C++ normally practices value semantics for all variables: The value of the variable (or expression) on the right of the assignment is copied into (the storage of) the variable on the left side of the assignment. In contrast, Eiffel only applies value semantics to a variable as a storage optimization when the size of its value is less than or equal to the size of a computer word.

We have discussed instantiating objects by variable declaration. There are a number of other ways of instantiating objects in C++. The **new** built-in operator returns the address of an object dynamically allocated in heap storage. The slots in an array of any type are each objects. Each object is "named" by its index into the array, as in the example below.

```
Frog kermit;
Frog pond[100];
int index = 4;

pond[index] = kermit;
```

Finally, each data member and base part of an instantiated object of user-defined (class)  type is also an object.

```
class Frog {
public:
    ...
private:
    String name;
    int distance;
};

Frog kermit;
```

In the example above, not only is kermit an object, but so is kermit's name and distance data members.

## 1.4 Object and Type

Let's reverse the order of definition of object and type. Let the definition of object be as before in the rough definition cited above. That is,

*Definition:* an *object* is an entity that

- *State:* Possesses a state and that exists for some period.

- *Interface:* Responds to messages. The set of messages to which an object responds is called its (public) interface.

- *Information hiding:* The only way to query or modify the state of an object is by sending it a message.

Now in terms of object, it is possible to define type

*Definition:* A *type* is the collection of all objects in a system that responds in the same way to the same set of messages. That is, a type is a collection of objects with the same public interface.

The order of definition selected—type-object, object-type—has a subtle effect on object-oriented design philosophy. The order type-object has an a priori flavor. That is, this order encourages the designer from the outset to decompose a system into *types* of objects, where all instances of a type share the same behavior (public interface) and implementation. Thus, the a priori concept of type helps the designer to factor out common behavior in the system. Furthermore, the types of one system or program may be reusable in another program. On the other hand, the order object-type simply informs the designer that his or her system is a collection of *objects* with no necessary relationship between their behaviors. On further reflection however, the designer might notice commonalities in the behavior of a set of objects in his or her design, and a posteriori deem that set a type. However, the objects in that set deemed a type need not share implementation.

Factoring common behavior is a benefit in either order or definition. However, the order object-type, which expresses the primacy of object, points us in the direction of viewing everything as an object, even types themselves. That is, a type has a state, independent of its instances; and a type has a public interface, independent of the public interface of its instances. Type as object is central to many object-oriented languages, such as Smalltalk and objective-C. Type as object is not central to C++; however, C++ does provide some support for the idea, which we will explore in Chapter 5.

Let's summarize the effect of the order of the definitions on the interaction model.

- *Type-object:*  A system (program) is a collection of one or more instances of different types of objects that get the work done by sending each other messages.

- *Object-type:*  A system (program) is a collection of objects that get the work done by sending each other messages.

## 1.5   Interaction between Objects

Objects (of either the typed or typeless kind) communicate by sending messages to each other. A system or program is thus a collection of objects (possibly of different types) that get the work done by sending messages. We can identify object-oriented messaging with the invocation of a member function against a variable of some class. Here are its properties:

- A message may change the state of the receiving object.

- A message may take zero or more explicit arguments. In this context, the receiving object is an implicit argument that is always present.

- The message returns a value of some type, possibly void, to the sender of the message.

A simple way of creating an interaction between objects is with a main program in C++. Here is a main program that describes the interaction of a couple of `File` objects

```
main( int argc, char *argv[])
{
    File input( argv[1]);
    File output( argv[2]);

    while( !input.iseof() )
```

```
        output.put( input.get() );
}
```

What is the program doing? You'll notice that the program merely instantiates a couple of variables (input, output), and has them send messages to
each other. The shortness of main's body is typical in object-oriented programming, not only of main programs but also of member function bodies
in general. Here is the public interface and implementation of class File:

```
typedef int Boolean;
class File { // Implementation layered on FILE
public:
    // constructor
    File( char *name = "", char *mode = "r")
    {
        if( *name )
            fp = fopen( name, mode);
        else if( *mode == 'r' )
            fp = stdin;
        else
            fp = stdout;
        state = (int)fp;
    }

    // destructor
    ~File()             { if( fp) fclose( fp); }

    Boolean isok()      { return state; }

    Boolean iseof()     { return feof( fp); }

    int get()           { return getc( fp); }
    // unget and peek useful for lexical scanners
    void unget(int c) { (void)ungetc( c, fp); }

    int peek()  { int c = get(); unget(c); return c; }

    void put( int c)  { putc( c, fp); }
private:
```

```
    FILE *fp;
    int state;
};
```

Let's formalize a bit our notions of program and message expression. First a definition: The cartesian product of two sets $X$ and $Y$, denoted $X \times Y$, is the set of all ordered pairs $(x, y)$ where $x$ is taken from $X$ and $y$ is taken from $Y$. When $T$ and $S$ are types, we let $T \times S$ denote the cartesian product of their respective value sets.

```
T c;
X x;
Z z;

z = c.f(x);
```

In the code fragment above, c is an object of type T, x of type X is used as an argument to the message, and z is an object of type Z to which is assigned the return value of the message expression. We send the message f(x) to c by the member function invocation expression c.f(x). We can model the effect of the invocation by a mathematical function $\varphi$

$$\varphi : T \times X \to T \times Z$$

where the $T$ to the left of the arrow represents the state of c before the invocation, $X$ is the argument type, the $T$ to the right of the arrow represents the new state of c as a result of the invocation, and $Z$ is the type of the return value. Split $\varphi$ into its vector components,

$$\varphi(t, x) = (\sigma(t, x), \rho(t, x))$$
$$\sigma : T \times X \to T$$
$$\rho : T \times X \to Z$$

where $\sigma$ computes the new state of the object, and $\rho$ computes the return value. We can connect this mathematical machinery to C++ fairly easily. After all, the message expression c.f(x) denotes the return value, so

$$c.f(x) = \rho(c, x)$$

Let's use the following C++-like notation, [c.f(x)], to denote the new state of the object c, then

$$[c.f(x)] = \sigma(c, x)$$

Note that the pair (c.f(x), [c.f(x)]) completely describes the effect of the message expression. This model of the message expression works well under the assumption that the argument x is being passed by value, that is, the value of x in the above code fragment is not changed by the invocation of the member function. The model can be modified to account for call-by-reference semantics in the argument x by giving $\varphi$ the form

$$\varphi : T \times X \to T \times X \times Z$$
$$\varphi(t, x) = (\sigma(t, x), \eta(t, x), \rho(t, x))$$

where $\eta$ computes the new value of the object $x$, after member function invocation. We can also write this model as

$$\varphi : T \times X \times Z \to T \times X \times Z$$
$$\varphi(t, x, z) = (\sigma(t, x), \eta(t, x), \rho(t, x))$$

despite the fact that the computation of the return value by $\rho$ does not depend on the initial value of the variable z. The benefit of writing $\varphi$ in this way is that it makes the domain and range of $\varphi$ to be the same, $\hat{X}$

$$\varphi : \hat{X} \to \hat{X}$$
$$\hat{X} = T \times X \times Z$$

In this view, the message expression acts as a state transition operator $\varphi$ on a state space $\hat{X}$. This relates object-oriented programming nicely to the standard mathematical view that a program is a function relating initial states to final states, all in the same state space.

In the object-oriented model, a program is a collection of objects of different types that send each other messages to accomplish the work. Under the restriction that there is no concurrency, a program is essentially an ordered sequence of message expressions, if flow control constructs—*if .... while ...*—are ignored. The state of the program is an ordered tuple consisting of the states of all the objects in the program. Thus, the state space of the program is the cartesian product of the types of all the objects in the program.

For example, in the short program in this section there are four objects,

```
argc, argv, input, output
```

The state space for the program is

$$int \times char** \times File \times File$$

Admittedly this is a bit of a simplification—we have ignored exported environment variables and a few other things. Nonetheless, the example is instructive of how one can begin to apply mathematical ideas to programming.

I want the reader to leave this section with some food for thought. One of the nice things about the object model is its uniformity. That is, one can regard a system or program as just a large object composed of subobjects that interact. The design advantage of this point of view is that it leads us to ask the right questions: What is the "public interface" of the system? Because the system has an interface, is it at all necessary for its decomposition into component objects to be visible? Is the system itself a reusable component within larger systems? If it is not reusable, how can I make it so while still fulfilling its designed purpose? The Eiffel programming language [MEY] supports this uniform point of view that

> *Everything is an object.*

There is no main program; rather, there is a mechanism for selecting which object "runs" first.

## 1.6  Data Abstraction

*Definition:*   Data hiding is a practice wherein the programmer restricts herself or himself to the public interface of a type for purposes of inspecting or modifying the state of an object of that type.

The advantage of defining data hiding as a practice is that it encourages the programmer to do it, even in languages that lack syntactic support for it.

As we will see, C++ supports data hiding with **private** visibility of class members.

*Definition:* A data abstraction is a type together with data hiding.

In C++, the programmer creates user-defined types using the class mechanism. Class allows the programmer to glue together syntactically a description of the data structure together with the public interface. We call this gluing together encapsulation. A class consists of two kinds of members: data and function. All objects of a given class type share the member functions and share the data template. Each object, however, has its own storage for the data. Each member possesses a visibility: private or public. A public member is visible in much the same way as a data field in a C structure. A private member is only visible within the implementation of a member function. There is a third choice of visibility, protected, which provides a (base) class with a different interface to its derived classes than the face it shows to all other code. See chapter 2 for a discussion on responsible use of **protected** class scope.

## 1.7 Mapping Data Abstraction into C++

A data abstraction (finally!) in C++ is a class all of whose data members are private. The following table summarizes recommended visibilities of class members:

| Visibility | public | private |
|---|---|---|
| Member function | Public interface | Factor common Implementation from Public member functions |
| Data member | No! | Represent object state |

The values in the data members represent the state of class object instances. The public member functions constitute the public interface of the type. Private member functions are useful for factoring common code out of the implementation of the public member functions. Private member functions have nothing to do with the semantics of the type, because they are not visible outside of the type.

The only way to inspect or modify the state of a class instance object is to
invoke a public member function on it, because direct access to a private
data member is a syntax error, as in the example below:

```
class Object {
public:
    void set( int n)
    {
        val = (val + n >= 0) ? val + n : val;
    }
private:
    int val;  // invariant:  val >= 0
};
...
Object x;
x.set( 3);    // legally change state of x
x.val = -3;   // syntax error!!
```

One of the many advantages of data hiding is that it reduces the possibility
of corrupting the state of the object, because the only entities that get to
touch the state are its member functions. A necessary condition for object
state sanity throughout its lifetime is that each member function transits
the object from one sane state to another sane state, which is essentially a
restatement of the correctness of the implementation. With regard to state
sanity, data hiding helps localize bugs: If an object is in a corrupt state, it
could only have come about as the result of incorrect implementation or use
of some member function.

For example, in the code fragment above, let us posit that an object of type
`Object` is in a sane state if and only if its data member `val`) satisfies

$$val >= 0$$

at all times. In the literature, this is called a representation invariant. A
look at the code for `set()` shows that it preserves this invariant. If `val`
were public and thus the assignment `x.val = -3` were syntactically correct,
it would still violate the invariant and corrupt the state of the object. This
is not a small thing, for a program is in a sane state if and only if all of its
objects are sane.

From here on out, all types are assumed to be data abstractions. Here is a classical data abstraction, a stack of integers in C++:

```
typedef int Boolean;
const Boolean TRUE = 1;
const Boolean FALSE = 0;

const int size = 100;

class Stack {
public:                      // these members are public
        Stack() : sp(0)          {}
        void push( int x)        { elt[sp++] = x; }
        int pop()                { return elt[--sp]; }
        int peek() const         { return elt[sp - 1]; }
        Boolean isempty() const { return sp <= 0; }
        Boolean isfull() const  { return sp >= size; }
private:                     // these (data) members are private
        int sp;              // sp points to next available slot
        int elt[size];
};
```

peek() in class Stack is an example of a constant member function, that is, a member function that is not permitted to change the state of the object against which it is invoked. The const notation does two things, which correspond to the separation of interface from implementation *(interface)*: It assures the potential user of a Stack object that functions like peek inspect but never modify object state. Second *(implementation)*, any implementation of a constant member function that attempts to modify a data member will fail to compile.

How do we invoke a operation against an object? This is the message expression (this popular terminology comes from Smalltalk); in C++ it corresponds to invoking a member function - object.memberfunction(). In the code sample below, we send messages to a Stack object s:

```
Stack s;
...
if( !s.isfull())
        s.push( 3);      // invoke push against s
```

The advantages of data hiding are well known. They include

- Separation of interface from implementation

- Maintenance of object data integrity

The main pedagogical problem with data hiding is that a member function invocation looks suspiciously like a function call (well, sometimes it is ...), with all the associated overhead. This is anathema to the speed freaks among us, who are grimly determined to wring every last cycle out of their code. These are the kind of people who look askance on one-line functions. At this point, the wise language instructor explains that C++, along with a number of other well-designed languages (CLU [LSK], Eiffel [MEY] ) supports inlining; that is, the compiler, with a few hints from the programmer perhaps, generates the code for a member function invocation inline, without all that function call overhead. This is precisely to encourage the definition of short member functions. A wiser instructor goes further and points out that inlining has no effect on the semantics of the call, something that cannot be said for macro expansion [KR]. The point is to encourage programmers to write member functions with small bodies.

## 1.8   Change of Implementation

One of the much-touted benefits of data hiding is the separation of interface from implementation: A (client) programmer can reason about and use a type without knowing anything about its implementation; she or he just has to know the type's behavior (as described in a type manual page). To illustrate the point, let's reimplement **class Stack** with a singly linked list data structure. The way the game is played is that we must verify that the new implementation is correct, that is, stack objects still behave properly.

**class Node** is a helping type that we shall use in the construction of **class Stack**. A node is an object that contains a value of some type—say **T**—and a pointer to some other node or NULL. Node is the typical structure out of which linked lists are constructed. The **typedef** of the dummy parameter **T** parameterizes the implementation below by the type of value in the node, here **int**. Using this mechanism, **T** can be bound to any built-in or user-defined type.

```
typedef int T;
class Node {
public:
    Node( T x) :            // initialize node value
        val( x), Next(0) {}

    T value() const         // return value
    {
        return val;
    }

    Node *next()            // return address of next node
    {
        return Next;
    }
    void link( Node *p)     // link to p
    {
        Next = p;
    }
private:
    T val;
    Node* Next;
};


// equations satisfied by class Node:
//    for all x : Node( x).value() == x
//    for all n, p : [n.link( p)].next() == p
```

Notice that as simple a type as `Node` is, we strictly observe data hiding (all data members private). The constructor initializes the node's value. The `value()` member function allows inspection of the current value of the node. The `next()` function returns the address of the next node in the list or NULL. The `link()` member function links this node object to another node. The implementation satisfies the equations listed above. Indeed, in formal specification, the equations constitute the behavior of the `Node` type and thus are the (unambiguous) criteria against which the correctness of any implementation is judged. As before, the notation `[n.link( p)]` means the state of the `Node` object `n` after the invocation of the member function `link(p)`. You can think of it as if `link()` returned `*this` rather than `void`.

Here is an implementation of Stack in terms of Node:

```
typedef int Boolean;
const Boolean TRUE = 1;
const Boolean FALSE = 0;
const int size = 100;

class Stack {
public:                          // these members are public
    Stack() : head(0), sp(0) {}

    void push( int x)
    {
        Node *p = new Node( x);

        if( head != 0)
            p->link( head);
        head = p;
    }

    int pop()
    {
        int r = head->value();
        Node *p = head;
        head = head->next();
        delete p;
        return r;
    }

    int peek() const          { return head->value(); }

    Boolean isempty() const   { return head == 0; }

    Boolean isfull()  const   { return sp >= size; }
private:
    Node *head;
    int sp;
};
```

In the above design, `class Node` and `class Stack` are at the same level of
visibility: Any C++ program structure that can see the definition of `Stack`
can just as easily see the definition of `Node`. This is fine as long as we think
that we can reuse `Node` to build other types. But, if we are only interested
in `Node` as an artifact of the implementation of `Stack`, according to the principles of implementation hiding, we ought to hide `Node`'s definition, so that
no other part of the application knows it exists. This would certainly help
in keeping the global name space clean. In C++ 2.1, it can be accomplished
by embedding the definition of the helping type `Node` within the definition
of `Stack`:

```
class Stack {
public:
    void push( int x)  { ... }
    ...
private:
    class Node {
        // Node members
    };

    // Stack data members
};
```

Although the preceding syntax is accepted in C++ 2.0, it is deceptive: `Node`
is just as visible as `Stack`.

To demonstrate the correctness of the reimplementation (indeed of any implementation), we need a description of `Stack`'s behavior that is implementation free. The first thing that comes to mind is a manual page for the type,
that is, a set of manual pages, one per member function. Though useful,
the type manual page is intrinsically ambiguous—written as it is in human
language—and thus subject to multiple interpretation. Perhaps we can do
for `Stack` what we did for `Node`: come up with a set of equations relating
the member functions. Here is a set of equations that appeal to our usual
intuition about stacks:

```
for all s, x : [s.push( x)].pop() == x, and
    [[s.push( x)].pop() == s
for all s : let x = s.pop() in
    [s.pop()].push( x) == s
```

As before, [s.memberfunction()] means the new state of the Stack object s after the invocation of the member function. The equations say that push() and pop() are inverse to each other: If you push and then pop (or pop and then push), the resulting stack state is as if no operation was performed.

Node's operations can be invoked unconditionally. Intuitively we know that is not true for Stack. For example, before pushing a value onto the stack, we ought to confirm in advance that the push operation will not cause the stack to overflow by establishing

$$s.isfull() == FALSE$$

Similarly we ought to check for underflow

$$s.isempty() == FALSE$$

before attempting to pop a value off the stack or to peek at the top value on the stack. After all, these two operations make no sense if the stack is empty.

The boolean expression s.isfull() == FALSE is called the *precondition* for the member function push(). If the precondition is true, the member function can be invoked. If the precondition is not true, the behavior of the object, and thus the program of which it is part, is undefined from that point onward.

Often a predicate is associated with a member function that describes the desired state of the object after the member function has terminated execution. This predicate is called a *postcondition*. Of course, we are only interested in satisfaction of the postcondition in those cases in which the object's state satisfies the member function's precondition. The postcondition is important for practical as well as theoretical reasons. For if the programmer wishes to invoke two member functions from the public interface of a type in succession, she or he must ensure that postcondition of the first function implies the precondition of the second. This is called the chaining condition. Sometimes there is no need to waste machine cycles at runtime verifying the chaining condition because, as in the example below, the postcondition of the first function *implies* the precondition of the second.

```
Stack s;
```

```
if( s.isfull() == FALSE)  {
    s.push( 3);

    // postcondition of push:  s.isempty() == FALSE
    // precondition of pop():   s.isemtpy() == FALSE
    // postcondition of push  implies precondition of pop!

    printf( "%d\n", s.pop());
}
```

The table below summarizes the preconditions and postconditions for the member functions of **class Stack**. The entry **TRUE** signifies that the corresponding function can be invoked unconditionally, which certainly makes sense for the predicate functions **isempty()** and **isfull()**, for the preconditions and postconditions of push() and pop() are defined in terms of them. The table notes that invocation of **isempty()** or **isfull()** does not change the state of the stack object.

| function | precondition | postcondition |
|----------|--------------|----------------|
| push | !isfull() | !isempty() |
| pop | !isempty() | !isfull() |
| peek | !isempty() | no state change |
| isempty | TRUE | no state change |
| isfull | TRUE | no state change |

The preconditions and postconditions tell us for which **Stack** object states the equations must hold. The preconditions and postconditions together with the equations can be taken as the unambiguous specification of the behavior (semantics) of the **Stack** type.

Before leaving this topic, I would like to examine the reimplementation of **Boolean Stack::isfull()**. Given that nodes are being dynamically allocated and de-allocated (via the C++ built-in heap storage management operations **new** and **delete**), doesn't it make more sense to implement **isfull()** as

```
Boolean isfull() { return FALSE; }
```

for, after all, the stack object is represented as a linked list, which can contain an arbitrary number of nodes. That is, the stack is never full. Of course, this is a lie in the real world, because there is no such thing as an infinite amount of memory in the computer. Well, we can fix that with the implementation

```
Boolean isfull()
{
    Node *p = new Node( 0);
    delete p;
    return p == 0;
}
```

which checks if there is storage available for the next push(). The code depends on new returning 0 if there is no more heap storage—at least a chunk of the requested size (sizeof Node)—available. This implementation is correct, because the specification does not say *when* the stack will overflow. The Stack type specification simply mandates the provisioning of a mechanism (isfull()) for identifying an overflow condition when it occurs.

## 1.9  Specification and Correctness

In a previous section, we have modeled both program and message expression as a mathematical function

$$\varphi : X \rightarrow X$$

which associates initial states with final states. Often, we are less interested in the function $\varphi$ than in its behavior or properties, expressed usually in terms of predicate logic. Preconditions, postconditions, and equations are examples of properties. We can model properties as $n$-ary boolean-valued functions—predicates—on the above state space $X$. The most common forms for these predicates are unary (1-ary)

$$P : X \rightarrow Boolean$$

and binary (2-ary)

$$P : X \times X \to Boolean$$

A common way of formally specifying the behavior of a program $\varphi$ is the Hoare Triple [GRIES]. Let $P$ be a unary predicate and let $Q$ be a binary predicate. Then

$$\{P\}\,\varphi\,\{Q\}$$

is a boolean expression defined to mean that the program $\varphi$, begun in any state satisfying $P$, terminates in a state satisfying $Q$. In our model, this can be expressed as

$$\{P\}\,\varphi\,\{Q\} \equiv \forall x : P(x) \Rightarrow Q(x, \varphi(x))$$

A state $x$ is said to satisfy a predicate $P$ if $P(x) = TRUE$. In the Hoare triple, $P$ is called the precondition, and $Q$ is called the postcondition. The philosophy behind the Hoare triple, indeed behind specification, is that what is really important is the precondition postcondition pair of predicates $(P, Q)$. That is, we will accept any implementation (program) $\varphi$ that makes the Hoare triple true. The Hoare triple nicely captures the relationship between specification (interface, behavior) and implementation. This is reminiscent of the relationship between Captain Picard and his first officer on the new *Star Trek* series, when the captain says to him, "make it *so*, number one, make it so." The captain's job is to specify what the universe should look like by the end of the episode. The first officer's job is to accomplish the captain's wishes, by whatever means will work. Generally, the captain does not care what those means are.

It would be nice to incorporate the specification of types described as a triple

$$(ValueSet, OperationSet, EquationSet)$$

within the framework of the Hoare triple. The basic idea is to regard the precondition and postcondition of a type operation as being part of its signature in the *OperationSet*. The next thing is to distribute the equations over the postconditions of the various operations. We illustrate this with the example **Stack** of integers. Below, the equations are called out explicitly.

```
        typedef int Boolean;
        const Boolean TRUE = 1, FALSE = 0;

        class Stack {
        public:                    // these members are public
                Stack() : sp(0), size(100) {}
                // post:  isempty() == TRUE
                void push( int x)        { elt[sp++] = x; }
                // pre:  !isfull()
                // post:  !isempty()
                int pop()                    { return elt[--sp]; }
                // pre:  !isempty()
                // post:  !isfull()
                int peek() const        { return elt[sp - 1]; }
                // pre:  !isempty()
                // post:  peek() == pop()
                Boolean isempty() const { return sp <= 0; }
                Boolean isfull() const  { return sp >= size; }
// equations:
//           for all s, x :
//               [s.push( x)].pop() == x, and
//               [[s.push( x)].pop()] == s
//           for all s : let x = s.pop() in
//               [[s.pop()].push( x)] == s
        private:         // these (data) members are private
                int sp;  // sp points to next available slot
                int elt[size];
                const int size;
        };
```

In the class above, each member function is annotated with its precondition and postcondition. Note that the constructor Stack() does not need a precondition, but it does have a postcondition that guarantees that any Stack object is empty on instantiation. The class as a whole is annotated with equations that essentially say that push() and pop() are inverse to each other. The equations are assumed to hold whenever the appropriate preconditions hold. We can get rid of the equations section by distributing the equations over the postconditions in the following way:

```
typedef int Boolean;
const Boolean TRUE = 1, FALSE = 0;

class Stack {
public:                      // these members are public
      Stack() : sp(0), size(100) {}
      // post:  isempty() == TRUE
      void push( int x)        { elt[sp++] = x; }
      // pre:  !isfull()
      // post:  !isempty() &&
      //     for all s, x :
      //          [s.push( x)].pop() == x, and
      //          [[s.push( x)].pop()] == s

      int pop()                  { return elt[--sp]; }
      // pre:  !isempty()
      // post:  !isfull() &&
      //     for all s : let x = s.pop() in
      //          [[s.pop()].push( x)] == s

      int peek() const         { return elt[sp - 1]; }
      // pre: !isempty()
      // post:  peek() == pop()
      Boolean isempty() const { return sp <= 0; }
      Boolean isfull() const  { return sp >= size; }
private:               // these (data) members are private
      int sp;  // sp points to next available slot
      int elt[size];
      const int size;
};
```

In either style of specification, we have a way of rigorously describing the behavior of a type of object, independent of any implementation concerns. Consequently, we have an unambiguous criterion against which to measure the correctness of any particular implementation.

Let us prove that the implementation given above for Stack is correct. What does this really mean? It means to show that the implementation of each member function satisfies its precondition and postcondition in the sense of the Hoare triple, and to show that all the equations are satisfied.

Starting with the constructor `Stack()`, we must demonstrate that after a `Stack` object `s` has been instantiated

$$\text{Stack s;}$$

it satisfies `s.isempty() == TRUE`. By implementation, this can be so if and only if `sp <= 0`. But the constructor guarantees that `sp == 0` at instantiation. So, the constructor satisfies its specification.

`push()`: A `Stack` object is not full (`s.isfull() == FALSE`) if `sp < size`. Pushing an element onto the stack increments `sp` by one, so clearly `sp` must satisfy `sp > 0`, and so after the push `s` must satisfy `s.isempty() == FALSE`. One goes through a similar exercise for `pop()`.

To prove that the equations are satisfied, we must take a closer look at the state space of `Stack` objects. Our initial guess is that it is the cartesian product of the types of the non-constant private data members:

$$int \times Vector(int, size)$$

The `int` in the product above represents the stack pointer `sp`, and $Vector(int, size)$ denotes the type of the integer array data member `elt`. There is no need to include an `int` dimension for the `size`, because the `size` does not vary over the life of a `Stack` object. What do we mean when we say that two `Stack` objects are in the same state? The answer to this question tells us how to implement the overloaded comparison operator `==`

$$\text{Boolean Stack::operator == (const Stack\&);}$$

the simplest answer is bitwise equality of data structures, under which the overloaded comparison operator has the implementation

```
Boolean Stack::operator == (const Stack& s)
{
    Boolean r = (size == s.size) && (sp ==  s.sp);
    int j;
    if( r)
        for( j = 0; (j < size) && (elt[j] == s.elt[j]); j++)
            ;
    return r && (j == size);
}
```

This definition of equality is too strong. In truth, we don't care about the equality of corresponding elements in the `elt` arrays for `j >= sp`; we only care about what's going on for `j < sp`. After all, `sp` implements the stack pointer, and anything above the stack pointer might as well be garbage. The discussion leads to a refined notion of stack state equality, which we document in the following implementation of the overloaded comparison operator:

```
Boolean Stack::operator == (const Stack& s)
{
    Boolean r = (size == s.size) && (sp ==  s.sp);
    int j;
    if( r)
        for( j = 0; (j < sp) && (elt[j] == s.elt[j]); j++)
            ;
    return r && (j == size);
}
```

Let us take the above as the meaning of equality in the equation set of **class Stack** as well. Let us verify that the equation

$$[\texttt{s.push( x)].pop() == x}$$

is satisfied. The new state of s after the push, [s.push( x)], is ( sp', elt') where

```
sp' == sp + 1, and
elt'[sp] == x, and
for all j such that 0 <= j < sp
    elt'[j] == elt[j]
```

pop() decrements sp' by 1, with the result that the stack pointer has the original value sp. pop() returns the value elt'[sp], which is x. To show that

$$[[\texttt{s.push( x)].pop()] == s}$$

we have to show that the stack pointer is invariant under pushing and them immediately popping. We have done so above. Because the element arrays on both sides of the above equation are slotwise equal for slots $j$ < sp, the equation in fact holds under our refined definition of stack equality. That the equation

$$[s.pop()].push( x)] == s$$

holds, where x = s.pop(), is proven in a similar manner.

## 1.10    List Type

If we ignore the Stack::isfull() member function, the linked list implementation of the Stack type in the previous section (section 1.8) behaves a lot like a simple singly linked Lisp-like [HS, LISP] list type, which leads us to suspect that we could reuse much of the implementation. In the specification for type Simplist below we indicate to which Lisp functions the Simplist member functions correspond, in the comment on the same line as the function prototype.

```
typedef int T;
typedef int Boolean;
const Boolean TRUE =  1,
              FALSE = 0;

class Simplist {
public:
    Simplist(); // constructor
    // postcondition:  isempty() == TRUE

    T head() const;           // car
    // precondition:  isempty() == FALSE

    T remove();               // delete
    // precondition:  isempty() == FALSE

    Simplist tail();          // cdr
```

```
    void add( T x);              // cons
    // postcondition:  isempty() == FALSE

    Boolean isempty() const;  // null
// equations:
//    l.remove() == l.head()
//    [l.remove()] == l.tail()
//    l.tail().add( l.head()) == l
};
```

Note that the list type is parameterized by the type **T** of what it contains—here integers. The parameterization of the type is effected by binding **T** to **int** using **typedef**. The subject of parametry is given full treatment in chapter 4.

**head()** returns the value of the head element of the list without changing its state. **remove()** gets rid of the head of the list. **tail()** returns the tail of the list against which **tail()** was invoked, that is, all elements but the head. **add()** adds a new value, making it the head of the list. **isempty()** returns **TRUE** if the list is empty, otherwise **FALSE**. Here is a picture of a singly linked list:

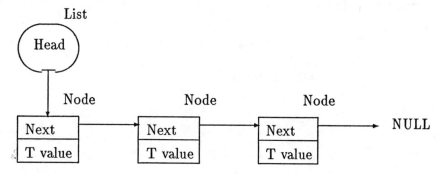

And here is an implementation of Simplist, which makes use of the Node type on page 18.

```
typedef int T;
typedef int Boolean;
const Boolean TRUE =   1,
              FALSE = 0;

class Simplist {
public:
    Simplist() : Head(0) {}

    T head() const                { return Head->value(); }

    T remove()
    {
        T r = Head->value();
        Node *p = Head;
        Head = Head->next();
        delete p;
        return r;
    }

    Simplist tail()
    {
        Simplist r;  // is empty now ...
        if( !isempty())
            r.Head = Head->next();
        return r;
    }

    void add( T x)
    {
        Node *p = new Node( x);

        if( Head != 0)
            p->link( Head);
        Head = p;
    }
```

```
    Boolean isempty() const  { return Head == 0; }
private:
    Node *Head;
};
```

I leave as an exercise to the reader that this implementation satisfies the specification. We shall make frequent use of the `Simplist` type throughout the rest of the book.

## 1.11 Initialization and Clean-Up

Earlier in the chapter, we discussed object state sanity and mentioned necessary conditions for it to hold

- *Data hiding*: All class data members private

- *Correct implementation*: All member functions implemented correctly

- *Correct use*: All member functions invoked correctly with respect to preconditions

Here is an example that shows that these conditions are not sufficient to guarantee object sanity. Imagine that `class Stack` has no constructors and that `foo()` is an external function with a `Stack` local variable

```
void foo()
{
    Stack s;  // no constructor
    if( !s.isfull() ) {
        s.push( 3);
        printf( "%d\n", s.pop() );
    }
}
```

What is the initial value of s? In the absence of a constructor (in particular one that takes zero arguments), its initial value is whatever garbage happened to be lying around on the runtime stack. This garbage state renders all further computation meaningless, for it is possible that `s.isfull()` will return TRUE. Furthermore, the behavior of `foo()` is nondeterministic; it may vary from program run to program run.

You may argue that this is only a problem for local variable objects; C++ guarantees that static variables are initialized to zero. But perhaps zero is not the correct initialization for a particular my program. The programmer needs to ensure that all objects—regardless of their storage class (local, global heap)—are properly initialized.

It looks like the missing ingredient to guarantee object state sanity is sane initial state. Indeed, one can prove inductively[1] that an object is in a sane state throughout its lifetime if

- *Data hiding*: All class data members private

- *Correct implementation*: All member functions implemented correctly

- *Initialization*: Object initialized to a sane state

- *Correct use*: All member functions invoked correctly with respect to preconditions

The problem with providing a type with an explicit initialization operation `init()` (as in `Stack` below)

```
class Stack {
public:
    void init();  // initialization
    ...
};
...
void foo()
{
    Stack s;
    s.init();
    ...
}
```

---

[1]Inducting over the number of member function invocations that the object suffers over its lifetime (I leave the proof to the mathematically inclined reader).

```
void bar()
{
    Stack s;
    if( !s.isfull() )
        s.push( 4);
    s.init();
}
```

is that the programmer must be disciplined enough to always initialize the object *immediately* after its instantiation, as in the function `foo()` above. That is, object instantiation and initialization need to be an atomic, indivisible operation, something akin to an atomic transaction against a data base. The alternative—letting some operation intervene between instantiation and initialization—illustrated in `bar()` above, is a recipe for disaster.

C++ provides support for atomic, simultaneous instantiation and initialization through special class member functions called constructors. Like any member function, constructors come in all signatures, from zero to one or more arguments. From a design perspective, constructors with zero arguments play a special role. Without looking at the `Stack` manual page or implementation, there is no way of telling whether

```
Stack s;
```

merely creates storage for an object named `s` of type `Stack`, or whether it creates storage for `s` and immediately initializes it with a constructor of zero arguments.

The wise class designer always provides a constructor of zero arguments (in addition to whatever other constructors seem necessary) to ensure that all instance objects start their lives in a state of grace and sanity. This step eliminates much of the chore of initialization from the hands of the client programmer.

A reasonable requirement on the `Stack` constructor is that after its invocation (postcondition!) the stack object is empty, that is,

```
s.isempty() == TRUE
```

This condition is satisfied by both of our **Stack** implementations on pages 17 and 20.

In practical terms, initializing an object often involves the allocation of scarce system resources, as well as ensuring the sanity of its initial state. Resources include heap memory, file descriptors, windows, and others. For example, the constructor in **class File** (page 11), opens a file object and assigns the file handle return value of the standard input/output (I/O) function **fopen()** to a data member. File opening involves the allocation of all manner of resources both in the data space of the requesting program as well as in the operating system kernel [BACH]. As any systems programmer knows

> *All system resources are scarce!*

Consequently, the object should relinquish the resource as soon as it no longer has any need for it. Certainly, the latest time to relinquish resources is when the object is about to go out of scope (pass on to the great container object in the sky ...). This is what is meant by the term *object clean-up.*

Here is a problem. The allocation of resources can be performed automatically and invisibly in a constructor, without the knowledge or explicit request of the client programmer. Indeed the rule of implementation hiding requires that this be so, because the resource allocation is an artifact of the current implementation of the type. Well then, if the client programmer is not responsible for initialization, neither should she or he be responsible for de-allocation.

Here C++ comes to the rescue of the type designer with the destructor class member function. The destructor—if it exists—is invoked automatically whenever an object of its type is about to die (go out of scope). Consequently, the body of the destructor is an ideal place to put clean-up actions and code for relinquishing resources allocated in the constructor. For example, the **File** destructor (page 11) closes the standard I/O **FILE** associated with the **File** object, thus de-allocating all kinds of operating system resources.

The **Node** implementation of **Stack** (page 20) presents a related problem. Here, resources—**Node** objects on the heap—are not allocated in the constructor, but rather are dynamically allocated (using the C++ built-in operator **new**) whenever a value is pushed onto a **Stack** object. In this implementation, when a **Stack** object dies, if it is not empty, all of the **Node** objects on its linked list become unrecoverable storage (i.e., garbage). It is easy to conceive of a scenario in which a program that makes use of this Stack implementation simply runs out of heap storage, and so cannot continue to execute. We can correct this problem by providing **class Stack** with a destructor that does the garbage collection

```
Stack::~Stack()
{
    Node *n;
    for( Node *p = head; p ; p = n)  {
        n = p->next();
        delete p;
    }
}
```

by walking the list and de-allocating each **Node**, using the C++ built-in heap storage de-allocator **delete**. We have only scratched the surface of the use of constructors and destructors, in particular with regard to per-class garbage collection. We have given an example of how to do garbage collection when the resources (here, **Nodes**) are not shared. That is, any given **Node** belongs to at most one **Stack** object. It is doable but more complicated to implement garbage collection schemes for shared resources.

## 1.12   List Iterators and Friend Functions

By definition in C++, A friend function of a class (say class B) is an external function or member function of some other class (say class A) that has direct access to the private members of class B. Here is a simple example of an external function, print(), which displays the value of an object capable of incrementing itself. Note that the declaration of friendship is found in the class Inc. That is, the class controls the set of functions with which it is intimate.

```
class Inc {
public:
    Inc( int n = 0)        { val = n; }
    void increment()    { val++; }
```

```
private:
    friend void print( Inc);
    int val;
};

void print( Inc i) { printf( "%d ", i.val); }

...
Inc i(3);
i.increment();
print( i);
```

Friend functions establish implementation relationships between classes. For when the data structure of class Inc changes, it is likely that the code of the friend function **print()** must be rewritten. Thus, untrammeled friendship is a violation of implementation hiding.

Are there situations that require friend functions? In those situations, is there a way of using friendship responsibly so as to preserve implementation hiding? To both these questions I answer: yes. There are cases in which several programming entities (functions and/or objects) require privileged access to common private data structures. Languages like Modula-2 [WIRTH] and Ada handle these situations with a programming language construct called a module (package in Ada), which allows the programmer to encapsulate together private data structures with precisely the functions that require access to them. Functions outside the module have no direct access to objects of type defined private in the module. Thus, modules support implementation hiding. *Caution*: A module is not an object!

The second question asks if friendship can be used so as not to violate implementation hiding. Let me sketch out an answer. If a class B has friend functions, provide B with a special interface of private member functions. Implement the friends of B strictly in terms of this private interface, taking care not to let the friend functions touch private data members in B. Note that nobody else in the universe knows anything about this private interface. Also, when it comes time to reimplement class B, recode the private interface along with the rest of B. The implementations of the friend functions change not one iota.

Here is a somewhat more challenging example of responsible friendship along the lines suggested above. **class Simplist**, discussed in section 1.10, defines a list of integers, implemented as a linked list of **Nodes**.

The public interface of **Simplist** provides Lisp-like list semantics. That is, we can insert or delete elements only at the head of the list. We would like to iterate over all the elements in a given **Simplist** object. One way is to view the iterator as a type of object in its own right with the following public interface:

```
class It {
public:
    It( Simplist &);
    Boolean isend() const;
    T get();      // precondition:  !isend()
};
```

The **It** constructor associates an iterator object with the list it iterates over. The boolean function **isend()** returns **TRUE** when iteration is completed, and **FALSE** otherwise. **get()** returns the next value in the list and prepares to fetch the value after it. For example, the following code fragment prints out all of the values in a list of integers:

```
Simplist l;
// fill the list with integers using Simplist::add()
...
It i( l);     // bind the iterator to the Simplist l
while( !i.isend() )
    printf( "%d\n", i.get() );
```

The interesting question is how to implement class **It**. The simplest approach is to make **It** a friend of **Simplist** so that **It**'s member functions can directly access the linked-list-of-nodes structure of **Simplist**, as follows:

```
class Simplist {
    friend It::It( Simplist &);
    // the rest of class Simplist as above
};
```

The above declares that the **It** constructor, and only that member function, is a friend of class **Simplist**. Why is this sufficient?

```
class It {
public:
    It( const Simplist &l) : current( l.Head) {}
    Boolean isend() const { return (current == 0); }
    T get()
    {
        T r = current->value();
        current = current->next();
        return r;
    }
private:
    Node *current;
};
```

The implementation of It is fine as far as it goes. But it depends painfully on the current implementation of Simplist. When the implementation of Simplist changes, so must It's. Another maintenance disaster!

In the following solution, I still implement It using friendship, but now the member functions of It depend only on a private member function of Simplist—tail()—which returns a new Simplist object that is the tail of the list!

```
class Simplist {
public:
    Simplist() : Head( 0)       {}
    Boolean isempty() const { return Head == 0; }
    T head() const          { return Head->value(); }
    void add(T x)           { /* as before */ }
    T remove()              { /* as before */ }
private:
    Node *Head;

    friend It;              // wholesale friendship
    // tail returns the tail of the List.  cdr in LISP.
    Simplist tail()
    {
        Simplist r;
        if( !isempty() )
```

```
                    r.Head = Head->next();
            return r;
        }
};
```

Above I am being sloppy by declaring that every member function of It is a friend of `Simplist`. This is more than enough. Can this friendship be limited to a select few?

```
    class It {
    public:
        It( const Simplist &l) : current( l) {}
        Boolean isend() const { return current.isempty(); }
        T get()
        {
            T r = current.get();
            current = current.tail();
            return r;
        }
    private:
        Simplist current;
    };
```

The latter implementation of It completely parallels the former; yet the latter is invariant under changes in the data structure of `Simplist`. It suffices for the owner of `Simplist` to properly rewrite the member function `tail()`. By the way, both implementations perform equally as speedily, because of inline optimization of function call overhead, which the C++ language provides by default (in many but not all cases) for member functions whose bodies are found within the class template.

Note in the above that nothing in the C++ language prevents It member functions from direct access to the data members of `Simplist` objects. Rather, the benefits of implementation hiding motivate us to practice this form of safe(r) programming.

## 1.13   Layering and Dummy Proofing

Layering is an implementation technique. It simply means that we *use* other
types to construct a given type ([LSK2]). Here is how layering maps into
C++ for a given class T;

- The data structure of **T** consists of data members of types **T1** ...
  **Tn**, where the **Tj** can be either user-defined types or built-ins of the
  language.

- The member functions of **T** use local variables and arguments of types
  taken from the list of types **T1** ... **Tn**.

Layering of data is the primary meaning of layering. Thus, in the implementation of **class Stack** above, we can say that **Stack** is layered on **Node**.
When we use a type **T1** to construct a given type **T**, we automatically have
access to the public member functions of **T1** within the bodies of the member
functions of **T**. This observation provides some insight into the implementation of **T** in that it paradoxically limits the number of functions (i.e., the
public member functions of **T1**) that we have to think about. At design
time, we can exploit layering in the reverse direction, using the specification
of **T** to provide constraints on the specification of **T1**, that is, constraints on
what services (member functions) **T1** must provide to implement **T**.

We can use layering to provide a nice solution to the following general
design problem. For concreteness, let's assume that the manual page for
**class Stack** includes preconditions and postconditions for each member
function, and the equations that the member functions satisfy. Following Meyer [MEY], the manual page establishes a *contract* between the de-
signer/implementor and the user (application programmer) of the type that
goes as follows:

- The designer is responsible for ensuring the correctness of the implementation of the type with respect to its specification. She or he must
  make sure that the type manual page exists (in real projects this is not
  to be assumed!) and accurately reflects the behavior of the type. The
  manual page ought to be so well written that a type user feels no com-
  pulsion to peruse the implementation of the type to reverse-engineer
  their understanding of what's going on.

- The user—who can be regarded as a client of the designer—is responsible for reading and understanding the type manual page. For it constitutes the behavior of the type (this is nothing more than a restatement of the principle of abstraction). Here comes the contractual part: The type will always work as advertised, as long as the user holds to his or her part of the bargain. Generally, this means checking preconditions before invoking member functions. If, conversely, the user does not use the type in a legal way—for example, by not verifying preconditions—the type is under no obligation to behave rationally.

Now, the contractual school of programming described above is daunting for real software projects for a couple of reasons:

1. No one writes type manual pages.

2. No one reads type manual pages.

3. The manual page is always incorrect and out of date, because the system requirements are changing so fast. So why bother reading it?

I exaggerate, of course. But ask yourself, honestly, how far does your project deviate from this description? Many designers, when faced with this unfortunately common state of affairs, abandon the contractual school and resort to a school of programming variously called "robust" or "dummy proofing." In dummy proofing, the designer attempts to implement the type in such a way that misuse of the type on the part of a client programmer will not put objects of the type in an irrational state and thus will not harm the program of which the object is a part. As we shall see, dummy proofing has an effect not only on implementation, but also on the behavior and the public interface of the type.

Here is a dummy proofing of `Stack` that makes nice use of layering. The heart of the dummy proofed design is to

> *Decouple safety from correctness.*

That is, our `Stack` class satisfies all our concerns for correct behavior, but it is viewed as unsafe. Let's make the rule that only responsible software citizens like designers get to use contractual classes like `Stack`. Let us design and implement `class Safestack` for safe use by the broader programming community. At the same, we want savvy client programmers, who are

aware of such things as preconditions and postconditions, to be able to use
SafeStack pretty much in the same way as Stack. We intend to implement
SafeStack using Stack.

```
class SafeStack {
public:
    SafeStack();

    void push( int x)
    {
        if( !s.isfull() )
            s.push( x);
    }

    int pop()
    {
        if( !s.isempty() )
            return s.pop();
    }

    Boolean isempty()    { return s.isempty(); }

    Boolean isfull()     { return s.isfull(); }
private:      // Safestack data structure layered on Stack
    Stack s;
};
```

In the above implementation, isempty() and isfull() just pass the buck to
their counterparts in class Stack. SafeStack push() and pop() explicitly
invoke the appropriate Stack precondition. If it is satisfied, then and only
then is the corresponding Stack function invoked.

The above implementation guarantees that the state of a SafeStack object—
which after all is the state of its Stack data member—will always be sane.
However, that is not the same as guaranteeing the sanity of a program that
uses a SafeStack object. For, imagine a scenario in which a huge sequence
of integers is pushed onto the object without the program explicitly checking for stack overflow (object.isfull() == TRUE). All pushes of integers
after overflow are lost—they go to the great big bit bucket in the sky! The

program probably depended critically on the lost information, so now the program is in a corrupt state.

We attempt to correct this problem by changing push()

```
Boolean Stack::push( int x)
{
    Boolean r = TRUE;
    if( !s.isfull())
        s.pop( x);
    else
        r = FALSE;
    return r;
}
```

Now the programmer can check the return value of push() after the fact to see if it succeeded, and if it didn't, to take corrective action. However, this is strange. It takes just as much code to check the return value of this version of SafeStack::pop() as it does to check the precondition of Stack::push() in advance of its invocation!

SafeStack::pop() presents an even greater challenge. Its implementation certainly prevents popping the real stack in the event that it is empty. But there remains the question: what value to return? In case of stack underflow it doesn't make sense to return anything, but if we want the signature of SafeStack::pop() to be the same as that of Stack::pop(), then it must return an integer value. The implementation returns whatever garbage is found in the runtime stack frame, which although poetically justified, is not good programming.

We can get rid of the garbage return by drastically changing the signature of SafeStack::pop()

```
Boolean SafeStack::pop( int *p)
{
    Boolean r =  TRUE;
    if( s.isempty() )
        r = FALSE;
    else
        *p = s.pop();
}
```

In the above implementation, pop() returns TRUE if the operation succeeds and FALSE otherwise. The programmer must provide the address of an integer object p as the explicit argument to pop(). If the operation succeeds, *p contains whatever was popped off the stack.

This solution is even less satisfactory than the one we came up with for SafeStack::push(): Its signature does not remotely resemble the traditional one. Moreover the argument p is a source of potential error; for it can be set to 0 or some other illegal address. So, in our attempt at dummy proofing, we have, at best, traded one kind of trouble for another. In sum, I recommend: Stick with the contractual school of programming!

It should be mentioned that there is a third school of programming, let's call it the exception handling school, which happens to be supported by the Eiffel language [MEY]. One can write in Eiffel preconditions and postconditions (required and ensure clauses) for each class operation (exported feature). By definition, an exception is the violation of the precondition of some class operation. In addition, a class designer may write a handler for each exception recognized by the class. An Eiffel program can be compiled in one of two ways. In the first, the exception handling code for all classes is compiled in. If an exception is encountered at runtime, the appropriate exception handler runs. This mode of compilation is recommended for debugging. The second mode of compilation leaves out all the exception handling code. In the second mode it is assumed that the program is written according to the contractual model, that is, the programmer has explicitly written code to check preconditions and take evasive action on violation.

The draft ANSI standard commits C++ in the future to a form of synchronous exception handling (see [ARM] or [EXC]). As of this writing, there are no commercially available C++ compilers that support this feature. The proposed exception handling scheme introduces three new keywords into the language—catch, throw, try—which enable parts of an application distant from each other to throw and catch values of arbitrary type. These values represent different types of exceptional conditions. The feature is intended to supplant the library functions setjmp() and longjmp() in that it takes care to destruct local objects in the scope of the throw. longjmp() knows nothing of destructors; it blindly leaps stackframes to the location of the setjmp(), which could easily put the program in an uncertain state. The feature is orthogonal to C++ support for types and objects. This is in marked contrast to Eiffel, where exception handling is intimately related to classes, objects, and preconditions for invocation of class operations.

To summarize, there are three schools of programming: contractual, dummy proof, and exception handling. All the schools can be built in terms of contractual types. The advantage of doing so is that the contractual type is typically simpler to understand and implement. By layering, we can separate our concerns of correctness and safety, with the contractual type handling correctness, and the types layered on top of it handling safety.

## 1.14 Summary

Here is a summary of the benefits of data abstraction:

- *Conceptual simplicity (abstraction)*: It is easier to reason about, design, and implement systems that are built out of entities that observe implementation hiding. For, all we have to discuss are the properties of the procedural interface of the various entities. These properties are typically far simpler (more abstract) than the algorithms that implement them.

- *Reuse*: The decoupling of the interface from the implementation allows program entities to be reimplemented without having to modify any other part of the program. This modularity also enhances the portability of software across operating systems and hardware platforms. In other words, implementation hiding allows us to reuse more of the code that we write, which decreases the cost of maintenance, now well over half the cost of any software product. These are important benefits in the 1990s when computers are cheap and programmer salaries high!

- Object and program state integrity.

# Bibliography

[ARM]  Margaret Ellis and Bjarne Stroustrup, *The Annotated C++ Reference Manual*, 1990, Addison-Wesley.

[BACH]  Maury Bach, *Internals of the UNIX System Kernel*, 1987, Addison-Wesley.

[BERN]  David Bern and Tsvi Bar-David, "Using References in C++," *C Users Journal*, pp. 21–25, volume 7, number 7, October 1989.

[CHJ]  B. Cohen, W. T. Harwood, M. I. Jackson, *The Specification of Complex Systems*, 1986, Addison-Wesley.

[CLEAVE]  J. Craig Cleaveland, *An Introduction to Data Types*, 1986, Addison-Wesley.

[EXC]  Dan Saks, "ANSI C++ Update: Exceptions Accepted," *The C++ Report*, volume 3, number 2, February 1991.

[GEH]  Narain Gehani (ed.), *Software Specification Technology*, 1986, Addison-Wesley.

[GRIES]  D. Gries, *The Science of Programming*, 1981, Springer-Verlag.

[HS]  Ellis Horowitz and Sartaj Sahni, *Fundamentals of Data Structures*, 1983, Computer Science Press.

[JSL]  Jonathan S. Linowes, "It's an Attitude," *BYTE Magazine*, August 1988.

[KL]  Karl Lieberherr, "Object-Oriented Programming: An Objective Sense of Style," *OOPSLA Conference Proceedings*, 1988.

[KP]       B. W. Kernighan and P. J. Plauger, *Software Tools in Pascal*, 1981, Addison-Wesley.

[LIP]      Stan Lippman and Bjarne Stroustrup, "Pointers to Class Members in C++," *Usenix Proceedings: C++ Conference*, Denver CO, 1988.

[LISP]     Robert Wilensky, *LISPcraft*, 1984, Norton.

[LIPS]     John Lipson, *Elements of Algebra and Algebraic Computing*, 1981, Addison-Wesley. (Defines type morphism.)

[LSK]      B. Liskov and J. Guttag, *Abstraction and Specification in Program Development*, 1986, MIT Press. (Addresses design of abstract data types.)

[LSK2]     B. Liskov, "Data Abstraction and Hierarchy," addendum to *Conference Proceedings: Object-Oriented Programming Systems Languages and Applications* (OOPSLA), 1987. (Liskov's approach to object oriented design, specifically addresses inheritance.)

[MEY]      Bertrand Meyer, *Object-Oriented Program Construction*, 1988, Prentice Hall. (Addresses object-oriented design, including parametric types.)

[MUR]      Bob Murray, personal communication, 1988. (I would like to acknowledge a debt of gratitude to Bob for the many conversations we had together refining the design framework.)

[SIM]      David Simen, personal communication, December 1988.

[SHO]      Jonathan Shopiro, personal communication, November 1988.

[SNY]      Alan Snyder, "Encapsulation and Inheritance in Object-Oriented Programming Languages," *Proceedings of the ACM Conference on Object Oriented Programming Systems Languages and Applications* (OOPSLA), SIGPLAN Notices 21, November 1986.

[SP]       Edwin Spanier, *Algebraic Topology*, pp. 14–21, 1966, McGraw Hill. (A brief review of category theory.)

[STR]      Bjarne Stroustrup, *The C++ Programming Language*, 1987, Addison Wesley.

[STR2]  Bjarne Stroustrup, "Parameterized Types for C++," *Usenix Proceedings: C++ Conference*, Denver CO, 1988.

[TBD]   Tsvi Bar-David, "Teaching C++," *Usenix Proceedings: C++ Workshop*, Santa Fe, NM, 1987.

[TBD2]  Tsvi Bar-David, "The C++ Column: Formal Specification and Object-Oriented Design," *The C Users Journal*, July 1990.

[YOU]   Tom DeMarco, *Structured Analysis and System Specification*, 1978, Yourdon. (The heuristic was suggested by students who had an understanding of structured analysis.)

# Chapter 2

# Inheritance

## 2.1 Introduction

Inheritance is a relationship between types that deals with sharing. The many definitions of inheritance seem to fall into two categories.

- Sharing of behavior (semantics)

- Sharing of implementation

The two categories correspond to two major activities that programmers are involved in: design and implementation. Identifying shared behavior between types is a form of intellectual reuse at design time, which sometimes—but not always—translates into code reuse. Conversely, there are definitions of inheritance that are not concerned in the least with the sharing of behavior; rather they view inheritance as a software packaging technique for easy code sharing. All object-oriented languages support the sharing of implementation; it is called class derivation in C++.

In this chapter, we shall discuss several flavors of inheritance, concentrating on the intuition behind the definitions. Much of the chapter is occupied with the question: What is the relationship between behavioral and implementation inheritance? Are the terms synonymous? The answer is that the two kinds of inheritance are not synonymous, and several C++ examples are developed to demonstrate the point. However, one can implement behavioral inheritance in terms of class derivation, and rules are presented for doing so. In all honesty, one can also implement behavioral inheritance in non object-oriented languages—such as C—using the layering of data structures, however; it is much easier to implement behavioral inheritance in languages that do support implementation hierarchy (class derivation).

## 2.2   Behavioral Inheritance

What is behavioral inheritance? This section presents an intuitive definition of the concept.

*Definition (behavioral inheritance):*  Given two types S and T that practice data hiding, we say that S *inherits* from T if all T operations can be invoked on all S objects with similar effect. It is as if the public interface (operations) of the base type T is a subset of the public interface of the derived type S

$$PI(T) \subseteq PI(S)$$

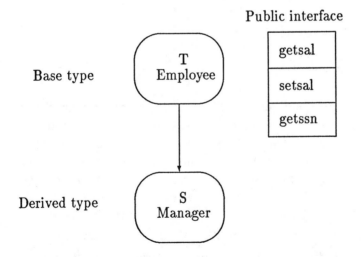

Although the definition is rough, it is immediately clear that this is a definition relating together the behaviors of two types, and not necessarily their implementations. The type T is called the base or parent type. The type S is called the derived or child type. A derived type may have additional properties and operations that have nothing to do with its base type. Behavioral inheritance is often called the *isakindof* relationship. For example,

I think that we would all agree (perhaps managers would not!) that a **Manager** isakindof **Employee**, because all the properties and operations that we think of as pertaining to employees also pertain to managers, such as name, address, phone number, social security number, the ability to get and set salary, and so on.

In the mammal hierarchy depicted below, the base type **Mammal** factors out properties or operations common to all kinds of mammals: The females of all mammalian species **suckle** their young. All mammals eat, and all mammals move *in some fashion*. **suckle** is an example of an operation whose implementation—as well as semantics—can be inherited from the base type into all derived types. This reflects the fact that breast structure, milk chemistry, and the suckle reflex on the part of baby mammals is pretty much the same for all mammals. After all, the name of the base type is derived from the latin word for breast—*mamma*.

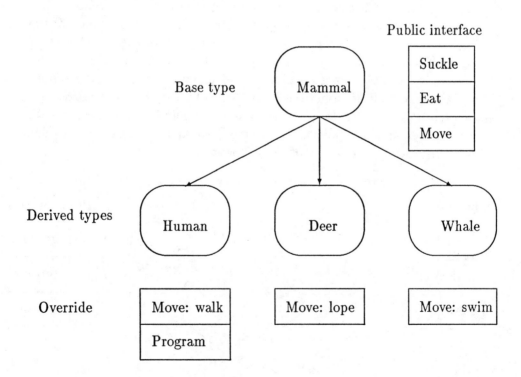

The **move** operation, however, partakes of a different character entirely. Whereas all mammals are characterized by the ability to move from point A to point B, *how* they do it (i.e., how each species implements the move property) depends on the species, the "derived type," if you will. For example, humans walk, deer lope, and whales swim. In object-oriented jargon, the various derived types *override* the implementation for **move** that they by default would have inherited from the base type **Mammal**.

**program** is an example of an additional operation—not found in the repetoire (public interface) of **Mammal**—whereby the derived type **Human** extends the base type. That is to say, not all mammals can program. Humans can. I was tempted to use **speak** as an example of an operation whereby a type extends its base type. However, it has become apparent in recent years that humans are by far not the only species capable of intraspecies as well as interspecies communication; primates and cetaceans can and do communicate. And I wouldn't be surprised if we find out in the future that other species can program, given an appropriate computer interface!

Our rough definition of behavioral definition can easily accommodate multiple (behavioral) inheritance. The result of having multiple parents is that the public interface of a derived type contains, as it were, the union of the public interfaces of its parent types. For example, the navy employs porpoises (a kind of mammal) for a variety of underwater tasks. It is perfectly legitimate to posit the existence of a type—**Mammemp**—which is derived both from **Mammal** as well as from **Employee**. All instances of type **Mammemp** (including porpoises, seals, etc.) have social security numbers, salaries, and are also capable of moving about and having other mammalian properties. The navy's porpoises are instances of the **Mammemp**.

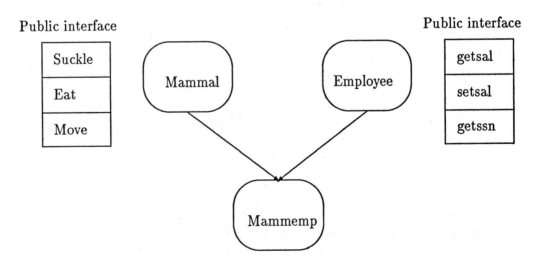

## 2.3  Inheritance of Implementation

C++ supports implementation inheritance with a mechanism called class derivation. Similar mechanisms for the sharing of software exist in other object-oriented languages, such as Smalltalk and Eiffel.[1]  C++ does not directly support the inheritance of behavior. However class derivation is commonly and effectively used to implement behavioral inheritance.

Rather than trying to come up with a language-independent definition of the inheritance of implementation, we will simply use as our definition public class derivation in C++.

*Definition (implementation inheritance):*  To say that type S is derived from type T means that

- *Inheritance of data structure:* Every S object has an "anonymous" data member of type T, in addition to the explicit data members.

- *Inheritance of algorithms:*  Any (public) T member function can be invoked against any S object.

- *Override:*  The derived type S may override any base type member function by explicitly declaring a derived type member function of the same name and signature.

Here is an idealized version of the data layout of a derived type object. It assumes that base parts and derived class data members are layed out sequentially in memory.

---

[1]The reader may notice that the book takes a definite viewpoint: I am not much interested in class derivation for its own sake. Behavioral inheritance is the point of interest. Therefore, I am mainly interested in class derivation only in so far as it is an efficient language mechanism for minimizing the amount of time that the programmer has to spend implementing behavioral inheritance.

```
┌─────────────────────────┐
│                         │
│                         │
│     Base data—T         │
│                         │
│                         │
├─────────────────────────┤
│                         │
│   Additional derived    │
│       data—S            │
│                         │
└─────────────────────────┘
```

The code fragment below is an example of class derivation. `class Manager` is derived from `class Employee`.

```
class Employee {
public:
    Employee( int n = 0)  { salary = n; }
    void setsalary( int n)  { salary = n; }
    int getsalary()  { return salary; }
private:
    int salary;
};

const int Max = 20;
class Manager : public Employee {
public:
    Employee *get( int n)  { return group[n]; }
    void set( Employee *ep, int n)  { group[n] = ep; }
private:
    Employee *group[Max];
};

Employee ed( 20000);

// give ed a raise
ed.setsalary( 25000);
```

```
Manager mary;

// class derivation and behavioral inheritance
mary.setsalary( 35000);  // void Employee::setsalary(int)

// additional member function
mary.set( &ed, 0);
```

As indicated, we can invoke the `Employee::setsalary()` member function against the `Manager` object `mary` because `Manager` is derived from `Employee`. The `Manager` type extends `Employee` precisely in that managers have other employees reporting to them. In this case `ed` reports to **mary**. This relationship is established with the invocation of the member function `Manager::set(Employee *)`.

## 2.4  Substitution Principle

Our behavioral definition of inheritance (page 54) is based on a substitution principle presented by Barbara Liskov in her keynote address to the OOPSLA conference of 1987:

> A type hierarchy is composed of subtypes and supertypes. The intuitive idea of a *subtype* is one whose objects provide all the behavior of another type (the *supertype*) plus something extra. What is wanted here is something like the following substitution property: If for each object $o_1$ of type $S$ there is an object $o_2$ of type T such that for all programs P defined in terms of T, the behavior of P is unchanged when $o_1$ is substituted for $o_2$, then S is a subtype of T.

In C++ terms, the substitution principle places restrictions—in the same spirit as Dijkstra's admonition [DIJ] to forgo the use of goto's—on our design and coding style, in particular in our use of class derivation and overrides.[2] The substitution principle mandates that much—but not all—of the manual page for a derived class override is already determined by the

---

[2]Recall that an override is a member function in a derived class with exactly the same signature as some member function in the base class.

manual page of the base class function it shadows. This is not such a totally horrible restriction; after all, the base class function and the derived class override share the same name. There ought to be some relationship in the behavior of the two functions, else why the same name? Psychologically, the reader of the program should be granted clemency for assuming that the two functions do something similar!

For every restriction that I voluntarily impose on my programming style, I want there to be a corresponding benefit, else why bother? One of the advantages of building C++ programs according to this substitution principle is that it is possible to read and reason about programs written in terms of objects related by (behavioral) inheritance without perusing source code, neither for base nor for derived types. That is to say, a team of programmers can *reuse* all of their understanding of the behavior of a base type when they read (or, indeed, write) derived type code. This is an "at-least" design principle: A derived type object behaves *at least* like base type objects and may have additional behaviors whereby it extends the base type. The uniform imposition of this principle gives a program a coherence and consistency that it otherwise would not have.

When Liskov says that S is a *subtype* of T it is the same as when we say that S behaviorally inherits from T. The key idea is that derived type objects *behave* like base type objects. This means that we can invoke any base type operation against any derived type object and obtain similar behavior. The term *behavior* right now is very fuzzy. The challenge is to define the term more rigorously. Here we take the position of the algebraic school of formal specification (see chapter 1 and [CHJ]): Namely, the behavior of a type is specified by a set of equations (axioms, if you will, for the type as an algebraic system just like a group or vector space) that relate the operations in the public interface of the type.

In light of this definition of type behavior, we could read the substitution principle as saying that all derived type objects must satisfy all base type equations. A derived type may have *additional* operations and equations, and, of course, the base type says nothing about them. Such a reading constitutes a very strong formal definition of behavioral inheritance. In what follows we shall employ a somewhat weaker definition that demands that only certain equations satisfied in the base type need be satisfied in the derived type. The heuristics and programmer guidelines presented later in the chapter are based on a theoretical model of behavioral inheritance as a species of data refinement (see [MORRIS]).

We shall use the following program to discuss behavioral inheritance as a substitution principle:

```
Employee e1, e2;
int salary = 30000;

e1.setsalary( salary);
printf( "%d %d\n", salary, e1.getsalary());

e2.setsalary( e1.getsalary());
printf( "%d %d\n", salary, e2.getsalary());

--------- Substitute m1 for e1 and m2 for e2 ---------

Manager m1, m2;
int salary = 30000;

m1.setsalary( salary);
printf( "%d %d\n", salary, m1.getsalary());

m2.setsalary( m1.getsalary());
printf( "%d %d\n", salary, m2.getsalary());
```

In the preceding program the dashed line is written in terms of `Employee` objects. The program below the dashed line is the result of substituting for each `Employee` object above the dashed line a `Manager` object whose `Employee` part has the same initial value as the object for which it is being substituted. The question is this: Under what circumstances is the substitution principle satisfied for this pair of programs? We can phrase the question more concretely: Under what conditions does class derivation of `class Manager` from `class Employee` also constitute behavioral inheritance of type `Manager` from type `Employee`?

To be able to answer the question, we need to specify the equations that describe the behavior of the `Employee` type. Let's keep things simple and specify just one equation, which we first state fuzzily in English:

> *Whatever I set the salary to I get back.*

To state the equation more rigorously, we avail ourselves of the notation discussed in chapter 1

$$[object.memberfunction( arguments)]$$

which denotes the new state of the object on return from the memberfunction. We can now unambiguously state the equation:

```
for all Employee objects emp and for all integers n:
         [emp.setsalary( n)].getsalary() == n
```

It is easy to show that the implementation of Employee as follows satisfies the equation.

```
class Employee
{
public:
     void setsalary( int n) { salary = n; }
     int getsalary()        { return salary; }
private:
     int  salary;
};
```

If setsalary() returned Employee, as in the implementation below,

```
Employee Employee::setsalary( int n)
{
    salary = n;
    return *this;
}

// Example:

Employee ed;
int n = 35000;

printf( "%d\n",
    ed.setsalary( n).getsalary());
```

The equation could be written more simply as

```
for all Employee objects emp and for all integers n:
          emp.setsalary( n)).getsalary() == n
```

Thus the state transition notation [e.setsalary( n)] is useful for those situations in which a member function changes the state of the object but returns a value of some other type, possibly **void**.

The next four sections examine four different derivations of **class Manager** from **class Employee** with Employee implementation and equation fixed as above. The four derivations are summarized subsequently.

1. No override in **Manager** to **Employee** member functions

2. Override **setsalary()** with a hidden bonus

3. Hidden bonus assigned to its own data member in **Manager**

4. Explicit bonus operations in **Manager**

The objective is to develop some insight into the relationship between behavioral inheritance and class derivation. As we will see, some of these class derivations constitute behavioral inheritance, some do not.

## 2.5  No Override to setsalary()

The implementation of Manager below

```
const int dim = 20;

class Manager : public Employee {
public:
    Employee* getemp( int n)    { return group[n]; }
    void setemp( int n, Employee *ep) {
        group[n] = ep;
    }
private:
    Employee* group[dim];
};
```

overrides none of the member functions of Employee. It is easy to show in this frequent and important boundary case that the Manager type satisfies the base type equation

```
for all Manager objects m and for all integers n:
        [m.setsalary( n)].getsalary() == n
```

Consequently, I can reason about the substitution of derived for base objects in the model program on page 61. For example, I can deduce from the equation that

```
m1.getsalary() == salary, and
m2.getsalary() == salary
```

## 2.6   Hidden Bonus

The implementation of Manager as follows provides an override for setsalary() and no other base class function.

```
class Manager : public Employee {
public:
    void setsalary( int n)
    {
        Employee::setsalary( n + bonus());
    }

    Employee* getemp( int n)     { return group[n]; }
    void setemp( int n, Employee *ep) {
        group[n] = ep;
    }
private:
    Employee* group[dim];
};
```

Manager::setsalary() consults a secret managerial bonus function that—depending on the profitability of the company during the past quarter and the phase of the moon—adds a positive increment to the explicit salary parameter n and passes the sum on down to the base class setsalary() operation. Does Manager satisfy the equation

```
[m.setsalary( n)].getsalary() == n
```

The answer in general is no because the `salary` data member of the `Employee` part of the `Manager` object after the `setsalary()` operation is

```
n + bonus() != n
```

which is not equal to `n` as long as the bonus is not zero (a consummation devoutly wished for by the manager). This implementation of `Manager` makes a shambles of attempting to reason about the model program on page 61 from specification (namely, the equation). For, having substituting `Manager` objects for `Employee` objects in the program, the first `printf()` will reveal a discrepancy between the `salary` variable and the actual salary of manager m1. Furthermore, setting m2's salary from m1's

```
m2.setsalary( m1.getsalary());
```

will result in m2 getting two bonuses, m1's and its own! None of which is apparent from knowing the equation or reading the program. The only way to understand what the program is doing is to cheat by studying the implementation of the derived class.

## 2.7  bonus Data Member in Derived Class Manager

Assuming we still want to to give managers bonuses, how can we do so and preserve semantic inheritance? In the implementation of `Manager` below

```
class Manager : public Employee {
public:
    void setsalary( int n)
    {
        Employee::setsalary( n);
        Bonus = bonus();
    }

    void addbonus()
    {
```

```
            Employee::setsalary( getsalary() + Bonus);
        }

        Employee* getemp( int n)    { return group[n]; }
        void setemp( int n, Employee *ep) {
            group[n] = ep;
        }
    private:
        int Bonus;
        Employee* group[dim];
    };
```

the `Manager::setsalary()` override assigns the bonus to a separate data
member—Bonus—in the derived class. At this point, the bonus is not yet
part of the salary, so it can be easily shown that **Manager** does satisfy the
equation

$$[m.setsalary( n)].getsalary() == n$$

This implementation of **Manager** provides an explicit function—addbonus()
—for making the bonus part of the salary. In any event, what with the equation being satisfied, the substitution principle holds for the model program,
and we can say that **Manager** behaviorally inherits from **Employee**.

## 2.8   Explicit Giving of Bonus

Finally, here is an implementation of **class Manager**, which satisfies the
equation,

```
    class Manager : public Employee {
    public:
        void addbonus( int b)
        {
            Employee::setsalary( getsalary() + b);
        }

        Employee* getemp( int n)    { return group[n]; }
```

```
        void setemp( int n, Employee *ep) {
            group[n] = ep;
        }
    private:
        Employee* group[dim];
    };
```

wherein bonuses are added into the salary explicitly with the `Manager::` `addbonus()` member function. Notice that there is no special data member in `Manager` for storing the bonus. Satisfaction of the equation means that the substitution principle holds for the model program, and again we can say that `Manager` inherits behaviorally from `Employee`.

## 2.9  Behavioral Inheritance Guidelines

How can we ensure that class derivation also constitutes behavioral inheritance? The following guidelines will ensure it. Namely, for each public member function in the base class

- No override is in the derived class.

- Override must return same value as base class function would when applied to base part of derived class object.

- Let b be base class object with same initial state as base part of derived class object d. Override must change state of base part of d in same way as base class function changes state of b.

We can express these criteria unambiguously with the help of yet another fake C++ built-in operator - `baseof()`. For simplicity, let us assume that all inheritance is single inheritance. Then, if `x` is an object of some type derived from the base type `Base`

> baseof( x) returns base part of x

`baseof()` is a demoter or upcaster. In the context of our ongoing example, `baseof()` could be implemented as follows:

```
class Manager : public Employee { ... };

Employee& baseof( Manager m)
{
    return *((Employee *)&m);
}
```

So, in terms of `baseof()` and the state transition notation `[obj.func( arg)]`
class derivation is semantic inheritance if

```
for any public Employee member function foo() and
    and for all Manager objects m:

    // identical return values
    m.foo() == m.Employee::foo() // or equivalently ...
    m.foo() == baseof( m).foo()

    // identical state change on base parts
    // commutativity of baseof and [obj.func( ...)]
    baseof( [m.foo()]) == [baseof( m.foo())]
```

Again, this condition relates semantic and implementation of derived class
override to base class function. Here are some guidelines for deriving a class
D from a base class B, so that D behaviorally inherits from B. Paradigmatically
your code should look like

```
class D : public B {
public:
    R foo(X x)
    {
        // may modify derived class data members
        // should not modify base part of object
        return B::foo( x);
    }

    void bar(X x)
    {
        // may modify derived class data members
```

```
            // should not modify base part of object
            B::bar( x );    // location in code irrelevant
            // may modify derived class data members
            // should not modify base part of object
        }
    };
```

There are two cases. `foo()` represents the case in which the base class member function returns a value. `bar()` represents the case in which the base class member function returns nothing but possibly modifies the state of the object. Of course, the derived class override must have an identical signature. It is a useful exercise for the reader to verify that the four implementations of `class Manager` conform to this paradigm.

The preceding condition

- Heavily constrains possible derived class implementations.

- Completely determines the return value of a derived class operation in terms of the return value of the corresponding base class operation.

- Derived class override must change the state of the base part of a derived class object in a manner congruent with which the base class operation changes the state of free-floating base class objects.

- Derived class override is free to change the values in the additional derived class data members in any manner it sees fit.

To summarize, when does the class derivation of `Manager` from `Employee` also constitute behavioral inheritance? Answer: Check the above criteria in terms of `baseof()` and the state transition notation `[x.f(...)]`. The list below indicates which of the four implementations of `Manager` satisfy the criteria:

1. *Implementation 1:* Yes.

2. *Implementation 2:* No.

3. *Implementation 3:* Yes.

4. *Implementation 4:* Yes.

## 2.10  Denver Syndrome

I would like to talk about a particular situation that can only arise in the context of multiple inheritance, which I term the Denver syndrome because I first explained these materials to my C++ students in Denver.

Imagine an inheritance lattice (directed graph) consisting of a base class B, two classes derived from it—D1 and D2, and a grandchild class C derived from D1 and D2. For concreteness, let's imagine that

- B is the class `City`.

- D1 is the class `State Capital`, denoted `Capital`.

- D2 is the class `County Seat`.

- C is the class of all cities that are both state capitals as well as county seats (`class SCCS`).

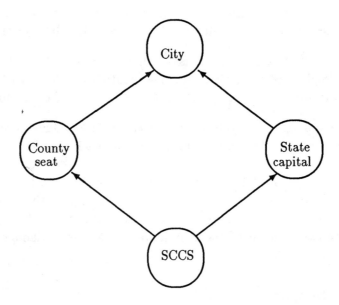

Doing the naive derivations in C++, we would obtain something like

```
class City {
public:
    void setname( String name)    { mayorname = name; }
private:
    String mayorname;
};

class CountySeat : public City {};

class Capital : public City {};

class SCCS : public CountySeat, public Capital {};
```

As indicated above, imagine that class City stores the name of its mayor using setname(). Now whether or not CountySeat or Capital override void City::setname( String), by the transitivity of class derivation, I should be able to invoke setname() against SCCS objects, should I not? In C++, the answer is in fact no, because as far as class SCCS is concerned, it is attempting to inherit two different member functions, one from class Capital and the other from class CountySeat that have the same signature

void setname( String);

This sort of name conflict is deemed a syntax error in C++. If it were legal syntax, what would it mean? Which setname() member function should be invoked, Capital's or CountySeat's? Worse, class derivation implies that both Capital and CountySeat objects have an anonymous data member of type City. Thus SCCS objects have two anonymous data members of type City and thus two places to store the mayor's name. Where should setname() store the name?

Symbolics Lisp solves this problem by selecting the setname() member function of CountySeat, which goes off and updates the mayor's name in the City part of a CountySeat object. That is, Symbolics Lisp's policy in case of member function name conflict is to select the first parent in the parentage "list" of a multiply derived class. This is called the *mix-in* policy. This is in marked contrast to the C++ policy that regards the parentage of a derived class as a mathematical set: no preferred order, no duplicate values.

Here are several different solutions to the Denver problem in C++. If we are
not concerned with having two `City` objects within an `SCCS` object, and are
only concerned with resolving the member function name conflict, we could
explicitly invoke the member function of our choice ( `setname()` in some
class derived from `City`) against an `SCCS` object using the scope resolution
operator

```
SCCS x;
String name( "mary");

x.CountySeat::setname( name);
x.Capital::setname( name);
```

Indeed, if `class SCCS` has an explicit `setname()` override, we may invoke it
by

```
class SCCS : public CountySeat, public Capital {
public:
    void setname( String);
    ...
};

SCCS x;
String name( "ed");

x.setname( name);
```

Of course, for `void SCCS::setname( String)` to be sensible, its body probably invokes one of its parent's `setname()`

```
void SCCS::setname( String n)
{
    ...
    Capital::setname( n);
    ...
}
```

If, on the other hand, we don't want to have two `City` objects within an `SCCS`
object, C++ provides us with an inheritance mechanism, called virtual base

classes, that will allow us to arrange for SCCS objects to have only one `City` base part and thus only one place for storing the mayor's name, which in the current example certainly seems like a more reasonable way to conduct business. Here is the syntax:

```
class City {};
class CountySeat : virtual public City {};
class Capital : virtual public City {};
class SCCS : public CountySeat, public Capital {};
// or optionally ...
class SCCS : public CountySeat, public Capital,
    virtual public City {};
```

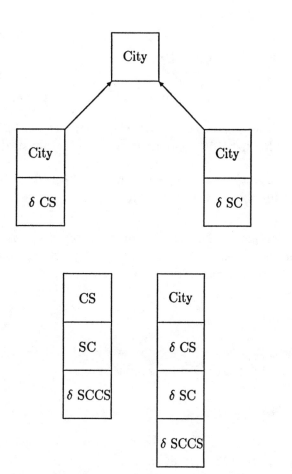

The preceding figure indicates how the data of an object of type SCCS is layed out in memory depending on whether the derivations involve virtual base classes or not. The upper picture describes the data layout of CountySeat and Capital objects. The lower-left diagram depicts the data layout of an SCCS object under the usual rules of class derivation. The lower-right diagram depicts the data layout of an SCCS object when City is a virtual base class.

From a design perspective, the problem with virtual base classes is that we have to decide to declare a class like City virtual very early in the design process, which completely eliminates the possibility of having two City base parts in its grandchildren (such as SCCS) or anything derived from its grandchildren. This is not so wonderful, for I can imagine scenarios in which it could be useful.

For example, a buffer in the UNIX block I/O buffer cache is always on two out of a possible three linked lists [BACH].

- *Free list:* Buffer is available for allocation to a hardware device.

- *Job queue:* One is associated with each disk device, for example. A buffer is on this list if it is currently undergoing physical I/O.

- *Hash list:* For ease of access, each buffer is hashed on the composite key (device number, block number).

In a manner analogous to the first implementation of class SCCS, class Buffer could be derived from two parent classes, each of which is singly derived from a class Linkable that looks like

```
class Linkable {
public:
    void set( Linkable* p)  { ngbr = p; }
    Linkable *islinkedto()  { return ngbr; }
private:
    Linkable *ngbr;
};


class LeftLink : public Linkable {};
```

```
class RightLink : public Linkable {};

class Buffer : public LeftLink, public RightLink {
    // buffer contents
};

Buffer b1, b2, b3;

b1.LeftLink::set( &b2);    // sets left link
b1.RightLink::set( &b3);   // sets right link
```

In the above example, the scope resolution operator (::) is effectively used to determine which `Linkable` base part of the `Buffer` object `b1` is set. For example, `b1.LeftLink::set( &b2)` sets the `Linkable` part of the `Left` base part of `b1` to the address of `b2`.

## 2.11  Private Class Derivation

This section discusses private class derivation and how it relates to behavioral inheritance and implementation hiding. We first review the semantics of public class derivation, which is all we have seen up until now. [STR]: if D is publicly derived from B,

```
    class D : public B { ... };
```

then all of the members of class B are members of D. In effect we can pretend that every D object contains an anonymous data member of type B. Furthermore, D objects inherit the implementation of B member functions. Thus, invoking a B member function against a D object is like invoking the function against D's anonymous data member of type B. By the way, this description applies equally to multiple inheritance as it does to single inheritance. A critical characteristic of public class derivation is that all `public` members of B become `public` members of D, that is, visible to users of D objects.

Here is a problem. Imagine a type queue of integers with the following public interface:

```
    class Queue {    // queue of integers
```

```
public:
    // initialize the queue to empty
    Queue();

    // returns TRUE if the queue is empty, else FALSE
    Boolean isempty() const;
    // returns TRUE if queue is full, else FALSE
    True isfull() const;

    // deletes and returns value at head of queue
    // precondition:  !isempty()
    int gethead();

    // make x the new head of the queue
    void puthead( int x);

    // delete and return the last element in the queue
    // precondition:  !isempty()
    int gettail();

    // make x the last element in the queue
    void puttail( int x);
private:
    ...
};
```

I won't trouble you with the implementation of class **Queue**. You can figure out the pointer gymnastics yourself. I can implement **class Stack** (page 17) by deriving it from **Queue**, so:

```
class Stack : public Queue {
public:
            Stack() : ();
            void push( int x)        { puthead( x); }
            int pop()                { return gethead(); }
            // Boolean isempty() is inherited
            // Boolean isfull() is inherited
    };
```

The beauty of this `Stack` implementation is that it reuses a great deal of `Queue`'s implementation, which presumably already exists. So there is a lot less work for me to do. The problem, however, is that `Stack` also inherits member functions that have nothing to do with the semantics of stacks. For example, I can

```
Stack stk;
...
stk.puttail( 37);
```

modify the base of the stack and thus corrupt its state. That is, successive popping will not reveal the very first element pushed on the stack but rather the number 37!

How can we resolve this conflict between class derivation and the intuitive semantics of `Stack`? The answer is by realizing the difference between behavioral inheritance and class derivation.

Applying behavioral inheritance to `Stack` and `Queue` earlier, it is clear that that `Stack` is not semantically derived from `Queue`, despite the use of class derivation, because `puttail()` and `gettail()` have no place in the public interface of `Stack`. What conclusions can be drawn from this? One conclusion is that class derivation does not always imply behavioral inheritance. Implementational inheritance (i.e., class derivation) is simply a way of building (implementing) new classes in terms of other classes. Indeed, language support for implementation inheritance does make it (relatively) easy to implement behavioral inheritance, but there is generally additional work left to do. Final conclusion: Because class derivation is an implementation technique, perhaps it should be hidden from view in a manner analogous to private data members. This approach is explored using the syntax of private class derivation in what follows.

All the inheritance examples seen so far have employed public derivation

```
class D : public B { ... }; // public derivation
```

which allows the sending of (public) base class messages to derived class objects. By contrast, in private derivation

```
class D : private B { ... }; // private derivation
```

which, unfortunately, is the default for class derivation

```
class D : B { ... };            // also private derivation
```

(public) base class operations cannot be invoked against derived class objects by other objects. However, in both visibilities of derivation, derived class member functions can invoke public base class member functions. What then is the use of private derivation, and how does it relate to the question at hand?

Private derivation is a means of hiding the use of implementation inheritance to construct new classes from old ones easily. Private derivation allows multiple classes to reuse implementation in an effortless manner. Here is an implementation of `Stack` that (privately) inherits the implementation of `Queue`. This solution solves the problem encountered in the public derivation of inheriting `Queue` member functions that have nothing to do with "stackness."

```
class Stack : private Queue {
public:
            Stack() : ();
            void push( int x)          { puthead( x); }
            int pop()                  { return gethead(); }
            Queue::isempty;
            Queue::isfull;
    };
```

Note the use of the scope resolution operator - :: - to render visible to `Stack` users the `Queue` member functions `isempty()` and `isfull()`, despite the privacy of the derivation. No other `Queue` member functions are accessible to `Stack` users.

One could just as easily have layered the implementation of `Stack` on top of `Queue`, as below:

```
class Stack {
public:
            Stack() : q() {}
            void push( int x)          { q.puthead( x); }
```

```
        int pop()               { return q.gethead(); }
        Boolean isempty() const { return q.isempty(); }
        Boolean isfull()  const { return q.isfull(); }
    private:
        Queue q;
};
```

That is, a `Stack` object has a single `Queue` data member, and the member functions of `Stack` are implemented (here trivially) in terms of the member functions of `Queue`. In fact, I can always convert the private derivation of a class D from a class B to a layered implementation

```
class D {
public:
    // member functions
private:
    B b;
    // other data members
};
```

wherein D contains a private data member of type B, and the member functions of D are implementated in terms of the member functions of B (and the other data members). Notice that layering is just a fancy word for data hiding, which is certainly a far more fundamental concept than private derivation. As a computer language instructor, I would expect most C++ programmers to master data hiding (and there are those who don't). Even experienced C++ programmers have trouble with private derivation!

This canonical conversion of private derivation into layering is troubling, because it leads to the conclusion that private derivation is excess baggage, which complicates a language that is growing evermore complex as the the years go by.

## 2.12   Protected Visibility and Class Derivation

Protected visibility is a C++ feature that allows a base class to present a different interface to derived classes from the usual interface presented by private-public visibility. By definition [LIP], a protected member m in a base class B

```
class B {
...
protected:
     int m;
...
};
```

is visible to any member function of any class derived from B (and, of course, to any member function of B itself). m is not visible (as if private) to anybody else.

Protected visibility is normally used to simplify the implementation of derived classes by permitting them access to protected base class data members. This usage is a *prima facie* violation of implementation and data hiding, for it couples together the implementation of base and derived classes. The situation is worse than it appears. From a design and reuse perspective, a good base class is one that is fruitful, that is, has many (children) classes derived from it. With the above usage of protected scope, when the data structure of a base class changes (and it will), potentially the code of each member function of every derived class may have to be modified. This is a maintenance nightmare!

What is a solution? Simply rigorously apply the principle of implementation hiding by forbidding the presence of data members in the protected portion of any class. Instead, provide a (base) class with an interface of protected member functions. Derived classes are thus insulated from changes of implementation in the base class, because they never directly access any data members—of any visibility—in the base class, only member functions of either public or protected scope. When the base class implementation changes, the protected interface is reimplemented along with the rest of the class.

To illustrate these and other problems and their solution, let's take a look at a hierarchy based on class File:

```
# include <stdio.h>
typedef int Boolean;
class File { // Implementation layered on FILE
public:
    File( char *name = "", char *mode = "r")
    {
```

```
        if( *name )
            fp = fopen( name, mode);
        else if( *mode == 'r' )
            fp = stdin;
        else
            fp = stdout;
        state = (int)fp;
    }

    ~File()                  { if( fp) fclose( fp); }

    Boolean isok() const     { return state; }

    Boolean iseof() const    { return feof( fp); }

    int get()                { return getc( fp); }
    // unget and peek useful for lexical scanners
    void unget(int c)        { (void)ungetc( c, fp); }

    int peek()  { int c = get(); unget(c); return c; }

    void put( int c)         { putc( c, fp); }
private:
    FILE *fp;
    int state;
};
```

class File is implemented on top of the standard I/O FILE abstraction [KR]. Opening a file is handled by the constructor, and closing a file is handled automatically by the destructor on the death of the File object.

Imagine two classes—Rfile and Wfile—derived from File. A Rfile object can only be opened for reading

```
    class Rfile : public File {
    public:
        Rfile( char *name = "") : ( name, "r");
    };
```

and a Wfile object can only be opened for writing

```
class Wfile : public File {
public:
    Rfile( char *name = "") : ( name, "w" );
};
```

The above implementations make deft use of constructors to ensure that a
Rfile object can only be opened for reading, and a Wfile object can only
be opened for writing. Both Rfile and Wfile objects are closed properly
because they inherit the (public) File destructor. However, one can still
attempt to write to a Rfile object

```
Rfile rf( "foo");
rf.put( 'a');
```

or read from a Wfile object

```
Wfile wf( "bar");
int c = wf.get();
```

both of which actions are nonsense at runtime, but nonetheless permissible
under the current scenario, because put() and get() are in the public portion of the base class File, and are thus visible to all users of derived class
objects. How can protected scope help solve this problem?

Place get() and put() (as well as peek() and unget()) in a protected
portion of class File

```
# include <stdio.h>
typedef int Boolean;
class File { // Implementation layered on FILE
public:
    File( char *name = "", char *mode = "r") {
                        /* implemented as before */ }
    ~File()             { if( fp) fclose( fp); }

    Boolean isok() const  { return state; }

    Boolean iseof() const { return feof( fp); }
protected:              // only visible to derived class
```

```
                         // member functions
    int get()                    { return getc( fp); }

    void unget(int c)      { (void)ungetc( c, fp); }

    int peek()  { int c = get(); unget(c); return c; }

    void put( int c)        { putc( c, fp); }
private:
    FILE *fp;
    int state;
};
```

and selectively override get() and put() in the derived classes

```
    class Rfile : public File {
    public:
        Rfile( char *name = "") : ( name, "r");

        int get()     { return File::get(); }
    };

    class Wfile : public File {
    public:
        Rfile( char *name = "") : ( name, "w" );

        void put( int c)     { File::put( c); }
    };
```

The use of the scope resolution operator— :: —above prevents recursion.
Note that it is now a syntax (compile time) error to write (put()) to a Rfile
object or read (get()) from a Wfile object, respectively.

I would like to summarize in tabular form recommended usage of protected
as well as public and private visibility under class derivation:

| Visibility | Member function | Data member |
|------------|-----------------|-------------|
| public | Public interface | **No!** |
| protected | Special interface<br>Visible to derived<br>Class member functions | **No!** |
| private | Factor common<br>Implementation from<br>Public member functions | Represent object state |

## 2.13  Summary

We have presented several different definitions of inheritance, all of which fall into one of the two categories:

- Inheritance of behavior (semantics)

- Inheritance of implementation

The message I want to leave you with is

> *Use class derivation to implement behavioral inheritance!*

Doing this requires us to be more precise in how we specify the behavior of a type. Our choice is algebraic (equational) specification. Guidelines have been presented for ensuring that class derivation is also behavioral inheritance. These guidelines constitute an infringement on the totally untrammeled freedom of the programmer to do what she or he wants! A benefit of this discipline is the ability to predict much of the behavior of programs written in terms of derived type objects from a knowledge of the behavior of the base type, without having to cheat by looking under the hem at implementation. Verifying that the guidelines have indeed been followed is a task eminently suited for mechanization. There is no such thing as a free lunch. If you want quality software, you have to build the quality in. I believe that behavioral inheritance ought to be part of the definition of quality for object-oriented software.

# Bibliography

[CHJ]     B. Cohen, W. T. Harwood, M. I. Jackson, *The Specification of Complex Systems*, 1986, Addison-Wesley.

[DIJ]     Edgsger Dijkstra, "Goto statement considered harmful," *Communications of the Association for Computing Machinery*, pp. 147–148, 11 March 1968.

[KR]      Brian Kernighan and Dennis Ritchie, *The C Programming Language*, second edition, 1988, Prentice Hall.

[MORRIS] Joseph Morris, "Piecewise Data Refinement," Edsger Dijkstra (editor), *Formal Development of Programs and Proofs*, pp. 117–138, Addison-Wesley, 1990.

# Chapter 3

# Dynamic Binding

## 3.1 What Is Dynamic Binding?

The purpose of this chapter on dynamic binding is primarily motivational. That is, I am more concerned with why dynamic binding is a useful software engineering concept—what problems it solves, both at design and implementation time—rather than with the mechanics of how it is accomplished. Nonetheless, this first section defines dynamic binding and shows how it can be implemented in C++ using `virtual` member functions.

Our working definition of dynamic binding is the ability of an object to bind—dynamically at runtime—a message to an action (or code fragment, if you will). The idea is that, in a given system, many different objects may respond to the same message—say `print` (i.e., display yourself to a display device); they just respond differently. Another way of putting it is that, although a collection of objects may all respond generically in the same way to a message (i.e., display yourself), the precise details of *how* a given object responds depends on its type. In most object-oriented languages (including C++, Eiffel and Smalltalk), dynamic binding is subject to the following restrictions:

- Every object is an instance of a type.

- All objects of the same type respond with the same action (code fragment) to a given message.

- The types participating in dynamic binding must share (inherit from) a common ancestor (parent, grandparent, ... ) type.

In summary, under dynamic binding

> *Every object knows its type at runtime.*

Dynamic binding is part of a spectrum of binding mechanisms that are characterized by the time at which the binding of code to name occurs. At one extreme, in languages like pascal or ada, all procedure names are bound to code by the end of compilation. This is called static binding. At the other extreme, deferred binding defers (symbol table) look-up of the code corresponding to a name until just before invocation. As we will see, dynamic binding in C+ is an (compiler) optimized form of deferred binding.

Deferred binding is the message-binding mechanism in Smalltalk. Furthermore, all types (user-defined or otherwise) are ultimately derived from an ur-type called `object`.

In contrast, in C++ there is no ur-type from which all types are derived. Indeed, one cannot derive a class from a built-in type—`char`, `int`, `float`, `double`, ..., as in the bad example below:

```
// this class has a syntax error!
class BadExample : public int {
public:
    void foo()  { x = 6; }
private:
    int x;
};
```

Furthermore in C++, the default-binding mechanism in the message expression is static binding—all message expressions are bound to a specific function address by the end of compilation, and it is the one that corresponds to the lexical type of the variable (or pointer) referring to the object.

```
class Frog {
public:
    void hop()  { ...; printf( "Frog\n"); }
    ...
```

```
private:
    ...
};

class TreeFrog : public Frog {
public:
    // override
    void hop()  { ...; printf( "TreeFrog\n"); }
    ...
};

Frog kermit;
Frog *p = &kermit;
TreeFrog lulu;
Frog *q = &lulu;

kermit.hop();       // kermit.Frog::hop()
lulu.hop();         // lulu.TreeFrog::hop()
p->hop();           // p->Frog::hop()
q->hop();           // q->Frog::hop() ... surprise!
```

In the preceding example, the smalltalker is unpleasantly surprised when she
or he discovers that the message expression q->hop() results in the runtime
invocation of the base class Frog::hop() function rather than the derived
class member function TreeFrog::hop().

The C++ programmer must explicitly request dynamic binding for a particular message (member function) by declaring it to be **virtual** in the base
class

```
class Frog {
public:
    // request dynamic binding
    virtual void hop()  { ...; printf( "Frog\n"); }
    ...
private:
    ...
};
```

```
class TreeFrog : public Frog {
public:
    // override
    void hop()  { ...; printf( "TreeFrog\n"); }
    ...
};

Frog kermit;
Frog *p;
TreeFrog lulu;

kermit.hop();      // kermit.Frog::hop()
lulu.hop();        // lulu.TreeFrog::hop()
p = &kermit;
p->hop();          // p->Frog::hop()
p = &lulu;
p->hop();          // p->TreeFrog::hop() ... as desired
```

It is a fact in C++ that a base class pointer (such as p) may point to any object of any type **publicly** derived from the base type. When a base class member function (such as `Frog::hop()` is declared **virtual**, the message expression `p->hop()` is interpreted in the following way:

> Invoke at runtime the `hop()` member function, which corresponds to the (derived) type of the object that the pointer p is pointing to currently. If the object's class has no override for `hop()` use the parent (base) class `hop()`.

Message expressions of the form `variable.f(...)` such as `kermit.hop()` and `lulu.hop()` are always statically bound in C++, owing to the fact that the lexical and dynamic type of the variable is always the same. With pointers like p there is a duplicity: The lexical type of the pointer is one thing (`Frog*` ), but the type of object that p points to can be anything derived from Frog.

## 3.2  Why Should You Care?

Now that we know what dynamic binding is, as well as how to accomplish it in C++, why should we care about the idea? For insight, let's look back again at our example of Frogs and TreeFrogs. In the dynamically bound message expression p->hop(), p can refer to any object of any type (publicly) derived from the base type **Frog** as well as to base type objects. The hop() code that is invoked depends on the type of object p points to.

Imagine the kinds of programs that can be written in terms of the dynamically bound message expression p->hop(). What is the dependency of such a program on the precise type of object that p points to? Very little. The only thing the program depends on is that the object p points to is a kind of **Frog** and that it is capable of hopping. Indeed if we focus our attention on the set of **virtual** member functions in the public interface of **Frog** and write programs in terms of dynamically bound message expressions in those member functions, those programs depend not a whit on the precise type of the objects, but rather on, as it were, a generic interface established in the **Frog** base class that describes all types that were, are, and ever will be derived from **Frog**.

Programs written in such a manner are open-ended and thus highly reusable. Today my program handles Frogs and TreeFrogs. Tomorrow, with little or no modification, it can additionally handle Toads, CaveFrogs, and who knows what other types as long as they are derived from **Frog**. A single such program in essence constitutes an entire infinite family of programs parameterized by the types in the inheritance tree stemming from **Frog**.

One of the fundamental challenges facing the software community is dealing with change [COX]. The incredible decline in the cost of computer hardware, the resulting change in the trade-off between the cost of programmers and the cost of hardware and software, and the accelerating demands of customers for increasingly sophisticated software to make use of powerful and relatively cheap hardware all require that an evolving software product must be able to handle the following kinds of change with minimal cost:

- Change in implementation (data structures and algorithms)

- Change in system requirements (behavior) demanded by our customers, most notably in the form of enhancement to existing system functionality

Chapter 1 discusses the principle of implementation hiding using types and objects to localize and compartmentalize changes in the implementation of an evolving system. Inheritance, conversely, is an excellent tool for managing change—notably enhancement—in the behavior of an evolving system. Typically, enhancement to the behavior of a system results in enhancing the behavior of existing types through inheritance as well as the creation of new types. Inheritance—even without dynamic binding—is an excellent technique for reusing existing types in the construction of new ones in a kind of incremental development that does not break existing code.

As described above, dynamic binding provides us with an additional tool for rendering a system implementation reusable in the face of changing requirements. The tricky part from a design perspective is figuring out just what generic (virtual member function) interface the various base types ought to have to accommodate expected changes (enhancements) in system behavior. Reuse has to be architected into a system design and implementation, and that is hard work, make no mistake. The consolation is that object-oriented programming provides a rich selection of tools—here specifically dynamic binding—for building reusable, easy-to-enhance system architectures. Furthermore, C++'s syntactic support for object-oriented concepts such as inheritance and dynamic binding greatly eases implementation of such robust system architectures.

What we are attempting to do in this chapter is to motivate dynamic binding and to provide some intuition and insight into its use and its consequences. The intuition of dynamic binding agrees nicely with the substitution principle used by Barbara Liskov [LSK2] to define semantic (subtype) hierarchy (see page 59 for a statement of the substitution principle).

## 3.3   Unions and Switch Case

Many a time, a thing is understood and appreciated more by contrast with its alternatives than from its intrinsic merits. It is in this spirit that I want to present several alternatives to dynamic binding as a central force in the architecture of a system. In summary, a problem is presented, that of sketching out the design of a graphics editor. An architectural solution is presented in terms of unions and switch-case statements. This solution is equivalent to a cascade of if ...  then ...  else's so nothing more need be said about if ... constructs. Another solution is presented that employs pointers to functions. The third solution is given in C++ employing inheritance and dynamic binding. All three solutions are discussed with particular attention paid to the languages in which they can be implemented.

Let us sketch out a portion of a graphics editor. This matter is discussed in great detail as a design case study in chapter 8. Following the heuristic

> *As you structure the data, so must you write the algorithms.*

We proceed to talk about data first. The picture managed by a graphics editor consists of different kinds of shape objects. Certainly one of the operations that we must implement is the display of each shape to the display device. It is certainly possible that each kind of shape may require special code that knows how to display it. How can we accomplish this? We could represent shape objects with the classical data structure of a discriminated union, which in general looks like

```
struct Shape {
    int typetag;  // small positive integer
    U u;
};
```

where the `typetag` is a small positive integer that tells which part of the union variable u is to be selected. The union U contains a member for each kind of shape, thus

```
// values for the typetag
const int POINT = 1,
          LINE  = 2,
          TEXT  = 3,
          BOX   = 4,
          // and so on ...

union U {
    PointData point;    // corresponds to typetag = POINT
    LineData  line;     // corresponds to typetag = LINE
    TextData  text;     // corresponds to typetag = TEXT
    BoxData   box;      // corresponds to typetag = BOX
    // and so on ...
};
```

where PointData, LineData, TextData, BoxData ...  are data structures (no member functions).  As indicated, a typetag value of LINE indicates that the union actually contains a LineData object and so on. Whenever a shape object is created, its data members must be initialized appropriately, for example, in the following manner in C:

```
Shape text;

text.typetag = TEXT;
text.u.text.x_position = ...;
text.u.text.y_position = ...;
...
```

For simplicity, let's imagine that the picture aggregate is represented by an
array of Shape's. Then we could certainly display a picture in the following
way:

```
    void display(Shape picture[ ], int numPicts)
    {
        int i;

        for (i = 0; i < numPicts; i++) {
            switch (picture[i].typetag) {
            case POINT:
                /* code to display a point */
                pointdisplay( picture[i].u.point);
                break;
            case LINE:
                /* code to display a line */
                linedisplay( picture[i].u.line);
                break;
            case TEXT:
                /* code to display a text */
                textdisplay( picture[i].u.text);
                break;
            case BOX:
                /* code to display a box */
                boxdisplay( picture[i].u.box);
                break;
```

```
        // and so on ...
        }
    }
}
```

Now this approach is fine as far as it goes. It solves the problem of displaying a picture. But what if our customer comes back three months later and says that she or he now wants to be able to manipulate triangles? She has just enhanced the requirements on us! Here is what has to be done:

- Select a small positive integer to represent triangles in the `typetag` in the discriminated union. Make sure that it does not conflict with the other typetags

  ```
  const int TRIANGLE = 5;
  ```

- Design a data structure for triangles `TriangleData` and add it to the union `U`

  ```
  union U {
      PointData point;       // corresponds to typetag = POINT
      LineData  line;        // corresponds to typetag = LINE
      TextData  text;        // corresponds to typetag = TEXT
      BoxData   box;         // corresponds to typetag = BOX
      TriangleData triangle;// corresponds to typetag = TRIANGLE
                             // and so on ...
  };
  ```

- Implement a function capable of displaying a triangle `triangledisplay()`

- Add to the switch-case statement in the picture `display()` function the case

  ```
      case TRIANGLE:
          triangledisplay( picture[i].u.triangle);
          break;
          ...
  ```

This architecture is a software engineering and maintenance nightmare for a variety of reasons. First, the programmer must implement the notion that the object knows its type explicitly with a typetag. Keeping the typetag integers straight after the number of types grows into the twenties is no small task. Whenever the graphics editor requirements are extended by a new kind of Shape, a tremendous amount of work has to be done, including adding a case for that type into the picture display() function. In other words we have to do surgery on a perfectly healthy function, running the risk of making it sick! Here I am reminded of Fred Brooks's dictum in *The Mythical Man Month* [BROOKS] that whenever you touch a correct piece of code, the odds are 50% that you will break it. For example, in the C++ and C switch-case statement, you must terminate each case with a break statement or you will drop through to the next case. Flexible as this is, most of the time we just want to execute one case and leave the switch-case statement. Many is the time that I have forgotten the terminating break; how many times have you? In contrast Pascal and ada have a switch-case construct in which the only thing you can do is execute the case and leave the construct.

This is not the end of the horror. There seems to be a software law of entropy that states: If there is one switch-case statement in an application, then there are probably ten! That is, switch case will be used to implement all the generic properties of the shape object, such as display, translate, rotate, scale.... Thus a system architecture based on discriminated union and switch case does not seem like a good bet for the long haul of the total system life cycle, the bulk of which is maintenance and enhancement. As we will see shortly, there are ways of programming that harken unto the wisdom of the aphorism

*If it's not broken, don't fix it!*

## 3.4   Solution with Pointers to Functions

As alluded to earlier, shape objects can do more than display themselves; they can also move in the plane, rotate, and scale. Here is a software architecture for the graphics editor based on pointers to functions that implement these behaviors in a manner consistent with our definition of dynamic binding. Imagine that the data structure for a shape is

```
struct Shape {
    PF *vtbl;
    // other data members
};
```

where `vtbl` is interpreted as the address of an array of objects of type `PF`.
`PF` is a pointer to a function taking `Shape` (and possibly other arguments)

```
typedef void (*PF)( Shape*, /* other arguments */ );
```

The reason that the first argument in the functional prototype above is
pointer to `Shape` is because the function needs to be able to change the
state of the shape object. Although the same effect can be accomplished in
C++ with an argument of type reference to `Shape`

```
typedef void (*PF)( Shape&, /* other arguments */ );
```

the pointer signature renders the design implementable in (ANSI) C. Let's
associate with each generic operation on shape objects (display, translate,
rotate, scale ...) a small non-negative integer

```
const unsigned int
            DISPLAY   = 0,
            TRANSLATE = 1,
            ROTATE    = 2,
            SCALE     = 3
            ...
```

and apply the following protocol to the `vtbl` pointer in any `Shape` object:
`vtbl` points to an array of function pointers. There is one such array for each
kind of shape. So, if for example, the editor supports point, line, text, and
box, then there must be 4 arrays. All the arrays are of the same dimension,
which is equal to the number of generic operations (here 4). All of the `Shape`
objects of the same kind point to the same array. The $j$th slot in any of
the arrays contains the address of a function that implements the generic
graphics operation appropriately for its kind. For example, the slot with
index `DISPLAY` in each array contains the address of a function capable of
displaying the object—appropriately as a function of the object's "type" to

the display device.  Thus the `vtbl` data member plays the role of object typetag at runtime.

As indicated in the following picture, here is how it works.  Say we have a pointer to a `Shape`, `shapeptr`, and we want to display the referenced object. We simply write

```
Shape *shapeptr;
...
shapeptr = /* address of any shape object */
(*shapeptr->vtbl[DISPLAY])( shapeptr);
```

We can now rewrite the picture display function in the following manner:

```
void display(Shape *picture, int numPicts)
{
    int i;
    Shape *p;
```

```
for (i = 0; i < numPicts; i++) {
    p = &(picture[i]);
    (*(p->vtbl[DISPLAY]))( p);  // dynamic binding
}
}
```

The preceding code is a good example of how dynamic binding is implemented in C using pointers to functions. Indeed, the original AT&T Bell Laboratories C++ compiler—cfront—which produces C code, implements virtual member functions (that is, dynamic binding) in a manner not far different from that described earlier.

Dynamic binding is not a new idea. The UNIX operating system kernel, which is written almost entirely in C, is and has always been chock full of function pointer tables [BACH]. In particular, the independence of UNIX from particular external devices (disks, terminals, network devices ...) is a result of the canonical interface that the operating system expects of any device. Very roughly, UNIX expects every device to make known to the kernel the addresses of four device-specific functions, which correspond to opening, closing, reading and writing the device. The kernel, at boot time, places the addresses of these functions in switch tables indexable by the type of device, which is represented by the major device number [BACH].

Notice something wonderful about the function pointer architecture: the picture `display()` function earlier is completely reusable; it never has to be rewritten as new shape types are added to the repetoire of the graphics editor. *Mirabile dictu*, the code of the `display()` function is also independent of additions to the generic set of operations supported by the graphics editor: Leaving out the details, simply tack the addresses of the functions corresponding to new operations onto the end of each array. However, here is what has to be done for each new kind of shape:

- Write the type-specific functions corresponding to the generic shape operations: display, move, rotate, scale ...

- Create a (global) array PF `type-specific-table[DIM]` (where DIM is the number of operations), and initialize it with the addresses of the new type's functions.

- Whenever instantiating a `Shape` object, make sure to initialize its `vtbl` field to the array that represents the object's type.

- For each generic `Shape` operation one writes a function similar in style to `display()` for performing that operation against the picture as a whole.

In sum, the function pointer architecture is quite robust in the face of changing system requirements. However, it involves its share of administrivia, namely the very fact that the programmer must implement dynamic binding (i.e., the concept that the object knows its type at runtime). The `Shape` object has an explicit typetag field `vtbl` that must be properly initialized. The programmer must establish a correspondence between small integers and the generic operation interface of `Shape`. The programmer must create function pointer arrays, one per type of shape, and properly initialize them.

This is a lot of work, all of which is subject to the possibility of error, of implementing it incorrectly. Wouldn't it be nice if there were a language that directly supported dynamic binding, for then there would be much less code for the programmer to write (and get wrong). In essence, the compiler writes the code (presumably correctly every time) for dynamic binding, not the programmer. This point fulfills the proverb

> *You can't put a bug in a piece of code that isn't there!*

As we see in the next section, the answer to our wistful prayer is yes in C++, where dynamic binding can be elegantly implemented via `virtual` member functions.

## 3.5   Solution to Problem in C++

C++ directly supports the concepts of inheritance and dynamic binding with class derivation and `virtual` class member functions, respectively, so we will make use of them here. Here is a summary of the graphics editor architecture to be presented. `Shape` is a base class from which are derived the various kinds of graphical objects, such as `Circle`, `Triangle`, `Box` in the picture on the following page.

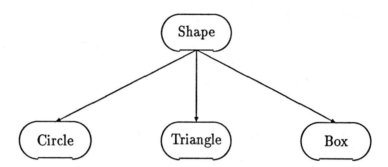

By declaring the generic graphics editor operations display, translate, rotate, scale ... as **virtual** member functions in the public interface of **class Shape**, we are at liberty to over-ride their implementations in the derived classes. Then at runtime, the message expression

```
Shape *p;
...
p = <address of object of type derived from Shape>;
p->genericfunction( ...);
```

is dynamically bound, that is, has the following interpretation: Invoke the derived class version of the generic function corresponding to the type of the object that the pointer p points to.

Because all graphics objects have a position in the plane, we can factor out the member functions and data structures that represent the position property into the base class **Shape**, as indicated below:

```
class Shape {
public:
    Shape(int x, int y) : pos( x, y) {}
    void move( int newx, int newy)   { pos.set( newx, newy); }
    int getx() const          { return pos.getx(); }
    int gety() const          { return pos.gety(); }
    virtual void display() { error( "display not overridden"); }
    virtual void rotate()  { error( "rotate not overridden"); }
```

```
    virtual void scale()   { error( "scale not overridden"); }
    // other member functions
private:
    Position pos;
    void error( char *p);  // display error message
        // appropriately for windowing system and
        // display device
};
```

Note above how the private member function `error()` factors common implementation out of the public member functions. In terms of a `Position` class, we can easily implement the `move()` member function, which translates the object to a new position. Similarly, we can query a shape as to its position by using its `getx()`, `gety()` functions. The design is such that all derived types are to inherit the `move()`, `getx()`, `gety()` functions—which represent the position property—without override. Conversely, a derived class is supposed to override any base class `Shape` member function tagged `virtual`, such as `display()`. Indeed, as indicated above, the base class virtual functions can serve a debugging function, reminding the developer to provide an override.

We have purposely posited the existence of a `Position` class, so as to be able to delay decisions about the precise details of the implementation of the position property for shapes. Nonetheless we have a pretty good idea of its interface:

```
class Position {
public:
    Position( int x, int y);  // initialize (x,y) coordinates
    void set( int x, int y);  // set coordinates
    int getx() const;         // get x coordinate
    int gety() const;         // get y coordinate
private:
    // data representation
};
```

The data representation could be a pair of integers representing the (x,y) cartesian coordinates, or $(r, \theta)$ polar coordinates. Developers of commercial graphics editors [CORELL] favor generalizing the `Position` type to representing the bounding box of the shape, that is, the smallest rectangle in the plane, with sides parallel to the $x$ and $y$ axes, respectively, which contains the shape. This makes it easy to map individual shapes to windows in some underlying windowing package. The public interface of such a **Position** type might look something like this.

```
class Position {
public:
    Position( int x, int y, int h, int w);
    void set( int x, int y, int h, int w);
    int getx() const;       // get x coordinate
    int gety() const;       // get y coordinate
    int geth() const;       // get the height h
    int getw() const;       // get the width w
private:
    // data representation
};
```

The constructor initializes the (x,y) coordinates of the lower left-hand corner of the bounding box, and its height h and width. The interpretation of the **set()** function arguments is the same; this function basically does what the constructor does, but at any time during the life of the object. The **get...** functions simply inspect the indicated values. To simplify the discussion, we shall use the first, simpler version of **Position**.

Here is a sketch of a derived class implementation for **class Circle**:

```
class Circle: public Shape {
public:
    Circle(int x, int y, int r) : Shape( x, y), radius( r) {}
    void display()   { /* Circle display code */ }
    void rotate()    { /* Circle rotate code */ }
    void scale()     { /* Circle scale code */ }
    int getradius()  { return radius; }
private:
    int radius;
};
```

In addition to overriding the base class virtual member functions, **Circle** has an additional property—the radius—mediated by the additional member function `getradius()`. In general, all of the classes derived from `Shape` will be of the same form as `Circle`: a constructor that invokes the base class constructor as well as initializing derived-class-specific data, implementation of the generic shape interface through overrides to the base class virtual member functions, and additional derived-class-specific member functions and data members.

We want to adhere to the design principle that

> *Everything in the system is an object.*

Consequently every function must find a home as a member function in the public interface of some class. Applying this dictum to the entire picture that the graphics editor manages, the picture itself must be a type of object. A little extra thought leads to the conclusion that `Picture` must be derived from `Shape`, because, after all, at a minimum it makes sense to invoke any generic `Shape` operation (such as display or rotate) against `Picture` objects, never mind what additional operations there are in the public interface of `Picture`. Below is a partial implementation of `Picture` in the spirit of this dictum:

```
const int DIM = 128;          // maximal number of shapes
    // in the picture
class Picture : public Shape {
public:
        Picture(int x, int y) : Shape( x, y), npics(0) {}

        void display()
        {
            for( int j = 0; j < npics; j++)  {
                Shape *p = picarray[j];
                p->display();
            }
        }

        void rotate()    { /* Picture rotate code */ }
        void scale()     { /* Picture scale code */ }
        // additional member functions
private:
```

```
        Shape *picarray[DIM];
    int npics;      // actual number of shapes in the picture
};
```

We represent a `Picture` as an array of pointers to `Shape` (`picarray[]`). I leave it to the reader to design and implement member functions for inserting and deleting shape addresses into a picture. The `Picture::display()` function walks the array and dynamically binds the `display()` message to each shape object whose address is contained therein.

The lovely thing about the `Picture::display()` function is that it *never* has to be modified as additional derived `Shape` types are added to the repetoire of the graphics editor. It depends on the generic fact that any object of type derived from `Shape` knows how to display itself appropriately. The same will hold true for all the member functions in `Picture` that override virtual member functions in the base class `Shape`. All of their implementations, if done in a manner similar to `Picture::display()`, are independent of the precise (derived) types of the objects "contained" in the picture. The *only* restriction is that the type be derived from `Shape`. So, for example, if we extend the graphics editor with a new type, say `Triangle`, the only thing we have to do is to declare that type is derived from `Shape` and implement it, as sketched out subsequently.

```
    class Triangle : public Shape {
    public:
        Triangle(int x, int y, int b, int h) :
            Shape( x, y), base( b), height( h) {}
        void display()   { /* Triangle display code */ }
        void rotate()    { /* Triangle rotate code */ }
        void scale()     { /* Triangle scale code */ }
        // other member functions ...
    private:
        int base;
        int height;
    };
```

This object-oriented design of the graphics editor in C++ exhibits a significant amount of code reuse, both in the factorization of the position property (both data structure and algorithms) of all shapes, as well as in the reusability of the implementation of the generic shape operations in `class Picture` through dynamic binding. Significant by its absence is any need on the part of the programmer to implement explicitly a typetag in the shape object, as we saw in the two previous designs. Here, by contrast

$$\boxed{\textit{The typetag of an object is its class!}}$$

and it is all taken care of by the C++ compiler.

## 3.6   Abstract Base Types and Pure Virtual Member Functions

A design question that arises in the context of inheritance is: Are there going to be any instances of the base type in a running program? If the answer is yes, then the implementation of the base class Shape given earlier is just fine.  Conversely, if it doesn't make sense to create base class objects at runtime, the C++ language provides compile-time checking for this notion in the form of pure virtual member functions.  The programmer needs to declare pure virtual at most one of the base class member functions (as shown in the modified implementation of **class Shape** subsequently)

```
class Shape {
public:
    Shape(int x, int y) : pos( x, y) {}
    void move( int newx, int newy)  { pos.set( newx, newy); }
    int getx() const          { return pos.getx(); }
    int gety() const          { return pos.gety(); }
    virtual void display() = 0; // pure virtual member function
    virtual void rotate()  = 0; // pure virtual member function
    virtual void scale()   = 0; // pure virtual member function
    // other member functions
private:
Position pos;
    void error( char *p);  // display error message
         // appropriately for windowing system and
         // display device
};
```

which has the following consequences: A pure virtual member function has no implementation in the base class. It must be overridden in each derived class. Not to do so constitutes a syntax error. The presence of at least one pure virtual member function in the base class renders it impossible to instantiate base class objects, except as one of the base parts of a derived class object.

In object-oriented parlance, a base class that is never to be instantiated is called an *abstract base class*. Its role is to server as the bearer for a generic interface (of (pure) virtual member functions), which remains to be implemented in the derived classes. If you will, an abstract base class establishes the semantics (specification, manual page) for the entire inheritance tree for which it is the root. Nonetheless, an abstract base class in C++ may have implementation, such as for the position property in `class Shape` earlier, which is shared by all of its derived classes in the usual way.

## 3.7  Summary

Dynamic binding, together with inheritance, has everything to do with the perception that object-oriented programming is stable: Small changes in the requirements for a system do not lead to large amounts of change in design and implementation. This was certainly seen to be the case in the graphics editor, where adding a new kind of shape to the editor's repetoire resulted in only a moderate amount of additional work, indeed an amount of work "linearly" proportional to the requirements for the new shape. Also the rules of class derivation ensure that adding new code in derived classes never requires modification of and possibly breaking old (base class) code.

I leave it to you, the reader, to judge between the three architectures presented (switch case, function pointer, virtual member function) as to which is superior from a software engineering viewpoint, that is from the viewpoint of reuse of design and implementation, ease of enhancement, and so on.

Finally, I would like to summarize the design heuristics sprinkled throughout the chapter:

- Every object knows its type at runtime.

- As you structure the data, so must you write the algorithms.

- If it's not broken, don't fix it!

- You can't put a bug in a piece of code that isn't there!

- Everything in the system is an object.

- The typetag of an object *is* its class.

# Bibliography

[BACH]  Maury Bach, *Internals of the UNIX System Kernel*, 1987, Addison-Wesley.

[BROOKS]  Frederick P. Brooks Jr., *The Mythical Man Month*, 1982, Addison-Wesley.

[CORELL]  Personal conversation with the vice-president of Research and Development for Corell.

[COX]  Brad Cox, *Object-Oriented Programming: An Evolutionary Approach*, 1986, Addison-Wesley.

[LSK2]  B. Liskov, "Data Abstraction and Hierarchy," addendum to *Conference Proceedings: Object-Oriented Programming Systems Languages and Applications* (OOPSLA), 1987. (Liskov's approach to object-oriented design, specifically addresses inheritance.)

# Chapter 4

# Parametry

## 4.1  Introduction

A parameterized type is roughly a one-parameter (possibly infinite) family
of types, where the parameter itself ranges over types. More to the point,
we are interested in parameterized types that possess a single manual page
(specification or behavior), which is—as it were—textually parameterized
by the same (dummy) type parameter as the family of types itself. The
benefit is implicit in our very definition of parameterized types: massive
reuse of specification. A single (parameterized) manual page serves to specify a (possibly infinite) family of types. Under many circumstances, we
can find a single parameterized implementation for a parameterized type.
With proper language support for parameterized types, the benefit is clear:
massive software reuse.

Parametrization is a fundamental mathematical concept. It simply means
that I have a function $f$ that maps each element $x$ of a domain set $X$ to
some element $y$ of a range set $Y$

$$f : X \to Y$$
$$f(x) = y$$

The benefit of parametrization includes both the reuse of design as well as
code. It identifies—in a compact manner—an entire family of computations
parameterized by the domain set $X$. Parametrization lifts the problem of
calculating a particular value (constant) $y$ to the problem of specifying and

111

implementing a function $f$ that will calculate potentially an infinite number of $y$'s corresponding to an infinite number of $x$'s. That is, we need not write a separate program to calculate $y$ for each $x$ in $X$. Rather we need only reason about and write a single program (select an algorithm) that implements $f$. So instead of specifying each relationship $(x, y)$ separately, we reason about and specify a single entity, the function $f$, which computes $f(x) = y$. And, instead of calculating each $y$ separately from each $x$, we provide a single algorithm for the function $f$, which performs the calculation.

Programming languages such as pascal, C, and C++ support parametrization (i.e., procedures or functions) when the range and domain sets are either built-in or user-defined types. In this chapter, we are interested in the case in which the domain $X$ of the function $f$ is a subset of the type system of a programming language, where type system denotes the set of all types that can be constructed in that language. Indeed we are interested in the more general case in which $f$ may be a function of several type parameters, as well as ordinary parameters. We may distinguish two possibilities for the range space $Y$: When $Y$ is the type system of the language, $f$ is then a *type*-valued function. This is essentially what is meant by a parameterized type. Another possibility for $Y$ is that it is a set of functions, whose signature is parameterized by $X$. Here $f$ is a procedure parameterized by type. Although the bulk of the chapter is devoted to parameterized types, parameterized procedures are a useful idea and will be discussed as well.

C++ 2.0 and 2.1 do not support parameterized types. For this reason, the last section of the chapter discusses a variety of ways to "fake" parameterized types using other language facilities. However, C++ 3.0 [STR, STR2] will support type parametrization. See [LIP] for a detailed discussion of the syntax and semantics of the feature. Eiffel [MEY] and CLU [LSK] already support parameterized types. Using the generic package feature of Ada [ADA], it is easy to create parameterized types.

## 4.2    Type System

### 4.2.1    Justification

We need to separate the parametrization of two kinds of things.

- Specification (behavior) of a type

- Implementation of a type

The specification or behavior of a parameterized type plays the leading role; its implementation is subordinate. For under the rules of data abstraction, it is the specification that the designer must make effort to create, and it is the specification about which client programmers must understand and reason. The goal is to find parameterized implementations that realize a particular parameterized type specification (see [CHJ, TURSKI]). Indeed, there may exist several different parameterized implementations that realize the specification.

To develop some insight into parameterized type specifications, let's begin by talking about the built-in parameterized types of C++. Several benefits accrue from this discussion. One, a parameterized type is a function that maps the type system of a language into itself. Thus, to understand parameterized types, we must first understand the concept of a type system. Two, the implementation of these types is hidden; they are artifacts of the implementation of the compiler. Therefore, our attention is less likely to stray away from the specified behavior of the types. Three, these built-in types generate the entire type system, which underscores the importance of thoroughly understanding their behavior. We transition from here to the next subsection on the built-in types of C++ with a definition.

*Definition:* The *type system* of a language is the set of built-in types together with all the user-defined types that can be constructed in that language.

## 4.2.2 Built-In Types

The built-in types of C++ fall into two broad categories.

- Integers of various sizes and sign (signed and unsigned `char`, `short`, `int`, `long`)

- Real numbers of various sizes (`float`, `double`)

The public interface of each of these basic language types consists of the built-in arithmetic operations and comparators

$$+, \ -, \ *, \ /, \ \%, \ ==, \ !=, \ <, \ <=, \ >, \ >=$$

Generally, the built-in operations can be applied either to objects or to values of a built-in type. However, the following operations can only be applied to objects (variables) of a type.

$$=, \; ++, \; --$$

In C/C++ integers masquerade as boolean values (zero is false, nonzero is true). As such their public interface includes the boolean operators

$$\&\&, \; ||, \; !$$

The integers, pesky polymorphic devils that they are, are also used as bit vectors; as such their public interface includes

$$\&, \; |, \; \hat{}, \; <<, \; >>, \; \tilde{}.$$

The built-in operators, themselves, are mildly polymorphic: That is, they may be used with objects of several different types. For example, + is meaningful for all the built-in types, such as

```
float f = 6.0;
int z = f + 6;
```

The compiler takes care of generating the correct addition code, as well as the various type conversions. C++ permits us to extend this operator polymorphism to user-defined types. That is, we can overload the meaning of any of the built-in operators of the language (with the exception of the member reference operator . ) when one of its arguments is of class type. For example,

```
String s = "hello, ", t = "world";
String sum = s + t;
```

Presumably, the addition here means concatenate s and t, so that the result in sum looks like

```
"hello, world"
```

The user-defined types of C++ are all constructed by application of the following built-in mechanisms to existing types, T and S, which can be built-in or user-defined:

- `Product<T,S>`

- `Array<T,n>`

- `Pointer<T>`

- `Union<T,S>`

- `Function<T,S>`

The preceding lists the generators for the type system of C, which is a subset of the type system of C++. Note that these very mechanisms are parameterized types! C++ possesses two additional mechanisms for constructing user-defined types.

- Class

- Class derivation

Notice, in the detailed description that follows, that for each of the built-in parameterized types listed above there is a single "manual page" in the C++ reference guide, and that manual page is—as it were—*textually* parameterized by the type parameters T or S.

### 4.2.3  Product

The notation `Product<T,S>` denotes the structure P with two data fields, one of type T and the other of type S:

```
struct P {
    T t;
    S s;
};

P p;    // instantiate an object of type P
```

It is called Product because the value set of P is the cartesian product of the value sets of T and S. In C++ a structure is a class with all members public. Although a struct may have member functions, we restrict our attention here to structures that only contain data members, just like struct's in C. In C++ the typedef keyword is, as it were, included in the keywords struct and class, so there is no need to say it explicitly, as one would in C. This, together with operator overloading, helps to give user-defined types the look and feel of built-in types.

The public interface (specification) of Product is

- Access or modify an individual data field

- Assignment (of structures to structures)

- Compute the size

- Take the address of an object

A simple example of a Product is

```
struct Position {
    int    x,
           y;
};

Position p;
p.x = 6;
p.y = -3;
```

Position is useful for representing the position of a window (in a windowing system like curses or X), or the position of a graphical object in a graphics editor.

### 4.2.4  Array

Array<T,n> denotes (contiguous) array of elements of type T of dimension n. In some sense, Array<T,n> is just a special case of Product<T,S>; that is, an array is just a structure with n data fields all of the same type, T. This observation ought, in principle, to yield the public interface of Array<T,n>.

It doesn't quite, so let's see what the public interface of array actually is in C++:

- Access or modify the $k$th slot in an array, where 0 <= k < n

```
T v[100];  // v is an array of T values
T t;
v[k] = t;
```

- Compute the size of an array

```
sizeof( v) == 100 * sizeof(T)
```

- Assignment: It is not supported by elementwise copy as for a struct, for C regards the name of an array of fixed size as synonymous with the address of its first element (i.e., an address constant)

```
v == &v[0]
```

### 4.2.5   Pointer

`Pointer<T>` denotes the type pointer to objects of type T, for example,

```
Frog kermit;
Frog *p = &kermit;
Frog *q = p;    // aliasing
```

A pointer variable can contain the address of any object of the type to which it is bound. The public interface of `Pointer<T>` is

- Completing the assignment (with concomitant aliasing of the referred-to objects)

- Using pointer arithmetic (including boolean operations)

- Dereferencing

- Taking the address of a pointer object

- Computing the size

### 4.2.6  Union

The notation Union<S,T> denotes the type U where

```
union U {
    S s;
    T t;
};
```

A union variable can contain values from two (or more) types. For example,

```
union U {
    int i;
    char *s;
} u;

u.i = 60;
u.s = "60";
```

For a critique against the use of unions (as well as switch-case statements) see page 92.

### 4.2.7  Function<T,S>

To complete our discussion of the types of (ANSI) C, let's look at the functions. The notation Function<T,S> denotes the collection of all functions that take a T value as an argument and return a value of type S. Of course T itself could be a (cartesian) product of other types. For example,

```
int getc( FILE *fp);
```

declares getc to be a function taking as its argument a pointer to a file and returning an int (actually a character). What is the public interface of Function<T,S>? Essentially, the only thing one can do with a function is to invoke it

```
int ch = getc(stdin);
```

The name of a function is its beginning address (a pointer constant) and can be stored in a pointer variable of the right type, for example,

```
int (*pf)(FILE *) = getc;
```

In this example, pf is a pointer variable capable of containing the address of functions with getc's prototype.

### 4.2.8 Type System of C++

C++ has two type-generation mechanisms in addition to those that it "inherits" from C:

- Class

- Derivation

*Class:*   The class mechanism enables the programmer to glue together syntactically the operations performed on a data structure, together with a C-struct-like description of the data. In other words, class expresses our definition of type. In addition, the programmer/designer has control over the visibility of class members—whether they be data or function—outside of the class. The programmer can easily construct a data abstraction out of a class by simply rendering all of its data members private (invisible). The public member functions then constitute the public interface of the abstraction.

Here is an example of a data abstraction implemented as a class:

```
class P {
public:
    void foo()
    {
        t.f();
        s.g();
    }
private:
    T t;
    S s;
};
```

Typically the member functions of P (foo) are implemented in terms of the member functions of T and S. This is the time-honored technique of layering. More on layering in the chapter on design, chapter 7.

*Derivation:*   The class derivation mechanism of C++ serves as means of implementing new classes in terms of old ones.

```
class D : <public> B {     // public keyword optional
    // stuff
};
```

The derived class D inherits the implementation (data and function members) of the class B that it is based on. As Liskov [LSK2] and Snyder [SNY] point out, this implementation hierarchy is something very different from behavioral inheritance, which could be implemented by class derivation or other means.

### 4.2.9   Type System of Fortran

The type system of C++ is infinite. In contrast, the type system of Fortran is finite and rather small. It consists of the built-in types: integer, real, logical, complex, and a brain-damaged (some say brain-dead) version of string—hollerith. There is one mechanism for constructing user-defined types: Array<T> where T is built-in.

### 4.2.10   Built-In versus User-Defined Parameterized Types

What is or is not a built-in parametric type depends on the language. The type generators for Pascal [WIRTH] are parametric types, most of which have counterparts in C. However, Pascal has I/O supported directly in the language, which is certainly not true for C. I/O is supported in Pascal by the parametric type (symbolically) File<T>, where T can be any built-in or user-defined type. File<char> (textfile) comes pretty close to describing the behavior of the UNIX file abstraction.

## 4.3   Stack<T>

The class template below is an implementation of the parametric type Stack-of-T-value in the proposed notation for parameterized types [ARM] for C++.

```
typedef int Boolean;
const int SIZE = 100;

template <class T> class Stack {
public:
    Stack()                    { sp = 0; }

    void push( T x)            { elt[sp++] = x; }

    T pop()                    { return elt[--sp]; }

    Boolean isempty() const    { return sp <= 0; }

    Boolean isfull() const     { return sp >= SIZE; }
private:
    T elt[SIZE];
    int sp;         // stack pointer, indexes into elt[]
};
```

The implementation satisfies the (parameterized) equations for all types T

```
for all s in Stack<T>, x in T :
    [s.push( x)].pop() == x,   and
    [[s.push( x)].pop() == s
for all s in Stack<T> : let x = s.pop() in
    [s.pop()].push( x) == s
```

As always, the expression [s.memberfunction()] denotes the new state of the Stack object s after the invocation of the member function. The above equations are a T-parameterized form of the equations discussed on page 21. The equations say that push() and pop() are inverse to each other: If you push and then pop (or pop and then push), the resulting stack state is as if no operation was performed.

Note the introduction of a new keyword to the C++ language—`template`.
Intuitively, the notation `<class T>` gives one the feeling that T is a param-
eter of type "type." T literally parametrizes both the public interface of
Stack as well as its implementation (data structure and code for member
functions). To instantiate a stack of integers and a stack of Frogs (where
Frog is a user-defined class) in the same scope, simply say

```
Stack<int> is;
Stack<Frog> fs;
```

And, of course, the compiler will ensure that you cannot push an integer on
a Frog stack.

```
fs.push( 3 );    // syntax error
```

## 4.4   Table<Key,Value>

A parametric type may be a function of more than one type parameter. An
example of such a parameterized family of types is a table of (`Key, Value`)
pairs. `Table` acts very much like an in-memory data base. It is also similar
to the AT&T C++ `Map` type [MAP]. The `Value` type ranges over the entire
type system of the language. The `Key` type, however, does not range over
the entire type system; it is subject to the restriction that it supports (key)
comparison. Let us assume that comparison is implemented by overloading
the comparison operator in the `Key` type.

```
Boolean Key::operator == ( Key&) const
```

Clearly the domain of the `Key` parameter is a proper subset of the type
system of C++, because comparison—unlike assignment—is not automatically provided by the language for all types. Here is a (more or less formal)
specification of the `Table` parameterized type:

```
template <class Key, class Value> class Table {
public:
    Boolean found(Key k)  const;
```

```
    Value get( Key k) const;
    // precondition:  found( k) == TRUE

    void put( Key k, Value v);
    // postcondition:  found( k) == TRUE && get( k) == v

    Value del( Key k);
    // precondition:   found( k) == TRUE
    // postcondition:  found( k) == FALSE
private:
    // data representation
};
```

Note that found() and get() are marked const; they do not change the state of the Table object against which they are invoked. The precondition for get() simply means that to get the value of a ( Key, Value) pair it has to be in the table! Note that put() has no precondition; one can always unconditionally put a (Key, Value) pair in the table. One can easily prove from the specification that if the key argument to put() is the same as the key of some key-value pair already in the table, then put() changes the value to its Value argument.

Here is an implementation of the Table type which satisfies the above specification.

```
template <class Key, class Value> class Table {
public:
    Boolean found(Key k)
    {
        for( p = 1; !p.isempty(); p = p.tail() )
            if( p.head().k == k )
                return TRUE;
        return FALSE;
    }

    Value get(Key k) { return p.head().v; }

    void put( Key k, Value v)
```

```
    {
        if( found( k) )
            p.head().v = v;
        else
            l.add( Pair<Key,Value>(k,v) );
    }


    Value del( Key k)
    {
        Value v = p.head().v;
        p = p.tail();
        while( !(l.head().k == k))
            p.add( l.remove());
        l = p;
        return v;
    }
private:
    Simplist< Pair<Key,Value> > l,   // head of list
                                p;   // p's head may match key
};
```

The `Table< Key, Value>` type is implemented in terms of the parameterized list type `Simplist<T>` where `T` is bound to the parameterized type `Pair<Key,Value>`. The specification and implementation of `Simplist<T>`—where `T` is bound to `int`—are discussed in section 1.10 beginning on page 30. The `Pair<Key,Value>` type is simply the cartesian product of the `Key` and `Value` types, and can be implemented by

```
template <class Key, class Value> class Pair {
public:
    Pair( Key kk, Value vv) : k( kk), v( vv) {}
    Pair() {}

    Key k;
    Value v;
};
```

An object p of type `Pair<Key,Value>` just contains a data member of type `Key` and a data member of type `Value`. A word about the publicity of the data members, which is something I have been telling you to avoid at all costs: I think of **Pair** as a cartesian product, namely I want to be able to get and set the individual data members separately. But, that is precisely the public interface of a C-style **struct**! Besides this implementation is a lot simpler than making the data private, and having a whole bunch of explicit set and get member functions!

Here is an example of a **Pair** where the **Key** type is **String** and the **Value** type is **int**.

```
Pair<String, int> p;
p.k = "hi, world";    // assume the constructor String( char *)
p.v = -6;
```

## 4.5   Container Types

A symbol table is a table of ( **String**, **Value**) pairs. We can easily implement a parameterized symbol table type by

```
template <class Value> Table<String,Value> class SymbolTable;
```

The symbol table type is parameterized by the type of **Value** it contains. **SymbolTable<Value>** and **List<T>** are examples of (parametric) container types. Array is an example of a built-in container type. Here's a rough definition:

*Definition:*   A type is called a **container type** if it *visibly* contains objects of other types.

It is important to regard containment and layered implementation of a type in terms of other types as separate concepts. For, layering is an artifact of implementation and thus hidden from the application programmer, whereas what the container type contains *must* be known (i.e., visible) to the programmer. It is literally part of the signature of the container. A container type is called *homogeneous* if all the objects therein contained are of the same type. **SymbolTable<int>** is an example of a homogeneous container type — it is a collection of name-integer pairs. Indeed, for any fixed **Value** type, **SymbolTable<Value>** is a homogeneous container type.

A container type is called *heterogeneous* if the objects contained therein are of different types. Heterogeneous containers pop up in all kinds of applications, ranging from lexical analyzers and compilers to graphics editors (see chapter 8). Implementing heterogeneous container objects depends very much on the target object-oriented programming language.

A way to implement heterogeneous container types in C++ is with the help of inheritance and base class pointers. For example, imagine that there exists a base class `BaseValue` and we want to construct a heterogeneous symbol table of objects of any type publicly derived from `BaseValue`. The solution is to instantiate a symbol table object **s** of type

```
SymbolTable<BaseValue *> s;
```

This design depends on the fact that the address of a publicly derived object can be used anywhere that the address of a base type object is formally expected. Any where includes assignment, arguments, and return values of functions. This design clearly restricts totally untrammeled heterogeneity by inheritance; in practice, for any particular application, this is not so restrictive. We just design the application so that all types of objects that need to put into a container are formally derived from a synthetic base class. And then we can recover the derived type nature of the objects through dynamic binding (virtual member functions).

What would happen if the pointer declaration were eliminated in the definition of the type of **s**?

```
SymbolTable<BaseValue> s;
...
class DerivedValue : public BaseValue { ... };

DerivedValue d;
s.put( "foo", d)
BaseValue b;
b = s.get( "foo");
DerivedValue d1;
d1 = s.get( "foo");  // syntax error!
```

We would be in for a surprise. `put()` above stores the base part of **d** in the symbol table, not the entire value of **d**. Thus the assignment to **b** only contains the base part of **d**. The assignment to **d1** is a syntax error because of the type mismatch, in that the return type of **get()** is **BaseValue**. There is no automatic promotion of base class to derive class values. If there were, what could it possibly be?!

The design of heterogeneous container types proceeds quite a bit more easily in most other object-oriented languages, such as Eiffel and Smalltalk. These languages do not provide the pointer type to programmers. Instead, object identifiers always have reference (pointer) semantics. Thus an assignment between two object identifiers constitutes aliasing. Furthermore, one can assign derived type objects to base type variables; after the assignment, the base variable simply refers to the derived object, all of it. So a parameterized type like **List[T]** in Eiffel can contain objects of any type derived from **T**, and that's the end of the story.

## 4.6   Parameterized Functions: Sorting

In a pure object-oriented design, all functionality is encapsulated as member functions of some class or another. C++ 3.0, however, supports both parameterized types as well as parameterized functions. For completeness of syntactic exposition, here is an example of a number of functions related to sorting vectors of **T** values.

```
// minindex returns index of minimum value in the vector v
template <class T> int minindex( T* v, int dim)
{
    int m = 0;
    if( dim > 1)
        for( int j = 1; j < dim; j++)
            if( v[j] < v[m])
                m = j;
    return m;
}

// min returns minimum value in the vector v
template <class T> T min( T* v, int dim)
{
    return v[ minindex( v, dim) ];
```

```
}
```

```
// sort sorts the vector v in place in ascending order
template <class T> void sort( T* v, int dim)
{
    int m;
    for( int j = 0; j < dim; j++)
        if( m = minindex( v + j, dim - j)) {
            T t = v[j];
            v[j] = v[j + m];
            v[j + m] = t;
        }
}
```

Both the signature and implementations of the above functions are parameterized by the type parameter T. Note that the parametric functions min(), minindex(), sort() are restricted to those types T that overload the comparison operator

```
Boolean T::operator < (T &) const;
```

Less obvious is the parametrization of the implementation by the assignment operation for T because it is automatically provided by the compiler if not explicitly supplied by type T.

## 4.7   Faking of Parameterized Types

C++ 3.0 supports parameterized types and functions. It is hoped, by the time this book is published, the 3.0 version of the language will be generally available. But even if it is, there are many C++ programmers who are using earlier versions of the language that do not support parametry. It is not clear how soon these people will upgrade to the latest version of the language. Given this situation, it is useful to be able to fake out parameterized types using version 2.0 or even 1.2 features of the language. This section discusses three ways to do it.

- Macros

- Template file

- Inheritance

## 4.7.1 Macros

We shall demonstrate how to fake parameterized types using class macros on the type `Simplist<T>` specified in section 1.10. A word of caution: Macros are difficult to debug. The thing is to debug the code before wrapping it in a macro. The trick is to bind the dummy type `T` to something simple, like `int`. If the code works for `int`, it is likely to work for all values of `T`.

Recall that the only data in a `Simplist<T>` object is a pointer to the first `Node<T>` object. First, here is the macrofied class definition for `Node<T>`:

```
#include <generic.h>
#define Node(T)    name2(Node,T)

#define MakeNode(T) class Node(T) {                        \
public:                                                    \
    Node(T) (T x) : val(x), Next(0) {}                     \
    Node(T) *next()              { return Next; }          \
    void link( Node(T) *neighbor)  { Next = neighbor; }    \
    T value()                    { return val; }           \
private:                                                   \
    Node(T) *Next;                                         \
    T  val;                                                \
};
```

The standard header file `generic.h` defines the macro function `name2`, which simply concatenates its arguments as strings (see the header file if you are interested in the hack). `Node(type)` creates an identifier suitable for naming a class. For example, if type is `int`, `Node(type)` returns `Nodeint`. To be able to use a `Node` of some type, you must invoke the macro `MakeNode(T)` before instantiating any objects of type `Node(T)`, like

```
MakeNode(int);
```

The invocation creates a definition for the class `Nodeint`. To instantiate a node object containing an integer, simply say

```
    Node(int) n(3);
```

Here is the macro class definition for Simplist<T> in terms of Node(T).

```
#define Simplist(T) name2(Simplist,T)
```

```
#define MakeSimplist(T) class Simplist(T) {          \
public:                                               \
    Simplist(T)() : Head(0) {}                        \
    T head() const  { return Head->value(); }         \
    T remove()                                        \
    {                                                 \
        T r = Head->value();                          \
        Node(T) *p = Head;                            \
        Head = Head->next();                          \
        delete p;                                     \
        return r;                                     \
    }                                                 \
    Simplist(T) tail()                                \
    {                                                 \
        Simplist(T) r;                                \
        if( !isempty())                               \
            r.Head = Head->next();                    \
        return r;                                     \
    }                                                 \
    void add( T x)                                    \
    {                                                 \
        Node(T) *p = new Node(T)( x);                 \
        if( Head != 0)                                \
            p->link( Head);                           \
        Head = p;                                     \
    }                                                 \
    Boolean isempty() const { return Head == 0; }  \
private:                                               \
    Node(T) *Head;                                    \
}
```

The way the code is written, we need to invoke MakeNode(T) before we invoke MakeSimplist(T). For example, to create a class definition for a list of integers, say

```
MakeNode(int);
MakeSimplist(int);
```

The invocation `MakeSimplist(int)` creates a definition for the class `Lispint`. To instantiate a list of integers, just say

```
Simplist(int) l;
```

What are the advantages and disadvantages of the macro class mechanism for implementing parametric types? First are advantages.

- There is a single source (header) file defining the parametric family. The implementer need implement and maintain but one file. The client programmer need only include this one header file.

- It is easy for client programmers to use, as we have seen.

- Client programmers get the benefit of compile time type checking. For example, you cannot add an integer to a `Simplist(Frog)`. However, the diagnostics will concern the class `SimplistFrog`. This requires that the client programmer have an understanding of the macro implementation.

Here are the disadvantages.

- For each kind of `Simplist` that the programmer needs, she or he must explicitly invoke the `MakeSimplist(T)` macro in addition to including the header file `list.h`. This essentially tells the compiler to prepare to generate code for the corresponding type of list. In languages that support parametric types, this is not necessary, for the compiler can infer from the declarations of variables of different `Simplist` types what code needs to be generated.

- `MakeSimplist(T)` does not work for arguments `T` that contain white space (blanks, tabs). This makes it difficult to bind `T` to pointer types. For example, `MakeSimplist(int *)` will yield compilation errors. This is because `Simplist(int *)` resolves under the macro preprocessor to

```
Simplistint *
```

which is not a class identifier, that is,

```
class Simplistint * { ...
```

is illegal. Removing the white space doesn't help because **Simplist(int*)**
resolves to

```
Simplistint*
```

which is also not a class identifier. A work-around is to **typedef** the
pointer type, for example,

```
typedef int* intptr;
```

Then, everything works just fine. That is, create a class definition for
list-of-integer pointers by saying

```
MakeNode(intptr);
MakeSimplist(intptr);
```

and instantiate such a list object by saying

```
Simplist(intptr) l;
```

- Experience shows that macros—in particular, multiline macros—are
  difficult to debug.

- Macro class definitions may be difficult to port to other machines because they depend on the robustness of C++ preprocessor. Some pre-
  processors can handle very long multiline macros; others cannot. The
  work-around is to decompose a long macro definition into a sequence
  of shorter ones. And that is just what we did for **MakeSimplist(T)**.

### 4.7.2 Template File

The template file technique [SHO] consists of textually parameterizing the file containing the class definition with a dummy-type parameter T. At the beginning of the file, the dummy T is bound to a real type with the a typedef. In fact, in section 1.10 we have already seen an implementation in this technique of the type Simplist<T>, in terms of the parameterized helping type Node<T>, whose template file implementation is found on page 18.

```
typedef int T;
...
class Node {
public:
    Node( T x) : val( x), Next(0) {}
...
private:
    T val;
    ...
};

class Simplist {
public:
    ...
    T head() const;
    ...
private:
    Node* Head;
};
```

Here is how to use the template file technique. Let's assume that the class definitions of Node and Simplist are in a header file list.h.[1] The first line in the file is

```
typedef int T;
```

Let's observe the convention that all subsequent references in the header file to the kind of values that the list manages are to T. Thus the **typedef**

---

[1]This is the AT&T suffix. Header file suffix varies as a function of the compiler manufacturer.

effectively parametrizes the entire header file in terms of the symbol T. In this case, by binding T to int in the typedef, we are implementing a list of integers. We could just as easily bind T to any built-in or user-defined type—say, Frog *—

```
typedef Frog* T;
```

and thus implement a list of Frog pointers.

The template file mechanism is easy to implement and use. When writing a program, if you need a list of something, you copy list.h to another (header) file and bind the symbol T there to whatever type of value you want the list to contain. For example, if T is bound to int, to instantiate an object of type Simplist<int> in a program, just say

```
    Simplist l;
```

The template file mechanism has its limitations. The main one is that there can be only one binding of T to an actual type per scope. The identifier Simplist simply refers to the class defined in the header file list.h. The compiler has no idea that Simplist really means list of integer or list of anything else. So we have to live with the annoying restriction that we cannot have both a list of integers and a list of strings (for example) within the same class or (external) function. However, the scoping rules of C++ do permit us to have a list of integers in one source file, and a list of strings in another source file. Here's how.

1. Make two copies of list.h.

2. Bind T in copy one to int.

3. Bind T in copy two to String.

4. Include the first copy in the first source file.

5. Include the second copy in the second source file.

### 4.7.3 Inheritance

This subsection deals with a use of class derivation to implement parameterized types. It is based on the notion that each type in a parametric family of types is derived from a common parent type. The central idea is that the child types not only share a common public interface, specified in the parent, but they also reuse as much of the parent's implementation as they can. In a strongly typed language like C++, most of the work in implementing a child type (corresponding to a type parameter value T) has to do with ensuring that the child's public interface is parameterized by T. For example, for `Simplist<Frog>`, this boils down to ensuring that only Frogs can be inserted or deleted in a list of Frogs, not integers.

Our implementational approach is to define a parent type for the parametric family (say `Simplist<T>`). Every time we want a particular kind of list (i.e., we want to bind T to a type), we will privately derive a type from the parent and use the parent member functions to help us implement the corresponding derived type functions. Let's apply this approach to the construction of `Simplist<Frog>`.

The data structure for the parametric family `Simplist<T>` is a singly linked list of nodes. In turn, each node has a data member containing the address of an object of type T. We select as the parent for the parametric family (conceptually at least) `Simplist<void *>`. This is a reasonable choice, because the address of any object of any type may be assigned to a void pointer without casting. To make life easy, let's implement `Simplist<void *>` using the macro class definitions developed earlier:

```
typedef void * voidptr;
MakeNode(voidptr);
MakeSimplist(voidptr);
// corresponds to Simplist<void *> Listbase
typedef Simplist(voidptr) Listbase;
```

`Listbase` corresponds to `Simplist<void *>`. Next we have to implement `Simplist<Frog>`. Let's define a class `ListofFrog` that corresponds to `Simplist<Frog>`:

```
class ListofFrog : Listbase {    // private derivation
public:
```

```
    ListofFrog() : Listbase() {}

    Frog* head() const { return (Frog *) Listbase::head(); }

    Frog* remove()     { return (Frog *) Listbase::remove(); }

    ListofFrog tail()
    {   // this is ugly ...
        return *((ListofFrog *)(&(Listbase::tail())));
    }

    void add( Frog* p) { Listbase::add( p); }

    Listbase::isempty;
};
```

The first thing we notice is that the derivation is private

```
class Listofchar : Listbase { ...
```

Why not public derivation? Because then the user of a **ListofFrog** instance
would have access to the public member functions of **Listbase**. For example,
she or he would be able to insert the address of a **int** into a **ListofFrog**

```
    class ListofFrog : public Listbase { ...

    ListofFrog l;
    int x = 6;

    l.Listbase::add( &x);
```

The insert is permissible because the functional prototype for **add()** is

```
    typedef void *voidptr;
    void Listbase::add( voidptr);
```

and one can assign the address of anything to a **void** pointer without coercion. But then ListofFrog would not be a homogeneous list of frogs, but

rather some kind of heterogeneous list of stuff. So the derivation must be private.

How can we reuse the code in the base class `Listbase`? One aid that C++ provides us is the notation

```
Listbase::isempty;
```

which renders the base class's `isempty()` (public) member function public in the derived class `ListofFrog`. We make `Listbase`'s `length()` function visible to `ListofFrog` clients in the same way.

Under private derivation, the base class public members are visible to derived class member functions. So, for example, we can easily implement derived class member functions in terms of base class member functions with the same name. However, the implementations are ugly in that they involve a lot of pointer casting.

As an exercise (and yet another way of implementing parametric types), you might try reimplementing `ListofFrog` using layering. That is, put a data member of type `Listbase` in the private part of class `ListofFrog`

```
class ListofFrog {
private:
    Listbase l;
public:
    // public interface
};
```

Compare your layered implementation to the inheritance implementation presented above. Which one is easier to write? Which one is easier to understand?

Historically, inheritance was the mechanism used (e.g., in Smalltalk [GOLD]) to implement parametric types. This alone is a reason for understanding this mechanism. C++ users can benefit from parametric types by exploiting language's support for inheritance. The advantages of this approach is that it is doable today and provides a moderate amount of code reuse. The major disadvantage is that, each time a programmer needs a member of a parametric family, she or he must define and implement a derived class. Which means writing code. This can quickly become a maintenance nightmare in a system that requires, for example, many different sorts of lists. For instance, the UNIX system kernel [BACH] employs a variety of lists including lists of inodes, lists of record locks, lists of blocks in the buffer cache, and so on. If the kernel were reimplemented in an object-oriented manner in C++ [JOY], the inheritance technique would lead to a derived class for each kind of list mentioned earlier. In contrast, with C++ 3.0 support for parameterized types or even macro class definitions, no additional code need be written!

The conclusion is: Don't use inheritance to implement parametry. Use the other techniques (notably macro class definitions), knowing that eventually the language itself will support parametric types.

# Bibliography

[ADA]     Nico Habermann and Dwayne Perry, *ADA for Advanced Programmers*, 1984, Addison-Wesley.

[BACH]    Maury Bach, *Internals of the UNIX System Kernel*, 1987, Addison-Wesley.

[CHJ]     B. Cohen, W. T. Harwood, and M. I. Jackson, *The Specification of Complex Systems*, 1986, Addison-Wesley.

[GOLD]    Adelle Goldberg, *The Smalltalk-80 Programming Language*, 1984, Addison-Wesley.

[JOY]     Bill Joy, keynote address, USENIX C++ Conference, Denver, CO, 1988.

[LIP]     Stanley Lippman, *C++ Primer*, 1989, Addison-Wesley.

[LSK]     B. Liskov and J. Guttag, *Abstraction and Specification in Program Development*, 1986, MIT Press. (Addresses design of abstract data types.)

[LSK2]    B. Liskov, "Data Abstraction and Hierarchy," addendum to *Conference Proceedings: Object-Oriented Programming Systems Languages and Applications* (OOPSLA), 1987. (Liskov's approach to object-oriented design, specifically addresses inheritance.)

[MAP]     "The Parameterized Map Type," AT&T Publication, 1992.

[MEY]     Bertrand Meyer, *Object-Oriented Software Construction*, 1988, Prentice Hall. (Addresses object-oriented design, including parametric types.)

139

[SHO]     Jonathan Shopiro, personal communication, November 1988.

[SNY]     Alan Snyder, "Encapsulation and Inheritance in Object-Oriented
          Programming Languages," *Proceedings of the ACM Conference on
          Object Oriented Programming Systems Languages and Applications*
          (OOPSLA), SIGPLAN Notices 21, November 1986.

[STR]     Bjarne Stroustrup, *The C++ Programming Language*, second edi-
          tion, 1991, Addison-Wesley.

[STR2]    Bjarne Stroustrup, "Parameterized Types for C++," *Usenix Pro-
          ceedings: C++ Conference*, Denver, CO, 1988.

[TURSKI] Władisław Turski and Thomas Maibaum, *The Specification of
          Computer Programs*, 1987, Addison-Wesley.

[WIRTH] Kathleen Jensen and Niklaus Wirth, *Pascal User Manual and
          Report*, 1974, Springer-Verlag.

# Chapter 5

# Type as Object

## 5.1 Introduction

The notion that types themselves are instances of a "metatype" has been around in the object-oriented world at least since Smalltalk [GOLD]. The notion is simple to state: Just as an object instance of a type has a state that varies over its lifetime and a set of messages (the public interface) to which it responds, similarly why not conceive of a type itself as having a state—separate from the states of any of its object instances—and an interface of messages—distinct from the public interface of its instances—to which *it* responds.

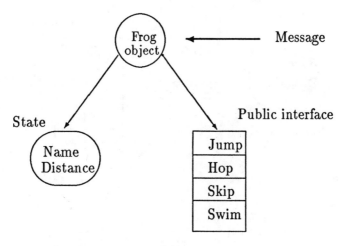

141

The picture above depicts a Frog object.  We see that it responds to the messages, jump, hop, skip, swim and that its state consists of its name and the distance the frog has traveled from the pond of its tadpolehood.

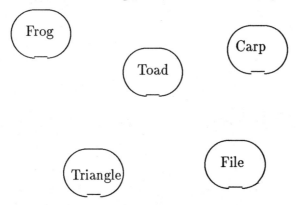

The picture above depicts some of the instances of the metatype **Type**, the instances being types including frog, other kinds of amphibians, and so on.

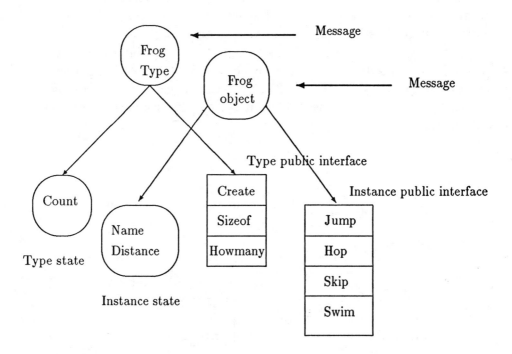

The preceding dual picture depicts both state and public interface of a frog instance object, as well as state and public interface of the frog type viewed as an object. The frog type's state (data) might include a count of all of the frog instance objects in a system, which, after all, varies over time as frog objects are created and destroyed. The public interface of the frog type as object includes

create-frog, howmany, size, ...

When the frog type receives the message `createfrog`, it creates a frog instance, initializes its name and distance (to zero) data, and returns (the address of) the frog object. On receiving the message howmany, the frog type returns an integer value denoting the number of frog instances in the system currently. On receipt of the size message, the frog type returns the size of a frog instance, which is presumably the same for all frog instances.

I would like to point out that one can choose to regard certain built-in operations in C++ as if they were part of the repetoire (public interface) of any type (or class) viewed as an object. For example, although notationally the `new` and `sizeof` operators are invoked as if they are procedures taking a type as an argument,

```
class Frog {
    // members
};
```

```
Frog *p = new Frog;        // poetically, p    = Frog.new()
int size = sizeof Frog;    // poetically, size = Frog.sizeof()
```

if I rotate my head 180 degrees, I can regard those invocations as message expressions against the frog type as an object.

There are object-oriented languages that provide direct support for type as object including Smalltalk, Objective-C [COX], and CLOS Lisp [KEENE]. In contrast, neither C++ nor Eiffel [MEY] provide direct support for type as object. However, as we will learn, C++ has a facility, `static` data and function members within a class, that can be used to provide partial support for the concept.

Why should a practicing and practical programmer care about this idea? There are several good reasons. Practically, the concept helps in "getting rid" of or at least hiding global variables (we will shortly see just how this is accomplished in C++) in a design or application. From a design perspective, the concept unifies type and object; a type is just a special kind of object that can create other objects that share an interface. This unification can simplify the way I reason about a system or application. As a design concept, type as object provides conceptual hooks on which to hang various "implementational" hats. For example, the return value of a message sent to a type could be a properly initialized object instance of that type. This is a nice way of modeling object creation and initialization, which can be done in C++ by instantiating a variable and simultaneously invoking its constructor. Finally, type as object provides a nice conceptual model (by no means the only one nor one that is universally loved) for using static class members in C++. Static data members represent the state of the type, and public static member functions constitute the set of messages to which the type responds. It should be pointed out that static class members also provide some degree of support for modular (Ada style) programming [BOOCH].

## 5.2   MegaBuzz Corporation

Before introducing the syntax for static class members, I want to describe a problem common to the maintenance and enhancement of large software systems. Joe, Mary, and Bobby all work for the MegaBuzz corporation, a large software and hardware development company. Mary and Joe—who are C programmers—report to Bobby. Mary is responsible for developing a data base of frammistans. One of the requirements on Mary's application is that it keep accurate track of the number of frammistans, because frammistans are inserted or deleted from the data base at arbitrary times throughout the day. Having attended a public seminar on object-oriented programming, Mary understands that `Frammistan` is a type, which she implements in her C application as a data structure together with a set of C functions that access the structure. Mary voluntarily abides by the rule of data hiding by ensuring that the only functions that access the `Frammistan` data structure are those in the above-mentioned set. She keeps track of the number of frammistans in a global variable called (for simplicity)

```
int count;
```

Joe—who works in a different building and on a completely separate project from Mary's—has the job of developing a data base of whipsidoodles that dynamically keeps track of the number of whipsidoodles as they enter and depart the data base. Because he attended the same course that Mary did on object-oriented programming, he too understands that `Whipsidoodle` is a type, and implements it in his application in a manner analogous to Mary's `Frammistan`. He too decides to keep track of the whipsidoodles in a global variable, which he, for simplicity, also calls

```
int count;
```

Of course, there is no harm in the count variables being named the same, because Joe and Mary are not working on the same main program, and in any event they have no idea what each other is up to.

Bobby attended the same course as Mary and Joe. Bobby knows what they are up to from their weekly status reports and is attuned to the importance of software reuse. Bobby has a customer who needs to keep track of *both* frammistans and whipsidoodles. Thinks Bobby: "I can quickly satisfy my customer and save a lot of software development money besides by linking together Mary and Joe's code!" So Bobby, unbeknownst to either Joe or Mary, goes and tries to compile and link their code together. The compile fails, leaving Bobby in a complete state of befuddlement, wondering if the money spent on object-oriented training was a complete waste!

The compilation may have failed because the two `count` variables are global, and the C linker deems it an unresolvable name conflict in the global symbol table. Calling Joe and Mary on the carpet, Bobby solicits their assistance. Promises have already been made to a customer, and they must be kept! Being good C programmers, Mary and Joe come up with the following solution: Mary will declare the frammistan count `static` at the top of the source file containing all of the functions that access frammistans

```
static int count;

struct frammistan {
  ...
};

/* frammistan access functions */
```

This way, the `count` variable is invisible to all of the application except for functions defined in the variable's source file. Joe will do exactly the analogous thing for whipsidoodles. And now the linker is happy (as will be the customer) and produces an executable program.

## 5.3   Static Class Members

For how to do it in C++, we turn from the world of frammistans and whipsidoodles to the world of amphibians.

```
class Frog {
public:
        Frog( char *Name)
        {
                name = Name;
                count++;
        }

        ~Frog()         { count--; }

        // instance interface
        void jump()     { distance += 100; }
        void hop()      { distance += 50; }
        void skip()     { distance += 25; }
        void swim()     { distance += 25; }
        void print()
        {
            printf( "Frog name is %s, distance from pond is %d\n",
                name, distance);
        }

        // type-as-object interface
        // new ...
        // sizeof
        static int howmany() { return count; }
private:
        // instance variables
        int distance;
```

```
    char *name;

    // type-as-object variables
    static int count;
};
```

In the preceding class definition, there are four kinds of members: ordinary data and function members, and static data and function members. The ordinary data members represent the state of `Frog` instances and are part of every `Frog` object. As all of the function members are public, the ordinary function members constitute the public interface to the `Frog` instances.

The static data member, `static int count`, represents the state of the `Frog` type viewed as an object. In C++ terms, `count` is shared data among all objects of type `Frog` and there is only one copy of it, regardless of the number of `Frog` objects in an application including the boundary case of zero frogs. Following the rules of data hiding, we make it private just like the ordinary data members. Were it to be public (a consummation devoutly to be unwished), it could be accessed as if it were a data field in a **struct** by using the scope resolution operator ::

```
              int n = Frog::count;
```

Whereas ordinary member functions can access ordinary data members (as well as static data members), the static member function **static int howmany()** can only access static members, here the static data member **static int count**. This latter remark make sense in terms of our use of static members to implement type as object. The static member function `howmany()` is invoked with the scope resolution operator, as in the program below

```
    ...
    Frog kermit( "kermit");
    ...
    printf( "there are %d Frogs in the program\n",
        Frog::howmany() );
```

Again, we can easily imagine `howmany()` as a message invoked against an object named `Frog`. Note that the preceding program fragment elegantly

handles the boundary condition: "no frogs exist at this moment."
`Frog::howmany()` simply returns zero.

## 5.4   Faking of Type as Object in C++ 1.2

Previous versions of C++ supported static data but not static member functions within a class. How best could we implement the concept of type as
object under this constraint? Not very well. As indicated below, we could
leave the `count` as a private static data member of `class Frog` and declare
the `homany()` function to be an ordinary public member function.

```
class Frog {
public:
    Frog( char *);
    // howmany() is ordinary member function
    int howmany() { return count; }
private:
    // ordinary data members
    static int count;
};

// Monitor is global variable
Frog Monitor( "monitor" );
        ...
        printf( "there are %d Frogs in the program\n"
            Monitor.howmany() - 1);

        Frog kermit( "kermit");
        ...
        printf( "there are %d Frogs in the program\n",
            Monitor.howmany() - 1);
```

But then the only way to find out how many frogs exist at some point in time
is to ask *some* frog instance: "How many of you fellows are there?" Several
unpleasant questions arise: What if there aren't any frogs? Should we count
in the census the one that we asked? In any event, all this presupposes that
there must always exist *at least* one `Frog` instance to ask the question of.

In the above program there is a global **Frog** variable—**Monitor**—whose sole purpose is to answer the **howmany()** question. The **Monitor** variable is an artifact of implementation that arises out of a lack in the programming language (C++ 1.2 and earlier). The variable's very existence renders obscure any source code of which it is a part. Let us be thankful that C++ 2.0 supports static member functions as well as static data members!

# 5.5 Modular Programming

Static class members provide some support for modular programming, which is the style of programming supported by Ada and Modula-2 [WIRTH]. Roughly, a module consists of two related pieces.

- Module specification (called the *spec*)

- Module implementation (called the *body*)

The module concept corresponds precisely to the well-known software engineering principle of the separation of the interface (module spec) from the implementation (module body). The module specification is a set of declarations of data structure and procedure signatures. There is no implementation in the module spec. A data structure signature is the name of a data structure type. A procedural signature consists of a procedure name, a return type (which can be void if the procedure does not return a value), and the types of the procedure arguments. Presumably the procedures access or modify the data structures declared in the module spec, but they don't have to. All entities declared in the spec are visible and available to client programmers.

The module body essentially contains the implementations of the entities declared in the module spec. All entities found in the module body are private, that is, not visible to clients of the module spec. The module body is a set of definitions (read implementations) of data structures and procedures. Each element declared in the module spec must have its implementation in the module body. However, the module body may contain additional data structures and procedures—completely unbeknownst of course to module clients—which are used to implement the visible entities declared in the module spec. For example, private static class data members —such as **static int Frog::count**—would find their place in the module body. Also private member functions would also be placed in the module body. The tt static int howmany() function would correspond to a procedure specified in the module spec, whose implementation in the module body returns the current value of the private count variable, which is also in the module body.

A fundamental use of modules in Ada and Modula-2 is the implementation of abstract data types. In this usage, the procedures in the module spec constitute the public interface of the type. All of these procedures manipulate a particular data structure named in the module spec. Canonically the data structure is the first argument to each of the procedures. Generally, this argument has call-by-reference semantics because the procedures in the public interface must be able to change the state of the object, which is represented by the specified data structure. The module body contains the layout of the data structure and the bodies of the procedures. In a C++ class, the data structure would be represented by private data members, and the procedures would correspond to public member functions, whose definitions are found outside the class template.

Can we come up with a use of a module for other than the implementation of a single abstract data type? After all, a module is simply a means of decomposing a system into subsystems with well-defined interfaces. The preceding thought points in the direction of another use of modules, namely, as a portability layer: Gather together in a single module all host system dependencies, such as operating system dependencies, and windowing or display device dependencies. This technique or decomposition makes it relatively easy to "port" an application from one environment to another: simply reimplement the module body that represents the portability layer. Because, presumably, its interface (the module spec) does not change, there is no need to reimplement any other part (or module) of the application. In passing, I would like to note that the "portability" module can be regarded as a collection of one or more abstract data types with related semantics as well as related implementation.

I would like to end the chapter exploring, just a bit, the consequences of the last thought—that a module is a collection of types with related semantics and implementation. If C++ possessed a module syntax in addition to its class syntax, it would radically reduce the need for friend functions. Just to hint at this, it is difficult to implement an iterator type, which provides iteration service for some other collection type, without making the iterator class a friend of the collection class. Clearly, both the collection and its iterator share semantics and, as indicated earlier, implementation.

If modules were available in C++, it would be possible to gather together the specification of both the collection type and its associated iterator type in a module spec, to hide the implementation of both types from client programmers in the module body, and for the collection type to share its implementation with the iterator type securely within the module body.

# Bibliography

[BOOCH]   Grady Booch, *Software Engineering with Ada*, 1986, Benjamin/Cummings.

[COX]     Brad Cox, *Object-Oriented Programming, an Evolutionary Approach*, 1986, Addison-Wesley.

[GOLD]    A. Goldberg and D. Robson, *Smalltalk-80: The Language and Its Implementation*, 1983, Addison-Wesley.

[KEENE]   Sonya Keene, *Object-Oriented Programming in Common Lisp: A Programmer's Guide to CLOS*, 1989, Addison-Wesley.

[MEY]     Bertrand Meyer, *Object-Oriented Software Construction*, 1988, Prentice Hall.

[WIRTH]   Niklaus Wirth, *Programming in Modula-2*, 1983, Springer-Verlag.

# Chapter 6

# Pointers to Member Functions

## 6.1  Introduction

I want to introduce a powerful feature of C++—pointers to member functions—in the context of an example taken from artificial intelligence (AI). The AI community makes heavy use of the Lisp language. Pointers to member functions make C++ an attractive AI language because they can be used to implement efficiently the various mapping operations (`mapcar`, `mapc ...`) available in Lisp. For concreteness, the word Lisp in this article means Franz Lisp as described in [WIL].

In that most AI work has been done in Lisp, the point of the exercise is to demonstrate that you *can* do AI work in C++, and that your reward (for battling the inevitable learning curve for this new language) is AI applications that run fast on general-purpose computing iron. I know that the Lisp community has attacked the performance problems of Lisp with semi-compiled versions of the language and special-purpose fast hardware (e.g. Symbolics Lisp machines). But I contend that for AI to enter into commercial maturity, AI 'smarts' must be integrated with other kinds of programs on general-purpose computers, and the composite system must perform well. C++ is a compiled language that provides the performance of C with support for the increasingly popular object paradigm. C++ may very well provide the bridge that AI needs to migrate into the programming mainstream.

The definitive reference here is the [ARM]. Those interested in implementation issues may want to take a look at the paper that Stan Lippman [LIP] delivered at the second C++ Conference in October of 1988.

## 6.2   Class Frog

Let's begin setting up the machinery for pointers to member functions with an example of a user-defined type, class `Frog`

```
const int neuter = 0,
          female = 1,
          male   = 2;

class Frog {
public:
    Frog( char *p = "the anonymous frog")
    {
        name = p;
        dist = 0;
        gender = neuter;
        printf( "BEGIN Frog %s\n", name);
    }

    ~Frog()                { printf( "END Frog %s\n", name); }

    char *Name()           { return name; }

    virtual void jump(int x) { dist += x; }

    virtual void croak()     { printf( "R-R-R-ibit\n"); }

    int distance()           { return dist; }

    int gender;     // values: (0) neuter, (1) female, (2) male
private:
    char *name;
```

```
    int dist;
};
```

# 6.3   Pointer to Data Member

C++ supports the notion of pointers to class members, either data or function.

```
Frog kermit( "Kermit");
int Frog::*pm;

pm = &Frog::gender;
```

In the fragment above, `kermit` is a frog, and `pm` is a variable of type pointer to data member of frog of type `int`. The expression `&Frog::gender` is a (address) constant of this type. A pointer to a data member has very much the flavor of an offset into the data structure of the class. That is, by assigning `&Frog::gender` to pm, pm can be used to refer to the gender data member of any frog. As in this example

```
kermit.*pm = male;
```

which has the meaning: assign the manifest constant 2 to the gender data member of the frog variable `kermit`. The type checking at compile time is strict. pm can only be used to point to integer data members of frog.

# 6.4   Pointer to Member Function

The syntax for a pointer to a member function generalizes the notation that we have just learned for a pointer to a data member.

```
int (Frog::*pf)() = &Frog::distance;
```

The expression `&Frog::distance` denotes the address of the distance member function of Frog and is a constant. In current implementations [LIP], in the case of static binding, the expression `&Frog::distance` compiles to an actual function address. Under dynamic binding, the expression compiles to the offset of the distance member function in the virtual function table of any class publicly derived from frog.

**pf** is a pointer variable that can contain the address of a member function of class **Frog** that takes no arguments and returns an int. As with pointers to data members, compile-time type checking is strict: pf may not be assigned the address of an external function, nor may it be assigned the address of a frog member function with a different functional prototype. For example, the following code fragment is in error

```
pf = &Frog::Name;     // syntax error:  type mismatch
```

because **Name** is a member function that takes no arguments and returns a **char *****. Here is how we invoke a pointer to a member function against an object of its type

```
int x = (kermit.*pf)();
```

For example, in the preceding code fragment, we are invoking whatever member function **pf** points to **Frog::distance** against the frog **kermit**. We can also invoke a pointer to a member function against a pointer to an object, as in the example below.

```
Frog *p = &kermit;
x = (p->*pf)();          // here, static binding
```

This supple notation permits a program to invoke an (almost) arbitrary member function against an arbitrary object of type frog. The best, however, is yet to come.

## 6.5 Compare C Syntax for Pointer to (External) Function

Let's compare the notation we have just learned for pointers to member functions with the notation for functions pointers in ANSI C [KR]:

```
void foo( int);
void (*pf)(int) = foo;
int x = 6;

(*pf)(x);
```

foo() is a function taking an integer argument and returns void. pf is a pointer to functions with such a prototype. We invoke the function whose address is stored in the pointer by dereferencing it. Thus (*pf)(x) means foo(6).

## 6.6 Mapcar

Now is a good time to define some of the Lisp mapping operations. mapc

```
( mapc function list )
```

applies the function to each element of the list and returns the argument list. In many Lisps, nil is returned. mapc is used when we are primarily interested in the side effects of applying the function. Conversely, mapcar

```
( mapcar function list)
```

returns the list of values produced by applying the function to each element of the list in turn. To implement mapc or mapcar in C++, we have to do some setup work, starting with the definition of a list of frogs.

## 6.7 Pond

Imagine that class Pond is a list of pointers to Frog. We can easily implement Pond

```
typedef Simplist<Frog *> Pond;
```

as a member of the parametric family Simplist<T> of list types, whose implementation is given in section 1.10. *Caveat:* The preceding uses the notation for parametrized types in C++ 3.0 and is not available in earlier versions. For more on parametrized types, see chapter 4. Here's a picture of the Pond:

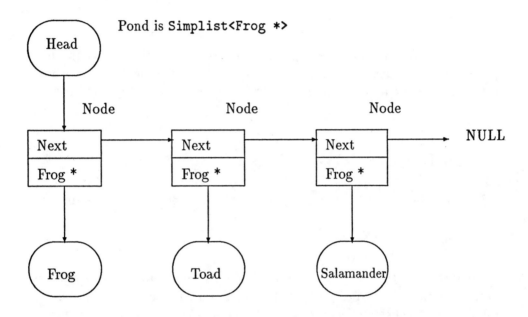

Now, what if we want to apply an arbitrary operation from the public interface of `Frog` to each frog in a pond? We could do it like this:

```
typedef void (Frog::*PF)(int );
```

`PF` is a convenient typedef for pointer to member function of `Frog` taking an integer argument and returning `void`. Here is `mapc()` as an external function:

```
void mapc( Pond pond, PF pf, int x)
{
    // for each frog in the pond ...
    for( Pond r = pond; !r.isempty(); r = r.tail())
        (r.head()->*pf)( x);
}
```

`r.head()` gets the address of each frog in the pond in sequence. The member function whose address is in `pf` is then invoked against that frog. Say we want all of the frogs in a pond to jump 3 units. Here's the code to do it.

```
Pond pond;
Frog kermit( "kermit"), lulu( "lulu");
// add Frogs into the pond
pond.add( &kermit);
pond.add( &lulu);

mapc( pond, &Frog::jump, 3);
```

What is the cost per frog of invoking mapc()? In this case of static binding [LIP], it is dereferencing a function pointer and applying the function to the frog. That is, (p->*pf)(x) translates to (*pf)(p) in C. The overhead of pointer dereferencing is small, and in any event, the code of mapc is compiled.

## 6.8 Polymorphism

One of the nice features of Lisp is the polymorphism of the built-in operations. Roughly, a function is polymorphic if its argument can be of any type. For example, the print function is capable of printing to the terminal any Lisp primitive and any list of heterogeneous elements. Thus, in Lisp one can map the print function over a heterogeneous list of frogs, integers, and strings.

```
(mapc 'print '( "print" 3 "frogs:" kermit lulu ))
```

So far, we have learned how to map a function over a homogeneous list of frogs in C++. Is there a way of mapping over a heterogeneous list in C++? The answer is yes, with restrictions imposed by class derivation. Roughly, all of the elements of a heterogeneous list must be of types derived from a common base class. Imagine that the types Newt, Toad, and Salamander are derived from class Frog. Furthmore let's assume that these types jump in different ways. Here's some C++ code to implement these ideas.

```
class Newt : public Frog {
public:
    Newt( char *n) : Frog(n) {}
```

```
        void jump( int x)
        {
            printf( "I'm a jumping Newt\n" );
            // invoke base class function against
            // this derived class object
            Frog::jump( x);
        }
};

class Toad : public Frog {
public:
        Toad( char *n) : Frog(n) {}

        void jump( int x)
        {
            printf( "I'm a jumping Toad\n" );
            Frog::jump( x);
        }
};

class Salamander : public Frog {
public:
        Salamander( char *n) : Frog(n) {}

        void jump( int x)
        {
            printf( "I'm a jumping Salamander\n" );
            Frog::jump( x);
        }
};
```

One of the nice things about public derivation is that the address of a publicly derived class object may be assigned to a base class pointer without type casting:

```
Salamander sally( "sally");
Frog *p = &sally;
```

Because a pond is just a list of `Frog` pointers, this means that a pond can contain the adresses of `Frogs`, `Newts`, `Toads`, `Salamanders`, and anything else derived from `Frog`. Thus any pond is potentially a heterogeneous collection of objects, whose heterogeneity is subject to the constraints of inheritance.

Now, what would happen if we invoked the `mapc` function we implemented earlier against a heterogeneous pond consisting of a `Frog`, two `Toads`, a `Salamander`, and a `Newt`?

```
Pond pond;
pond.add( new Frog( "kermit"));      // fill the pond ...
pond.add( new Toad( "toady"));
pond.add( new Toad( "minion"));
pond.add( new Salamander( "sally"));
pond.add( new Newt( "newton"));

mapc( pond, &Frog::jump, 3);
```

We want `mapc()` to invoke the jump function corresponding to the (derived) type of each object in the list. This is called dynamic binding, and is obtained in C++ by declaring jump virtual (as we did) in class `Frog`. If jump is not declared virtual in class `Frog`, then the effect is to invoke `Frog`'s `jump()` function against each object in the list—which is probably not what we want.

What is the cost per pond denizen of invoking `mapc`? Restricting ourselves to single inheritance [LIP], the member function identifier (e.g., `Frog::jump`) translates to a (constant) offset that is used to index into various arrays of function addresses.

`(p->*pf)(x) translates to (*p->vtbl[offset-of-pf])( p, x) in C`

Such arrays are called virtual function tables, and there is one for each class derived from `Frog`, as well as for `Frog` itself. It contains the addresses of derived class functions that override corresponding functions of the same name declared virtual in the base class `Frog`. Thus the overhead per denizen is an add plus a pointer dereference. This is cheap and, taken together with the fact that `mapc` is compiled, constitutes a high-performance implementation of a mapping operation over a heterogenous list.

There is a way in C++ of expressing the idea of a completely unconstrained heterogeneous list, namely a list of `void*` pointers. Indeed, the address of anything may be assigned to a `void*` pointer. However, such a list isn't very useful because it is a syntax error to invoke a member function against a `void*` pointer

```
void *p = new Salamander( "sally");
p->jump( 3);    // syntax error
```

even if the object pointed to by p can actually jump!

Strict type checking limits the use of mapping functions like `mapc()` in C++. That is, we cannot use mapc to map `Frog::croak()` across a pond because its functional prototype—void (Frog::*)()—is not what `mapc()` expects—void (Frog::*)(int). However, I think you can now see how to implement easily a separate mapping function for each functional prototype that occurs in the program.

# Bibliography

[ARM]    Margaret Ellis and Bjarne Stroustrup, *The Annotated C++ Reference Manual*, 1990, Addison-Wesley.

[KR]      Brian Kernighan and Dennis Ritchie, *The C Programming Language*, second edition, 1988, Prentice Hall.

[LIP]     Stan Lippman and Bjarne Stroustrup, "Pointers to Class Members," *USENIX Proceedings: C++ Conference*, pp. 293–304, October 1988, USENIX.

[WIL]    Robert Wilensky, *LISPcraft*, 1984, W. W. Norton.

# Chapter 7

# Design

## 7.1 Introduction

The heart of object-oriented design is the identification of the types in the program and the relationships between them. To identify a type is to specify its behavior (public interface). The behavior of a type is manifested by its public interface of operations (and, more formally, the equations that the operations satisfy). All this is under the absolute assumption of implementation (data) hiding. To identify relationships means bringing to light the relationships in the *behavior* of the types. One can then implement the behavior in many ways.

The kinds of behavioral relationships that we shall consider in this chapter are inheritance, parametric types, and has a component. I expect as the years go by that additional semantic relationships between types will be discovered. Recently the object-oriented community has also become interested in relationships between object instances. These relationships may be static (i.e., endure the life of the objects), or may only endure for some portion of the life of the objects or system. Consider the following example: Peter and Pat are both instances of type Human. Pat *owns* a 1989 Chrysler van (an instance of the type Car, and Peter does not own a car; he owns a twenty-year-old Schwinn bicycle. The relationship in question is ownership. It illustrates a trend in recent object-oriented literature, namely a desire to integrate data base design concepts, notably entity relation modeling [COAD], with "classical" object-oriented programming concepts into a unified object-oriented design framework. The design framework to be presented does not take into account object instance relationships, only static (lasting the life of the system) relationships between types. It seems to me that object instance relationships can be represented by predicates or assertions that describe the state of the system either at some point in time or for some duration. Viewing object instance relationships in this way will enable us to bring to bear the power of the formal methods of Dijkstra and Gries [GRIES]. I want to hint at the possibilities; to say more goes beyond the scope of this book.

C++ classes may have nonbehavioral relationships between them, typically implementational relationships. An implementational relationship is one in which the behavior of one class depends on the implementation of some other class (or classes), as well as its own. Friendship in C++ is an example of an implementational relationship. Another example is protected data members in a base class. The problem with implementational relationships between classes is, simply, that when the implementation of one class changes (as it often does) the implementation of the related class may change as well. This can create a maintenance nightmare. In this chapter, We will be taking a fairly hard-nosed position in restricting ourselves to behavioral relationships in the design framework to be presented. One benefit is the conceptual clarity of the resulting design. The other benefit is the decoupling of the behavior of one class from the implementation of any class, other than its own. All of these behavioral relationships can be implemented in C++.

A design framework is a way of using a set of tools to construct a system. Indeed, to build a system (whether it be a boat or a program), you need three things.

- A description of the properties of the system, how it behaves (a requirements document)

- A set of tools suitable for building the system (here, the concepts of object-oriented programming)

- A way of using the tools in an optimal manner to build the system (design framework)

The word design has two meanings. As a verb, it means the process of designing a system (i.e., a design framework). As a noun, it means the result of that process, usually some form of paper or electronic documentation (i.e., a design specification). A design specification can be divided into two parts, which correspond to the separation of interface (behavior) from implementation: the external spec and the internal spec. The external spec is essentially a collection of manual pages for each type. The manual page for a type discusses the behavior of the type by describing its public interface and the behavioral relationship of this type to other types. The internal design spec is a guide to implementing each type identified in the design process. For each type, the internal spec specifies a data structure and a set of algorithms (pseudocode) for implementing each operation in the public interface.

# 7.2  Requirements

Requirements describe the behavior of the system: *what* it does, not *how* it does it. One of the most difficult things for designers and programmers is to write requirements in an implementation-free manner, while simultaneously worrying about the technology needed to implement the system. This is a legitimate worry because just as there are theorems in mathematics that are not provable, so are there requirements documents that cannot be implemented, either for theoretical reasons or for reasons of the performance of current hardware. Nonetheless, the requirements constitute the starting point of the design process. It is all we have; from it we must be able to infer the types of objects in the system and how they interact.

Grammatical analysis [YOU] defines a mapping from the requirements document to a formal system specification. The nouns in the document name types of objects, and the verbs are operations in the public interface of one type or another. The mapping is ill defined, its fuzziness reflecting the inherent ambiguity of human language. Sometimes it is not clear to which noun a verb belongs. Sometimes it doesn't matter. A heuristic is to associate the operation with the object whose state it changes. For example, push and pop modify the state of a stack object. Unfortunately this heuristic is not always applicable. In graphics editors, the display message is traditionally conceived as being sent to shape objects. However, the object whose state is changed is the display device, not the shape object.

We take the viewpoint that the requirements for the system—at least an initial take on it—are (magically) given. We will not be discussing *how* to generate the requirements, usually termed requirements analysis, for this topic is covered elsewhere [YOU]. There are several recent books on object-oriented requirements analysis (OORA) [COAD], and we invite the reader to look there for further information on the subject.

Conversely, we are very interested in what happens to the design of a system when its requirements are modified, a common event in the real world of programming. This interest stems from the commonly held belief in the object-oriented community that object-oriented design is *stable*: that is, small changes in the requirements for a system lead to small changes in its design and implementation. This is contrasted with the belief that procedural design is unstable. I do not believe that object-oriented design is inherently stable. Rather, object-oriented programming provides a rich set of tools (object, type, implementation hiding, inheritance, parametric types, type as object) that will enable us to design stability *into* a system, indeed into the family of related systems supported by the types identified in the object oriented design process. The thought pattern comes by analogy from topology [KELLEY]. The system of interest is a point in a connected space of systems. As the requirements change in time, the system describes a continuous path through the system space "generated" by a collection of types. This notion of stability is related to Parnas's concept of program families [PARNAS] and merits further study.

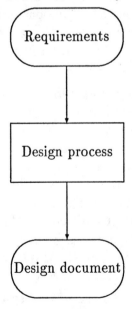

We can regard any design process as a procedure, whose input is system requirements and whose output is a design document (see the picture). Given an initial take on the requirements, we may wish to *iterate* the design process until both the requirements and the resulting design converge to the satisfaction of both client and designer-programmer, respectively. This iteration constitutes a form of prototyping that is cheaper than going all the way to full implementation of the system.

## 7.3  Interaction Model

As indicated in the picture, the input to the design process is a requirements document that describes the behavior of the desired system. The output of the design process is a design document that describes the types and their implementations, and the interaction model. Here order is important. The interaction model can only be specified *after* the types have been identified. Indeed, a given set of types can support an infinite family of related interactions. Following our object-oriented definition of a system, the interaction model describes how the highest-level objects in the system interact (send messages to each other). In many cases, the interaction model corresponds to the `main()` function of a program.

The system may, however, exhibit concurrency, for example, consist of multiple lightweight threads of computation within a single process or multiple-operating system processes across a network. Here each thread or process can be considered an object, where the message expression is actually implemented by interthread or interprocess communication facilities provided by the operating system. An example of such a system is a set of UNIX operating system processes that communicate via pipes or message queues [BACH]. A paradigmatic example of the interaction model is a remote procedure (system) call between client and server processes on different computers connected via some networking scheme such as RFS or NFS. Device drivers fit well into this concurrent interaction model. A device controller communicates (sends messages) with the host computer by sending it a hardware interrupt, which is perceived by the host as a small positive integer index into its interrupt table, which is an array of pointers to functions, one per type (major device number in UNIX terms) of device. The operating system kernel temporarily suspends whatever it is doing and invokes the indexed function to service the interrupt (i.e., respond to the message), and then resumes its activities. In turn, the host communicates with the device controller either with an interrupt or memory-mapped register.

Finally, many windowing systems for workstations, such as X windows, support the object model, though implemented in a procedural language such as C. Each window or more complicated entity derived from it is an object, capable of responding to messages or events. Events of interest include mouse motion and button selection. The designer of the window may specify the response to the event in a function (called the call-back function in Xtoolkit), which she or he associates with the window.

## 7.4    External Design Spec: Type Manual Page

As we have mentioned earlier, the external design specification consists of type manual pages. Ideally the manual page should reflect in human language as faithfully as possible the formal semantics of the type. However, in case of any doubt, the final arbiter of the type's behavior is the formal specification. A sample manual page for a parametric stack type follows. The corresponding formal specification is found in the last section of the chapter.

*Warning:*  Although the template notation for defining parametric types has been accepted into the ANSI standard for C++, as of this time there is no C++ compiler that implements the feature. On a more upbeat note, C++ provides excellent support for the design concept that a member function is an `inspector`, that is, does not modify the state of the object against which it is invoked. In C++, such a member function is called `constant`, an example of which is `Boolean isempty() const` in the following manual page. The `const` notation provides two very different benefits. In the type manual page, it immediately alerts the reader that the designated member function may inspect (return a value) but does not modify object state. At compile time, any implementation of a `constant` member function that attempts to modify object state—by assignment or invocation of a non-constant member function against a data member—is deemed an error.

```
STACK(3C++)   C++ USER-DEFINED TYPE   STACK(3C++)
NAME

       template <class T> Stack;


SYNOPSIS
```

```
typedef int Boolean;
const Boolean TRUE = 1;
const Boolean FALSE = !TRUE;

template<class T> class Stack { // Stack of T values
public:
        Stack();  // constructor initializes state
        // postcondition:  isempty()

        void push( T x);
        // precondition:   !isfull()
        // postcondition:  !isempty()

        T pop();
        // precondition:   !isempty()
        // postcondition:  !isfull()

        Boolean isempty() const;
        // no state change

        Boolean isfull() const;
        // no state change
private:
        // implementation
};
```

## DESCRIPTION

`Stack` is the parameterized type Stack-of-T-values. Stack objects are of finite capacity, that is, they can only contain a finite of values of type T. Stack has value semantics; that is, when a value or object of type T is pushed (`push( T x)` onto a stack object, its value (not its address) is copied into the storage of the stack. Stack objects of any particular type, say `int`, may be instantiated, for example, via

`Stack<int> istack;`

Stack overflow is detected by invoking the member function `isfull()`, and underflow is detected by invoking `isempty()`. Detailed description of the public member functions follows.

PUBLIC INTERFACE

Stack(); The constructor initializes the state of a stack object
on creation so that it comes into existence in the empty state
(i.e., satisfying the predicate isempty() == TRUE).

void push( T x); push permits the user to push a value of type
T onto a stack object. Before the operation, the stack object
must not be full. After the operation, the stack is not empty.
This operation changes the state of the object. Here is a code
fragment indicating proper use of push

```
Stack s;
...
T x;
if( !s.isfull() )
      s.push( x);
else    // error ...
      printf( "stack overflow\n" );
```

T pop(); pop() pops the top value off the stack object. Before
the operation, the stack object cannot be empty. After the operation, the stack is not full. This operation changes the state of
the stack object. Here is a code fragment indicating proper use
of pop

```
Stack s;
...
T x;
if( !s.isempty() )
      x = s.pop( x);
else    // error ...
      printf( "stack underflow\n" );
```

Boolean isempty(); // no state change. This predicate function returns TRUE if the stack object is empty; otherwise, it
returns FALSE. This operation does not change the state of the
stack object.

`Boolean isfull();` This predicate function returns TRUE if the stack object is full; otherwise, it returns FALSE. This operation does not change the state of the stack object.

## FILES

/usr/local/lib/Stack.h

## DIAGNOSTICS

This stack type follows the contractual school of programming. That is, the client programmer must *explicitly* check the precondition before invoking the associated member function. If the precondition is true, the associated member function may be invoked. If the precondition is false, the client programmer should take appropriate (evasive) action. If the precondition is false—whether or not it is checked—and the associated member function is invoked in any event, nothing sensible can be said about the program from that point onward. The state of the stack object is probably corrupt. Other objects in the program may also have their states corrupted (silently). With luck, the program will abort and dump core.

## BUGS

Falsification of a precondition should be caught by language-provided user-defined exception handling syntax, regardless of whether or not the client programmer explicitly checks the precondition. Unfortunately, C++ currently does not provide this feature.

# 7.5 Internal Design Spec

The internal design specification guides the implementation of each type identified in the design process. For each type, the internal spec specifies a data structure—private data members—and a set of algorithms (pseudocode) for implementing each member function in the public interface. If the type under design is derived (using C++ class derivation) implementationally from several parent types, it can be regarded as having an anonymous data member of each parent's type. Thus the data structure to be selected is modulo whatever is inherited. The goal to strive for is short member function bodies. The reward for brevity is often little difference between pseudocode and actual implementation. Here is an implementation of the parametric stack type.

```
typedef int Boolean;
const Boolean TRUTH = 1;
const Boolean FALSE = 0;

const int dim = 100;

template<class T> class Stack { // Stack of T values
public:
        Stack()                        { sp = 0; }

        void push( T x)                { elt[sp++] = x; }

        T pop()                        { return elt[--sp]; }

        Boolean isempty() const   { return sp <= 0; }

        Boolean isfull() const    { return sp >= dim; }
private:
        T elt[dim];
        int sp;
};
```

## 7.6   Design Process

So far we have viewed object-oriented design as a black box: We have described its input (a requirements document) and its output (a design document). At this point we have little idea what is in the box, so to speak how it is implemented. Is it possible to reverse-engineer the box from a description of its input and output and first principles? The principles that I have in mind are the key concepts of object-oriented programming: type,

implementation hiding, object model of a system, and semantic relationships between types (inheritance, parametric types, has a component). The
benefit of deriving the design process from first principles are

- The derivation reinforces the concepts of object-oriented programming, because the design process depends intimately on them.

- There is little need to memorize anything, because the design process
  is constructed from the principles of object-oriented programming.

- The reader is motivated to use the design framework, because she or
  he sees that it is reasonable given the assumptions from which it is
  derived.

The design framework presented below is not unique; it merely attempts to
map system requirements into a design. Experience with it indicates that
it seems to work. It is largely based on Barbara Liskov's methodology for
design in the context of abstract data types [LSK], that is, in the absence of
inheritance. For Liskov, all design is decomposition and subsequent recom-
position of the identified components *(divide and conquer)*. This methodology extends Liskov's by considering semantic relations between types. The
design framework is not complete; as new software engineering concepts are
discovered, they need to be integrated into the design framework. With all
these caveats behind us, let's begin the derivation.

A system in the object model is a collection of objects of different types that
get the work done by sending each other messages. So at the very least,
the design process should generate an initial decomposition of the system
into types, together with a model that identifies instances of these types
and specifies how they interact. For each type in the initial decomposition,
the next job is to specify its behavior by identifying the operations in the
public interface of the type. Following Liskov, we call this step abstraction.
Formalists will write a formal specification of the type. The rest of us
will sketch out the type's manual page. Now that we know how each type
behaves, we can ask the question: Are there any semantic relationships
between the types? Now it's time to implement the type. In this step,
called type decomposition, we must select a data structure to represent the
state of objects of this type, and we must select algorithms to implement the
operations (member functions) in the public interface. Both of these last
two steps—type relationships and decomposition—may generate new types

that are grist for the mill. That is, the new types also need to undergo the design steps: abstraction, type relationships, and decomposition. We say that a type is designed if it has undergone the aforementioned three steps. It appears that the design process is iterative, stopping when all types generated by the process have been designed.

We can view the design process as a procedure that manages a working list of types. The list is initialized by the initial decomposition on the requirements. The type relationship and decomposition steps may add types to the list. A type may be removed from the list once it has been designed. In terms of the list, the design process terminates when the list is empty.

Here is a pseudocode description of the design framework [MUR, SIM]; a detailed description of each step follows.

```
initial decomposition(on requirements document);
while( stopping condition has not been met )
        for( each type in working list) {
                abstraction;
                type relationships;
                type decomposition;
        }

return design specification;
```

### 7.6.1   Initial Decomposition

We summarize several points mentioned earlier in the chapter. Taking the requirements document as a guide, identify the major types in the system. The heuristic of grammatical analysis [YOU] suggests taking the nouns as identifying types, and the verbs as identifying operations. The art is in associating the verbs with the right nouns! A heuristic coming right out of the object model is to associate the operation with the object whose state is modified. This is not always the best choice. There are cases in which the object whose state is to be modified is a reference argument to a message dynamically bound to some other object, whose state may not change at all. The following chapter, a case study design of a graphics editor, will provide opportunities to practice this art.

Based on the requirements document, establish the high-level interaction model. That is, name instances of the major types, and specify how they send messages to each other. As mentioned earlier, the interaction model may be implemented by a short main program. The implementation of concurrency will require operating system or language support.

C++ does not provide support for (concurrent) lightweight tasks. However, there is interest in the C++ community in concurrency extensions to the language. In [GEH], Narain Gehani discusses concurrency extensions to C and C++. Bill Joy [JOY] has called for concurrency extensions to C++ as a means of improving its support for the implementation of operating systems. His precedent is sound: C itself was invented as the target implementation language for the UNIX operating system.

In contrast to C++, there is no such thing as a main program in the Eiffel language [MEY]. At the operating system command-line interface, the user specifies a type of object. The first piece of code to run is the create function for this type, which corresponds roughly to a constructor in C++. The create function, in turn, instantiates objects of various types and has them send messages to each other. Thus in Eiffel, the concept of a system is encapsulated in a type. That is, a system is an object. From this viewpoint, there is no difference between initial decomposition and type decomposition.

I mention Eiffel here because its syntax—no main programs—paradoxically encourages the designer to think in terms of families of related programs supported by a judiciously designed collection of reusable types.

## 7.6.2  Abstraction

Abstraction is the process of identifying the essential properties of a situation or entity, while ignoring the details. What is essential about a type is its behavior; implementation, though important, is secondary. So the abstraction step consists of specifying the behavior of the type by listing the operations in its public interface. Again, the formalists will want to write a formal specification of the type. Informally, we want to sketch out the type's manual page. At this stage of the game, it suffices to provide an informal and brief description of the (externally perceived) behavior of each operation. More detail would be a waste of time, because we might end up throwing away this part of the design. We want to do just enough work here so that the design process continues and doesn't grind to a halt. The result of this step forms the basis for the type manual page.

The following list of categories of operations may serve as an aid in identifying the public interface of a type:

- *Initializer:* Initializes state of object on creation. Initializers map most elegantly to constructors in C++.

- *Clean-up operation:* Clean-up object just before its demise. These functions map nicely to destructors.

- *Inspector:* Does not modify state of object but may return a value of different type. This category maps to `constant` member functions.

  A large subcategory of inspector operations is the predicate functions, namely, those inspectors that return a boolean value. Preconditions, postconditions, and assertions are all members of this category.

- *Changer:* Changes state of object. These may return a value.

- *Creator:* Returns value of same type.

A useful exercise is to determine the category each member function belongs to in `class Sequence` defined subsequently. The information we have to go on is the functional prototype of each member function and the comments embedded in the class template. As an overview, `Sequence` is the container type sequence of integer. It has operations for concatenation and subsequencing, as well as random access operations for getting and setting the element of a sequence object at an index.

```
// Sequence is a parameterized type with value semantics,
// designed according to the contractual school
typedef int T;

typedef int Boolean;
const Boolean TRUE = 1;
const Boolean FALSE =  0;

class Sequence {
public:
    // postcondition is initial condition:  isempty() == TRUE
    Sequence() : Length(0),  store(0) {}
```

```
// create singleton sequence of single value x
// postcondition:  length() == 1 && get(0) = x
Sequence(T x) : Length( 1), store( new T(x)) {}

// create an sequence of storage dimension l;
// all set to the same value x
Sequence( int l, T x) : Length(l), store( new T[l])
{
    for( int j = 0; j < l; j++)
        store[j] = x;
}

~Sequence()          { delete store; }

Boolean isempty() const    { return length() == 0; }

int length() const    { return Length; }

// precondition:  0 <= n && n < length()
T get(int n) const    { return store[n]; }

// precondition:  0 <= n && n < length()
// postcondition:  newstate.get( n) == x
void put( int n, T x)    { store[n] = x; }

// concatenate this sequence with argument
// to produce new sequence
Sequence cat( const Sequence& s) const
{
    Sequence r( length() + s.length(), 0);
    for( int j = 0; j < s.length(); j++)
        r.store[j] = store[j];
    for( j = 0; j < s.length(); j++)
        r.store[length() + j] = s.store[j];

    return r;
}

// return subsequence of this sequence at offset off
```

```
    // of length len
    // precondition:  off + len <= length()
    Sequence sub( int off, int len) const
    {
        Sequence r;
        r.Length = len;
        r.store = new T[len];
        for( int j = 0; j < len; j++)
            r.store[j] = store[off + j];
        return r;
    }
private:
    int Length;
    T *store;
};
```

The table summarizes the categories that the various member functions of
Class Sequence belong to.

| Member function | Category |
|---|---|
| Various constructors | Initializer |
| Destructor | Clean-up |
| isempty | Predicate |
| get | Inspector |
| put | Changer |
| cat | Creator |
| sub | Creator |

Up to now, we have been discussing individual operations in the public
interface of a type. Are there any global criteria for the goodness or quality
of the public interface of a type as a whole? A notion of global goodness
is admittedly a fuzzy concept, and is certainly different from the equations
(axioms) section of the formal algebraic specification of a type [CHJ], which
relates the behavior of one operation to another. Nonetheless, there are
several benefits to grappling with this issue, which we will enumerate after
discussing the following criteria:

- Correctness

- Completeness

- Minimality

- Orthogonality

- Convenience

- Performance

*Correctness:* The implementation of a type—which includes the implementation of the operations—should be faithful to the type manual page. In the words of Captain Picard of the new Startrek series to his first officer: "make it so, number one, make it so." Formalists simply say that the implementation should be correct regarding the formal specification of the type. At the risk of belaboring the point, the advantage of writing a formal specification—in addition to the usual manual page—is that it constitutes an unambiguous standard against which to measure the correctness of an implementation.

*Completeness:* Here is a user-oriented definition: The client programmer can do all the things she or he expects to be able to do with objects of this type. The criterion is inspired by the concept of a spanning set in a vector space [HERST]. That is, every vector can be written as a linear combination of vectors in the spanning set. By analogy, client programmers can do whatever they need to do with an object by writing simple expressions in the public interface of the object's type. The simplest expression is just to invoke an operation. The acid test of the completeness of a public interface is the extent to which client programmers observe data hiding by using it. Completeness discourages (though cannot prevent—at least in C++) the programmer from wanting to access the data structure of an object directly. The data of a class object can always be exposed by coercing its address to (char *) and then mucking about at will. This is not recommended practice!

*Minimality:* No operation can be implemented in terms of the rest of the public interface. Again, this concept comes by analogy from vector spaces. A basis for a finite-dimensional vector space is a minimal spanning set. Types with small public interfaces are easier to invent, reason about, and maintain. We can build more complicated types and operations in terms of minimal ones.  A design heuristic: Lurking inside every fat type with a large public interface is a minimal type yearning to be free! This is an interesting area of research, because I do not know how to prove minimality, though I believe that, with experience, one can recognize a minimal interface when one sees it. I conjecture that minimality is provable in the context of formal type specification and implementation languages possessing formal semantics, like Dijkstra's little language [GRIES]. Intuition tells me that the parametric `Stack` type, which we talked about earlier in the chapter, has a minimal public interface. In contrast, it is easy to prove nonminimality: demonstrate a single nonminimal implementation.

Nonminimality has some curious advantages.  Member functions implemented solely in terms of other member functions are portable. That is, they do not have to be re-implemented when the data structure is changed. Sometimes, such implementations can be read right out of the formal specification of the type—in particular, the equations section—which permits a degree of rapid prototyping. The designer must trade off portability against performance: It may be more efficient to implement the operation directly in terms of the data structure of the object.

*Orthogonality:*  Make the overlap in behavior of any two operations as minimal as possible. The operations will be easier to understand and easier to implement. Here the inspiration comes both from vector spaces with inner products as well as from reduced instruction set computer (RISC) architectures. The parameterized type array of T values (e.g., `double vector[100]` ) has an orthogonal public interface. After all, the only operations that can be performed on an array are getting and setting the value at an integer index, and operations at one index have no effect elsewhere. Conversely, the traditional file abstraction (e.g., `FILE` in `stdio.h`) does not have an orthogonal interface because it is possible to effect the file offset either by getting a character ( `getc()` ) or by random access ( `fseek()` ).

*Convenience:*  This criterion runs counter to the others. It says that type designer should provide operations, hallowed by custom, even if their inclusion renders the public interface nonminimal or nonorthogonal. `Class Sequence` above is not minimal, because the `isempty()` member function can be implemented by comparing the `length()` to zero.

*Performance:*  The demands of performance may require that the designer add operations into the public interface that violate minimality or orthogonality. The reason is that the operation can be implemented more efficiently directly in terms of the data structure of the object, despite the fact that it could also be implemented in terms of the rest of the public interface. This issue is clouded by the `inline` optimization feature provided by several object-oriented languages, including C++ [ARM]. That is, in many cases, the compiler optimizes out the function call overhead of the message expression. Thus the expense of invoking a member function is no more than that of executing its body.

For example, say we want to add a `void print()` member function to `class Stack`, capable of displaying to standard output the contents of a stack object in order from its top to its base. It is required that the print function not change the state of the stack. If we insist on implementing `print()` in terms of the existing public interface, the only way to view the contents of a stack object is to pop each element off. Assuming that the `Stack` is a stack of integers, the implementation might look like

```
void Stack::print()
{
    Stack t;
    int val;
    while( !isempty() ) {
        val = pop();
        t.push( val);
        printf( "%d\n", val);
    }
    while( !t.isempty() )
        push( t.pop() );
}
```

Despite the fact that `print()` leaves its object in the state that it found it, we cannot declare it to be constant—`void Stack::print() const`— because it does modify the state of its object during intermediate steps. `print()` has a far more efficient implementation directly in terms of the data structure.

```
void Stack::print() const
{
    for( int j = sp - 1;j >= 0; j--)
        printf( "%d\n", elt[j]);
}
```

Notice that this implementation can be declared constant, because it does not modify the state of the stack object.

In summary, the benefits of the preceding criteria include ease of understanding and implementation of a type. I suspect that a system that consists of types with quality public interfaces is stable.

### 7.6.3  Type Relationships

The designer looks for behavioral (semantic) relationships between types, (static) relationships that hold throughout the life of the system. Note that this step can only be performed after the abstraction step. For, it requires that we already have some idea of the behavior of the types identified up to now. Arming ourselves with rigorous definitions of the various concepts in the object universe makes identifying the relationships a lot easier. We are motivated to search for these relationships because of the big payoff in software and design reuse. We will be discussing three semantic relationships between types

- Inheritance (is a kind of)

- Parametric types (stack of integers)

- Containment (has a component)

In the above list, an indicative phrase is associated with each type relationship. The phrase permits extending the grammatical analysis of the requirements document by enabling us to identify these type relationships. For example, if the requirements for a graphics editor talks about the picture as a list of shapes, we may easily conclude that the programmer must either build or find in a component library the parameterized type `List<T>`, where the type parameter `T` is going to be bound to `Shape` (or `Shape *`).

### Inheritance

This section reviews inheritance-related design concepts that we have discussed in previous chapters. There are three items I want to discuss.

- A priori inheritance

- A posteriori inheritance

- Pitfalls of multiple class derivation in C++

*A Priori Inheritance:* Intuitively, under a priori inheritance, the base type establishes a generic interface for all types derived from it. That is, the base type acts as a repository for a manual page (semantics), which all derive types inherit and thus must implement correctly. In practice, we often already have in mind several types that we want to derive from the base type. So we want to make the base type manual page "weak" enough so that the derived-type manual page contains it and does not contradict it. For example, in a graphics editor, the manual page for the base class `Shape`'s `display` function states that when a `Shape` object receives the `display` message, it paints itself to the display device in some fashion. This specification is certainly weak enough to be satisfied by the manual pages for the `display` function override in the derived classes `Text, Circle, Box,` ...

Often when we work with a priori inheritance, the base type is so abstract that there are no instances of it in the system. Such a type is called an *abstract* base type. In the graphics editor example, `Shape` is an abstract base type. There are no `Shape` objects in a picture, only objects of types derived from `Shape`, such as `Text, Circle, Box,` ... An abstract base type is created in C++ by declaring at least one of its member functions to be *pure virtual*, such as `display` in `class Shape`.

```
class Shape {
public:
    virtual void display() = 0;
    // the other members
};
```

A pure virtual member function has no implementation. No objects can be instantiated of a class with a pure virtual member function. Furthermore, any class derived from `Shape` *must* override the `display` function—not to do so is a compilation error.

One might conclude that an abstract base class has no implementation. This is not necessarily true. We can factor the position property out of the `Shape` hierarchy into the base class.

```
class Shape {
public:
    virtual void display() = 0;

    // move the shape to new coordinates
    void translate( int X, int Y);

    // return x coordinate of shape position
    int getx();

    // return y coordinate of shape position
    int gety();

    // other member functions
private:  // coordinates of center of shape
    int x,
        y;
};
```

Generally, all the member functions in an abstract base class are declared **virtual**, but not necessarily pure virtual. In this design, classes derived from **Shape** may simply inherit its position data structure and the code of the position-related member functions **translate()**, **getx()**, **gety()**, and still satisfy the semantic definition of a priori inheritance. In addition, a derived type may have additional member functions, which do not override anything in the base type. For example, **Text** objects can be displayed in a variety of font styles and sizes. Clearly the **void Text::setFontStyle()** member function has nothing to do with the base class **Shape**.

A priori inheritance can be used to distinguish between different technologies used to implement a given abstraction, such as **Window** for workstations with high-resolution display devices [LIP2]. **Window** is an abstract base, from which are derived classes that encapsulate such windowing technologies as X windows, NeWs, MicroSoft windows, and so on. Here there may very well be few additional member functions in the derived type, beyond those that override member functions declared in the base class **Window**. This scheme can be used to render a windowed application independent of the actual windowing technology in the following way. All member functions in base class **Window** are declared **virtual**. The application developer instantiates a window object of a particular derived type and assigns its address to a base class pointer. All of the rest of the code of the application consists of sending dynamically bound messages to the window pointer, which invoke the appropriate derived class override.

```
class X_window : public Window { ... };
...
Window *wp = new X_Window( /* constructor arguments */ );
...
wp->getnextevent();
...
wp->move( x, y);
...
```

Most of the code of the application is independent of the windowing technology; the only line of code that needs to be altered is the assignment of the address of a derived class object to the base class `Window` pointer. Furthermore, an application designed in this way can handle multiple windowing technologies simultaneously, by simply instantiating objects of several types derived from `Window`. It bears repetition that the primary advantage of the scheme is conceptual uniformity and simplicity. The developer writes the same line of code (the dynamically bound message expression `wp->windowfunction()`) regardless of the complicated technology needed to implement it. The scheme depends critically on the assumption that all of the windowing technologies can be regarded as sharing a single common interface, which requires different implementations.

*A Posteriori Inheritance:* This kind of inheritance describes situations in which the designer notices, after the fact, that several types have some common behavior. The common behavior is identified by looking in the corresponding type manual pages for operations with common descriptions. That the names of two operations in different types are the same is a good hint at similar behavior, but is not necessary. Regard the set of operations so identified as the public interface of a *synthetic* base type, viewing the other types as derived from it. Often, the derived types can inherit implementation from the base type without recourse to override. However, as we saw in the chapter on formal definitions of inheritance, there may be restrictions on the use of the operation in the derived type that do not obtain in the base type. This *factorization* of the public interfaces of a set of types has the flavor of determining the intersection of two sets in a Venn diagram.

*Pitfalls of multiple class derivation in C++:* The C++ syntax for multiple inheritance lays traps for the unwary.

```
class Child : public Parent1, public Parent2, ... {};
```

Lexically it would appear that the comma-separated list of parents of a derived class is indeed a list: Order counts, and a base class may be mentioned more than once. Nothing could be further from the truth. The lexical list is in fact a set. That is, the order of the parents is irrelevant, and duplicates are not permitted. In contrast, in Common Lisp [KEENE], the parent collection is a list: Duplicates are permitted, and the order of the parent classes determines from which parent the derived class inherits code in the event that two or more parent classes have operations with the same names.

## Parametric Types

Applications with a sophisticated windowed user interface constitute an increasing percentage of all applications being written today. This category is essentially that of object editors, which enable a user literally to view an object visually and possibly to modify its state in a what-you-see-is-what-you-get (WYSIWYG) manner. The category includes text editors, graphics editors, network management systems, and others. Two kinds of types are needed to build such applications.

- User interface types including windows, pop-up menus, scroll bars

- Structure types used to represent the internal state of the object being displayed

Here we are going to concentrate on the structure types. Often the object being displayed is a collection or aggregate of other types of objects. Such an object is an instance of a *container* type, which by definition is some kind of collection of other types of objects. For example, a text editor like emacs or vi manipulates a buffer, which is a homogeneous sequence of characters. Conversely, a graphics editor manipulates a picture, which is a heterogeneous set or list of different kinds of shapes.

Many of the classical structure types of computer science and mathematics are parametric container types. Here are a few examples

- `Array<int,T>` - e.g. `Frog Pond[100];`

- `List<T>` with public interface: get, insert, delete, tail ...

- `Stack<T>` with public interface: push, pop, isempty, isfull ...

- `Table<Key,Value>` with public interface: isin (find), get, put ...

- ...

An interesting issue with parametrized types is the domain of the type. That is, given a parametrized type `F<T>`, for what types `T` is `F<T>` defined? In the list above, `Array<int,T>` , `List<T>` and `Stack<T>` are defined for any type `T`. However, table of key-value pairs is only defined `Table<Key,Value>` for those `Key` types that support comparison, say, as an overloaded comparison operator

```
Boolean Key::operator == ( const Key &) { ... }
```

for, after all, `Value` objects are placed and looked up in a table based on a unique, comparable key.

As alluded to earlier, there are two kinds of container types: *homogeneous* and *heterogeneous*. In a homogeneous container, all of the objects are of the same type. An array of integers is the homogeneous container par excellence, as is a list-of-frogs `List<Frog>`.

In a heterogeneous container, the objects are of different types. A common form of heterogeneity is where it is constrained by inheritance (e.g., list of amphibian, i.e., a list of objects of any type derived from amphibian). One can insert frogs, as well as toads or salamanders, into such a list.

Our first attempt at implementing an inheritance-constrained heterogeneous container type in C++, such as stack of amphibian, might result in

```
typedef Stack<Amphibian> Stack_of_Amphibian;
```

however, this will not work for some subtle reasons. When I push Kermit onto the stack

```
class Frog : public Amphibian { ... };
```

```
Frog kermit;
Stack<Amphibian> stk;

// push Amphibian( kermit) on stack where
// Amphibian::Amphibian(const Frog& );
stk.push( kermit);
Amphibian k;

// k is assigned the Amphibian base part of kermit
k = stk.pop();
```

what actually ends up on the stack is Kermit's amphibian base part since the code generated by `stk.push( kermit)` is actually

```
stk.push( Amphibian( kermit))
```

In the absence of an explicit definition, the C++ compiler automatically generates a constructor with the footprint (prototype)

```
Amphibian::Amphibian( const Frog & );
```

which *demotes* a `Frog` to its `Amphibian` part. In fact, C++ will automatically generate such a demotion constructor for every type (publicly) derived from `Amphibian`. Then when we pop Kermit off the stack, we don't get all of Kermit, just his base part. Which certainly violates the stack axiom: pop returns precisely whatever was pushed last. What to do?

The type definition

```
typedef Stack<Amphibian *> Stack_of_Amphibian;
```

comes closer to solving our problem, for now we can push and pop the *address* of any object of any type publicly derived from `Amphibian`. How do we know that we have just popped the address of a `Frog` off the stack, and not a `Salamander`? After all, the signature of pop is

```
Amphibian *Amphibian::pop();
```

which is a bit vague. All we know is that pop returns the address of an object of *some* type derived from `Amphibian`. Answer: We can implicitly recover the derived-type information by dynamic binding, that is, by invoking against the address member functions that are declared `virtual` in the base class `Amphibian`.

The type definition

```
typedef Stack<Amphibian& > Stack_of_Amphibian;
```

is problematic. True enough the expression `stk.pop().jump()` below

```
class Amphibian {
public:
    virtual void jump();
    ...
};

Stack_of_Amphibian stk;
Frog kermit;

stk.push( kermit);
stk.pop().jump();
```

binds dynamically to the derived type of object that `stk.pop()` refers to. However the fact that C++ does not permit arrays of references severely limits the space of implementations for the parametric stack type. In particular, it invalidates the simple array implementation for `Stack<T>` given earlier in this chapter. In honesty, a linked list implementation of `Stack<T>` wherein each node contains an `Amphibian` reference [ARM] would work. Nonetheless, because of the severe limitations on the use of references in C++ (they must be initialized, and can never be reassigned), I prefer the `Amphibian` pointer approach.

How can we implement in C++ container types with completely unrestricted heterogeneity, that is, containers that contain objects of any type? It is difficult to do in C++ for reasons that contrast interestingly with Smalltalk [GOLD]. In Smalltalk, every class is derived eventually from the ur-class Object including so-called primitive types such as integer. Thus, by virtue of inheritance, a list of object in Smalltalk can contain any kind of object!

In contrast, there is no such ur-class in C++. That is, a C++ class need not be derived from anything; it can stand alone, so to speak.

What about containers of void pointers such as

```
typedef Stack<void *> Vstack;
```

Indeed we can push the address of any type of object onto such a stack, because ultimately the implementation of push assigns the address to a **void** * pointer. The problem arises when we pop an address off the stack

```
void *Vstack::pop();
```

pop returns a **void** * address **p**, and there is no way in the C++ language of recovering the real type of the object! Indeed, no operations of any type may be performed on **p**.

The best one can do in C++ to implement containers of unconstrained heterogeneity is to emulate Smalltalk and create a large inheritance hierarchy derived from an artificial ur-class called, say, `Object`. Then `Stack<Object *>`, `List<Object *>` ... are capable of containing any object of any type derived from `class Object`. This is precisely what Keith Gorlen [GORLEN] did in porting the Smalltalk environment to C++ in his National Institute of Health (NIH) class library.

### Has a Component

In recent years the object-oriented community has been experimenting with integrating data base concepts with "traditional" object-oriented concepts. An important data base concept is the has a component or containment relationship: the notion that an object consists of a collection of component objects, each of which may be further decomposed until one reaches the atomic (indecomposable) types of objects supported by the data base. For example, a Boeing 747 jet *has* three landing gear. In turn, the type landing gear can be decomposed into its parts.

Has a component is problematic. From a data base viewpoint, the decomposition of an object is visible and constitutes the bulk of the semantics of the object. The decomposition is viewed as fixed and changes little over time. Data base objects are fairly static: That is, the only operations against an object are to get or set the value of one of its components. This view conflicts mightily with the object-oriented view, wherein objects are dynamic, that is, they respond in complicated ways to messages, and data decomposition is hidden, being viewed merely as an artifact of the current implementation of the object's type.

The challenge, then, is to reconcile these two conflicting views of an object. Tom Wheeler [1] suggests that objects have no intrinsic type. That is, the only things that really exist are objects. A type is a view of an object; a given object can be viewed in many ways. Views are related to multiple inheritance: Each view can be regarded as a base type from which the object is derived. The object's type can be regarded as the union of all of its views. How an object is viewed depends on the viewer's needs and perspective. The pilot of a 747 jet views it as a kind of (derived from) flying machine capable of responding to the messages

```
take off, fly, land, ...
```

Conversely, an aircraft mechanic views the jet as some kind of heterogeneous collection of parts that she or he must maintain. In C++ notation

```
class Boeing747 : public FlyingMachine,
    public List<Component *> { ... };

class FlyingMachine {
public:
    void takeoff();
    void fly();
    void land();
    ...
};

class LandingGear : public Component,
    public List<Component *> { ... };
```

I think of the various derivations above from Component as being semantically a priori and the derivations from List<Component *> as being semantically a posteriori. The conflict over the visibility of the components

---

[1] I am indebted, as ever, to my colleague Tom Wheeler of the Software Engineering Program at Monmouth College for creatively rattling my cage when I get stuck!

is resolved here by deriving `Boeing747` from `List<Component *>`, which permits the insertion (or deletion) of (the address of) any kind of object derived from aircraft `Component`. *Caveat:* There is nothing about the list type that requires that it contain (pointers to) landing gear objects. Thus it is the responsibility of the `Boeing747` type to maintain the consistency of that relationship.

A related point of view: In the sense of model-based formal specification [CHJ], we may model the jet as having an abstract decomposition (fuselage, landing gear, etc.) without committing ourselves in the least to a real data decomposition of `class Boeing747`. As Liskov [LSK2] points out, you don't need class derivation to implement semantic hierarchy. So it really doesn't matter how `Boeing747` is implemented, as long as it gives the *appearance* of being a collection of *visible* components. That is, as long as I can find the second landing gear, inspect its part number, and modify a strut, the implemented data decomposition is of no semantic importance.

A way of implementing the model-based viewpoint in C++ is *not* to derive `Boeing747` from `List<Component *>` but rather to enrich its public interface with member functions that support the aircraft mechanic's view of the jet as a collection of components, as follows:

```
class Boeing747 : public FlyingMachine {
    LandingGear& getlg( int n);
    Wing& getw( int n);
    // other component-related member functions
};
```

For example, `getlg(1)` returns a reference to the first landing gear of the jet, thus permitting the mechanic to inspect, modify or replace the component. And so on: For each component in the model of the jet, there corresponds a `Boeing747` member function that returns a reference to the component's type.

### 7.6.4   Type Decomposition

Following Liskov [LSK], sketch out an implementation for the type. First, select a data structure (in programming, function follows form, in contrast to the Bauhaus school of architecture, where form follows function). If the type inherits from a couple of parent types, the designer can regard the target type as containing an anonymous data member of each parent type. Thus, the designer need only select the ADDITIONAL data members that she or he feels are needed to implement the type. Sketch out (pseudocode) each operation in the public interface. The heuristic is that the implementation of an operation on the target type should consist of a sequence of invocations to the operations of the following:

- Data members that constitute the structure of the target type

- Parent types from which the target inherits

- Explicit arguments to the operation

Karl Lieberherr [KL] calls this heuristic the law of Demeter. Paradigmatically,

```
class D : public B {
public:                 // public interface of D
        foo()
        {               // PI means public interface
            bar();  // in PI(B)
            a.f();  // in PI(A)
            c.g();  // in PI(C)
        }
private:            // additional data members of D
        A a;
        C c;
};
```

For example, the D member function foo() consists of an invocation to bar() (from the public interface of the base type B), an invocation of f() against the data member a, and an invocation of g() against the data member c. This is where object-oriented design includes procedural design, precisely in the sketching out of the operations in the public interface of a type.

## 7.6.5  Stopping Condition

*Stopping condition:*  One can view the design framework as a procedure that manages a working list of types. The list is initialized by the initial

decomposition step. New types are added to the list as a result of the type
relationship or decomposition steps. A type is deleted from the working list
on completion of the three steps (for it): abstraction, type relationships, and
type decomposition. So, a simple way of stating the stopping condition for
the design process is that the working list is empty. Another way of stating
the stopping condition is that all of the types remaining in the working list
are either

- Types built into the language

- Types supported in a runtime library, either standard or project specific

- Types that we have already encountered as a result of the design process

## 7.7  Performance

The performance of an object refers to its consumption of computer resources, typically memory—related to the size of the object—and CPU
cycles—related to the time it takes to invoke an operation. Throughout
the book, we have emphasized the behavior (semantics) of types and consequently their correct implementation. Where does the performance of types,
programs, and systems fit into design?

Following Brad Cox [COX], performance should be mentioned in the manual page of a type when it constitutes part of the behavior of that type
perceptible to the user. However, performance should only be discussed in
terms of the public interface of the type, never in terms of an implementation. For example, the manual page for a table type T1 may state that
table storage consumption is linearly proportional to the number of records
in the table. Similarly, the time it takes to look up a record on a key is linearly proportional to the number of records. This is fine as long as the table
type has a (constant) member function that returns the number of records
currently contained. Conversely, in the very same type library, there can be
another table type T2, with essentially the same public interface but totally
different performance characteristics. Namely, nothing is said about storage
consumption, but look up on a key occurs in constant time. Thus discussion of performance in the type manual page provides the programmer with

some of the information needed to make intelligent selections out of a type library, in much the same way that electrical engineers consult catalogues of integrated circuits (ICs) to build electronic devices.

Often, the requirements for a system specify a performance budget that must be met. These requirements may place severe constraints on the data structures, algorithms, and even hardware selected for an implementation, the discussion of which is well beyond the scope of this book. Nonetheless, Barbara Liskov [LSK] provides an excellent suggestion for mapping performance requirements into an implementation: *factorization*. Namely, assign a portion of the performance budget to each object in the high-level decomposition of the system. From there, proceed recursively to assign a portion of each object's performance budget to its data components that come out of its data decomposition. This is all based on the assumption that the performance of an object is some simple function of its data members, for example, the sum.

# Bibliography

[ARM]        Margaret Ellis and Bjarne Stroustrup, *The Annotated C++ Reference Manual*, 1990, Addison-Wesley.

[BACH]       Maury Bach, *Internals of the UNIX System Kernel*, 1987, Addison-Wesley.

[CHJ]        B. Cohen, W. T. Harwood, M. I. Jackson, *The Specification of Complex Systems*, 1986, Addison-Wesley.

[COAD]       Coad and Yourdon, *Object-Oriented Requirements Analysis*, 1990, Prentice Hall.

[COX]        Brad Cox, *Object-Oriented Programming: An Evolutionary Approach*, 1986, Addison-Wesley.

[GEH]        Narain Gehani (ed.), *Software Specification Technology*, 1986, Addison-Wesley.

[HERST]      I. N. Herstein, *Topics in Algebra*, 1964, Blaisdell.

[GOLD]       Adelle Goldberg, *The Smalltalk-80 Programming Language*, 1984, Addison-Wesley.

[GORLEN]     Keith Gorlen, *Data Abstraction and Object-Oriented Programming in C++*, 1990, Stuttgart.

[GRIES]      D. Gries, *The Science of Programming*, 1981, Springer-Verlag.

[JOY]        Bill Joy, keynote address, USENIX C++ Conference, Denver, CO, 1988.

[JSL]        Jonathan S. Linowes, "It's an Attitude," *BYTE Magazine*, August 1988.

[KEENE]          Sonya Keene, *Object-Oriented Programming in Common Lisp*, 1989, Addison-Wesley.

[KELLEY]         John L. Kelley, *General Topology*, 1955, Van Nostrand.

[KL]             Karl Lieberherr, "Object-Oriented Programming: An Objective Sense of Style," *OOPSLA Conference Proceedings*, 1988.

[LIP]            Stan Lippman and Bjarne Stroustrup, "Pointers to Class Members in C++," *Usenix Proceedings: C++ Conference*, Denver CO, 1988.

[LIP2]           Stan Lippman, personal communication, 1988.

[LIPS]           John Lipson, *Elements of Algebra and Algebraic Computing*, 1981, Addison-Wesley. (Defines type morphism. Proves type morphism respects type equations Eq(T).)

[LSK]            B. Liskov and J. Guttag, *Abstraction and Specification in Program Development*, 1986, MIT Press. (Addresses design of abstract data types.)

[LSK2]           B. Liskov, "Data Abstraction and Hierarchy," addendum to Conference Proceedings, *Object-Oriented Programming Systems Languages and Applications (OOPSLA)*, 1987. (Liskov's approach to object-oriented design, specifically addresses inheritance.)

[MEY]            Bertrand Meyer, *Object-Oriented Software Construction*, 1988, Prentice Hall. (Addresses object-oriented design, including parametric types.)

[MUR]            Bob Murray, personal communication, 1988. (I would like to acknowledge a debt of gratitude to Bob for the many conversations we had together refining the design framework.)

[PARNAS]         David L. Parnas, "On the Design and Development of Program Families," *IEEE, Transactions on Software Engineering*, volume SE-2, number 1, March 1976.

[SIM]            David Simen, personal communication, December 1988.

[SHO]            Jonathan Shopiro, personal communication, November 1988.

[SNY]    Alan Snyder, "Encapsulation and Inheritance in Object-Oriented Programming Languages," *Proceedings of the ACM Conference on Object-Oriented Programming Systems Languages and Applications (OOPSLA)*, SIGPLAN Notices 21, November 1986.

[SP]    Edwin Spanier, *Algebraic Topology*, pp. 14–21, 1966, McGraw-Hill. (A brief review of category theory.)

[STR]    Bjarne Stroustrup, *The C++ Programming Language*, 1987, Addison-Wesley.

[STR2]    Bjarne Stroustrup, "Parameterized Types for C++," *Usenix Proceedings: C++ Conference*, Denver, CO, 1988.

[TBD]    Tsvi Bar-David, "Teaching C++," *Usenix Proceedings: C++ Workshop*, Santa Fe, NM, 1987.

[TBD2]    Tsvi Bar-David, "The C++ Column: Formal Specification and Object-Oriented Design," *The C Users Journal*, July 1990.

[YOU]    Tom DeMarco, *Structured Analysis and System Specification*, 1978, Yourdon. (The heuristic was suggested by students who had an understanding of structured analysis.)

# Chapter 8

# Case Study: Graphics Editor

## 8.1 Introduction

This chapter deals with a small case study application of the object-oriented design framework that was presented in the previous chapter. The purpose of the chapter is to get the reader up and running as quickly as possible on a nontrivial design exercise. The example is that of a graphics editor. Of course, this example is sufficiently rich and complicated to serve as a full-fledged case study for this book or a semester-long course. Which means, as a mini-case study, we will be leaving out a great deal of detail, primarily concerning implementation. I will not adhere rigidly to the order recommended in the design framework, because the stream-of-consciousness discussion that follows is a taste of what actually happens in the real world. However, we will follow the ordered design rule: "first data structure (of private data members), then algorithms (of member functions)" because this seems to be an immutable law of the programming universe. The design of the graphics editor is nontrivial and interesting for yet another reason: In it we identify an inheritance diagram—the triangle paradigm—which, when abstracted and parameterized a bit, can serve as a general design paradigm in contexts far beyond the one in which it was discovered.

## 8.2   Graphics Editor Requirements

Here is a set of informal requirements for the graphics editor. It is expected in a real design that the requirements will be refined in a feedback loop responsive to the customer for the product and the needs for specificity engendered by the detailed design and implementation documents. The graphics editor is a program with a windowed interface, including a mouse, that permits the user to create, inspect, modify, and display pictures.

A picture is a collection of different kinds of shapes. Shapes supported by the editor include text in a variety of font styles and sizes, points, lines, boxes, circles, ellipses, and so on. A picture can be stored in a file for later retrieval, inspection, or modification.

The user of the graphics editor can create and destroy any kind of shape object. In general the graphics editor supports the following operations against the different kinds of shape objects: display, translate (in the plane), rotate, scale ... Particular types of shapes, like text, may support additional operations that manage additional properties, like font style (roman, helvetica bold, *italics*, `constant width`, *slanty*) and font size (6, 10, 12, 18, 24, 36 point) for text objects. In addition the user may temporarily group shapes together, manipulate the group as a single entity, and disband the group while preserving its individual elements, or delete the group wholesale.

Here is a bit more detail on the user interface of the graphics editor. The editor can be invoked from the command line with or without a command line argument.

```
$ graphed picture        # with an argument
$ graphed                # without an argument
```

The argument is the name of a file containing a picture previously saved by the editor. When the editor is invoked, it comes up with the screen of the display device divided into two areas: a large rectangular window (work area) in which the user draws, and a much smaller *palette* area from which the user selects different kinds of shapes—by clicking on them with the mouse—to put into the work area. When the editor is invoked on an existing picture stored in a file, the work area is initialized to that picture; in all other cases, the work area is empty. If the editor is invoked with a file name that does not correspond to an existing file, the work area comes up empty, but all subsequent saves of the work area are written to that file.

The user interacts with the editor in a very simple manner. She or he selects an object by clicking on it with the mouse, and subsequently selects an operation by depressing a mouse button, which causes a pop-up menu of operations to appear on the screen, and moving a cursor to the desired operation and releasing that mouse button. This complicated verbal description can be more simply described as: "The user sends a message to a shape object." The pop-up menu of operations displayed is the one appropriate to the type of shape selected.

## 8.3   Shape Type

In a procedural design, we would proceed to sketch out the main program (high-level inter-action) first. In an object-oriented design, we cannot quite do that, because the main program is a sequence of object instantiations and message expressions, and we don't yet know what the objects are, much less their public interfaces! So, let us first identify the major types that compose the editor and develop at least a rough idea of their public interfaces.

Grammatical analysis of the requirements suggests the following high-level types: `Editor, Mouse, Window, Picture, Collection, Shape, Text, Point, Line, Box, Circle, Ellipse, File, Group`.

The very use of the phrase "is a kind of ..." in the requirements leads me to conclude that the various kinds of shapes—Text, Point, Line, Box, Circle, Ellipse, File, Group—all inherit from Type Shape. This conclusion is reinforced by the requirements stating that there is a common set of operations—create, destroy, display, translate, rotate, scale—that all types of shapes enjoy. We posit that this common set of operations is the public interface of Type Shape. Here is what the public interface looks like in C++ for `Shape` and one derived type, `Box`:

```
class Shape {
        // read in picture from file
        Shape( String filename);
        Shape( File f);
        virtual ~Shape();
        virtual void display();
        virtual void translate( int x, int y);
        virtual void rotate( double theta, int x, int y);
```

```
        virtual void scale( double factor);
        ...
};


// Box must override inherited implementations
// of member functions
class Box : public Shape {
        // read in picture from file
        Box( String filename);
        Box( File f);
        ~Box();
        void display();
        void translate( int x, int y);
        void rotate( double theta, int Xctr, int Yctr );
        void scale( double factor);
};
```

## 8.4   Picture Type

Thinking ahead a bit to mapping the design onto an implementation, most windowing systems (X windows, Microsoft Windows, Curses) regard the window type as an abstraction for a rectangular region of the screen of the display device. Because all the different kinds of shapes mentioned earlier have a corresponding bounding box, we would not do badly to derive (via some flavor of inheritance) type Shape from type Window, for then shapes would inherit all the properties of Window, such as bounding box and a fortiori position in the plane, the ability to be moved (translated) in the plane, and so on.

Whatever other properties type Picture possesses, it seems to be the internal representation (in memory) of whatever is being edited in the work area on the screen. The requirements state that a picture is a heterogeneous collection of different kinds of shapes. Which leads to the conclusion that Picture is derived from some kind of parameterized container or collection type

```
class Picture : public Container<Shape *>  { ... };
```

That is, a Picture is some kind of collection of Shape pointers. I am being

deliberately vague as to the precise nature of the `Container` type; it will
be determined in the ensuing discussion. The angle brackets above denote
that Container is a parameterized type. (Recall that this is the proposed
notation for parameterized types in C++ 3.0.) Why does the derivation

```
class Picture : public Container<Shape>  { ... };
```

not work? Because `Picture` is a heterogeneous collection of different kinds of
shapes. A `Container<Shape>` is a homogeneous container of Shape objects
or values and thus cannot contain, for example, a `Text` object. More precisely in C++, the assignment of a `Text` object to a `Shape` variable would
leave only the `Shape` part of the object in the container, and that is not
enough. In contrast, the heterogeneity of a container of `Shape` pointers is a
consequence of the fact in C++ that the address of any object of any type
publicly derived from a base type may be assigned to a base type pointer
without coercion.

I must confess that the whole business of designing heterogeneous container
types is much easier in other object-oriented languages, such as Eiffel [MEY]
or Smalltalk [GOLD]. These languages do not have syntax for pointers. In
its place, the semantics of named variables is reference semantics. That is,
all variables can be thought of as pointers and thus assignment between two
variables of the same type results in aliasing, that is, both variables after
the assignment refer to the same object. Furthermore, derived-type objects
may be assigned to base type variables. Thus in Eiffel, a `List[Shape]` is
heterogeneous by default, and can potentially contain objects of any types
derived from Shape.

Are there any base type `Shape` objects in a `Picture`? I think not, for if there
were, what would they look like on displaying themselves to the screen? In
the object-oriented literature, a type of which there are no instantiated
objects is called an abstract base type (or class). The instances can only be
of derived type, as in our graphics editor. C++ enforces the semantics of
abstract base class with the syntax of pure virtual member function.

```
class Shape : public  Window {
public:
    virtual void display() = 0;
    ...
};
```

In the class fragment above, `display()` is pure virtual. By definition, this member function has no implementation. Any attempt to instantiate a `Shape` object

```
Shape s;     // syntax error
```

is a syntax error. For a class to be an abstract base class, it suffices for only one of its member functions to be pure virtual. Abstract base types are closely related to the concept of a priori (semantic) inheritance. Abstract base classes serve as a repository for semantics (member function manual pages, or a generic interface, if you will) that the derived types must implement and not violate via override. This is merely a restatement of a priori inheritance. I conclude, then, that the family of types derived from `Shape` are all, from a design perspective, derived (semantically) a priori. Nonetheless, in C++, an abstract base class may provide implementation to its derived classes. Indeed, in the above design, class `Shape` inherits much implementation from class `Window`, which is, of course, passed along to its children. Furthermore, `Shape` can factor additional implementation out of its derived classes by providing additional (beyond what is inherited from `Window`) private data members and protected member functions.

What kind of container or collection of `Shape` pointers is `Picture` derived from? In other words, what is the public interface of the container type? The answer depends on the designer's experience and, to some extent, on what's available in type libraries. We can deduce the public interface from the requirements, which state that the user of the graphics editor can essentially add and remove different kinds of shapes to the visible work area. Well, because the `Picture` is the internal representation of what's on the screen, we must be able to insert and delete `Shape` pointers correspondingly into a `Picture` object. Two parameterized types suggest themselves:

```
Set<Shape *> and Simplist<Shape *>.
```

The public interface of `Set<T>` is given in section 8.7 in this chapter. A description and implementation of the parametric list type `Simplist<T>` can be found in section 1.10. A finite-dimensional array, `Array<T,n>`, clearly won't do the trick because there is no way of knowing in advance how many shape objects the editor user is going to put in the picture. `Set<T>` is a good choice when there is no ordering between the shapes. However, in

many graphics editors, there is an ordering, and it is the order in which
the shapes are displayed to the screen. The order determines which objects
obscure other objects, which overlay the others. So, because we can always
use (view) a list as if it were a set—by ignoring the ordering property of
list—in the interest of generality, we choose to derive **Picture** from list of
shape pointers

```
class Picture : public Simplist<Shape *>  { ... };
```

Is there any need to override the member function implementations that
**Picture** inherits (via class derivation) from **List<Shape \*>**? I think not,
and thus claim that, from a design perspective, **Picture** is (semantically)
derived a posteriori from **List<Shape \*>**.

Might **Picture** be multiply derived and, if so, from what other parent types?
In many graphics editors, the entire work area (i.e., Picture) can be treated
like any other shape that is displayed, translated, rotated, and scaled as if it
were a single entity. Furthermore, **Picture** is a natural parent type for the
Group type, which is also manipulated as a single shape. All this evidence
from the requirements document leads to the conclusion that **Picture** is (a
priori) derived from **Shape**

```
class Picture : public Shape, public Simplist<Shape *>  { ... };
```

A subtle benefit of this multiple derivation is that (the address of sub-
)pictures may be inserted into pictures, for after all, a Picture is just a
kind of **Shape**. This benefit is known to be a cause for rejoicing in the
camps of CAD/CAM designers.

The requirements state that the user of the editor can load and store pictures
from a file. This requirement can be satisfied by load and store member functions in the public interface of **Picture**. By the way, in doing so, **Picture**
becomes a persistent object. By definition, a persistent object is one whose
lifetime is independent of the program that created it. The signature (prototype) of these functions look like

```
class Picture : public Shape, public Simplist<Shape *>
{
public:
```

```
    Picture( String filename, shape_args) : Shape( shape_args)
    {
        . . .
    }
    load( String filename);
    store( String filename);
    . . .
};
```

We could also provide the functionality of **load** in a **Picture** constructor, as indicated above.

## 8.5   Editor Type

At first glance, it may seem strange to regard the editor itself as a type of object, but that is precisely what must be done according to the object-oriented orthodoxy, which states:

> *Everything is an object of some type!*

If so, what is the public interface of the Editor type?

From the requirements it would appear that an editor object interprets the command stream—mostly a sequence of mouse clicks, with some ASCII characters thrown in—and performs actions against both the internal and visual representations of the work area (simply put, the picture). Note that the **Picture** type, through **Shape**, is a grandchild of **Window**. And, of course, a **Picture** object is also a list of **Shape** objects. Thus **Picture** can be used to represent simultaneously both the internal and visual representations of the work area. In brief, an **Editor** object edits (manages) **Picture** objects.

For simplicity of design, we assume that an editor object manages precisely one picture and that a picture corresponds to at most one file. Why do I say at most and not precisely one? Because the edit program can be invoked with no arguments. Presumably, in such a case, the program contains an editor object that is managing a picture, which currently does not correspond to any file. This is just like an anonymous buffer in a text editor. Shortly we shall see how to build an edit program easily, based on the **Editor** type, which manages multiple pictures and files.

We can represent (implement) the "has a" relationship that an editor object manages one picture by putting a `Picture` data member in the private part of class `Editor`. The editor object can also store the name of the file that the picture is associated with in a (private) `String` data member.

How does the `Editor` respond to user requests via mouse clicks and so on? Here we face the design choice of centralized versus decentralized control. In the centralized model, the editor object is responsible for detecting every window event (mouse clicks, ASCII characters—as they are called in commercially available windowing systems), parsing the event, that is, ascribing a meaning to it, and then taking some action against the corresponding `Picture` object.

To understand the decentralized model, it is necessary to describe the fundamental paradigm of many commercial windowing systems for high-resolution workstations (X, Microsoft, Sunviews), which happens to be quite object-oriented. Namely, a windowed application is a collection of objects of type derived from window.

Each such object obviously has a visual representation on the screen. As well, its internal state may be represented by data structures whose addresses are stored in the object. The designer can prepare such an object to respond to window events by associating with it a function (called the call-back function in X toolkit parlance), which is invoked whenever an event occurs within its window. The action taken is to effect the object's visual representation and internal state (shades of the object model!).

Assuming that `Shape` is derived from `Window`, and `Window` is implemented as in the previous paragraphs, each kind of `Shape`, such as `Text`, has some data structure associated with it—for `Text`, font information—and a call-back function. When the editor user selects, for example, a `Text` object in the work area, its call-back function has the responsibility of responding to operations selected in the pop-up menu (move, rotate, scale) in a manner appropriate to the type of the object.

Here is a possible implementation of the guts of the editor, which makes use of pointers to member functions dynamically bound. The selection of a `Shape` object corresponds to assigning the address of, say, a `Text` object to a `Shape` pointer, for example,

```
Shape *p;
. . .
```

```
p = picture.get( n);
```

The selection of an operation named in a pop-up menu (say, scale) causes the address of a Shape base class member function to be assigned to a member function pointer variable, thus,

```
void (Shape::*pf)();
...
pf = &Shape::scale;
```

We implement the object doing its thing (here the Text object scales itself) by invoking the pointer to the member function against the pointer to the object

```
(p->*pf)();
```

Declaring all member functions of class Shape **virtual** ensures dynamic binding, that is, ensures that the member function corresponding to the (derived) type of the object that the pointer p points to is invoked in the above expression (e.g., Text::scale).

In summary, here is a (partial) class template for the Editor type:

```
class Editor {
public:
        // converts named file into picture object
        Editor( String filename = "");
        // stores picture to file
        ~Editor();
        // parses command stream into actions
        // against picture and windows
        void eval();
private:
    Picture p;
    String fname;  // name of file picture is stored in
    ...
};
```

## 8.6  Interaction Model

Now that we know what the objects are and what they can do, we can write
the main program. It is quite short!

```
main( int argc, char *argv[])
{
    Editor ed( argc > 1 ? argv[1] : "" );

    ed.eval();  // manage an edit session
}
```

The program instantiates an `Editor` object and initiates an edit session.
In harmony with the requirements document, the edit program can be invoked with or without a file name. This feature is supported by supplying
class `Editor` with a constructor that properly initializes the `Editor` object's
`Picture` data member. If the command argument, `argv[1]`, is a non-null
string, the `Picture` data member is initialized from the file.

To get a feeling for how easy it is to accommodate changes in the requirements for the graphics editor, let's sketch out what happens if we require the
editor to handle multiple pictures. Although this is admittedly a pretty fuzzy
requirement as stated, an easy way to handle the family of applications that
satisfy it is to build them all around an object of type `Simplist<Editor *>`.
The main program might look like

```
Simplist<Editor *> l;

main( int argc, char *argv[])
{
    if( argc == 1) {
        Editor *pe = new Editor;
        l.add( pe);
        pe->eval();
    } else {
            // read in all the picture files
            for( int j = 1; j < argc; j++)
                l.add( new Editor( argv[j]));
            l.head()->eval();
```

```
        }
    }
```

To switch from picture to picture, the `Editor::eval()` member function has to know about the list `l`. There are many ways to accomplish this; one is shown above: make the list a global variable.

We can get rid of the global variable `l` by designing a multiple picture editor type, `Geditor`

```
class Geditor {
public:
    Geditor( int ac, char *av[])
    {
        if( ac == 1)
            l.add( new Editor);
        else for( int j = 1; j < ac; j++)
            l.add( new Editor( av[j]));
    }

    void eval()  { l.head()->eval(); }
private:
    Simplist<Editor *> l;
};
```

I leave it to the reader to ensure that `Editor::eval()` can "see" the list data member `Geditor::l`. In any event, the main program now simplifies to

```
main( int argc, char *argv[])
{
    Geditor ed( argc, argv);

    ed.eval(); // manage an edit session
}
```

## 8.7  Public Interface of Parameterized Set<T>

For reference, here is the public interface of a parameterized set type. Its implementation is left as an exercise to the reader. (*Hint:* Use a Simplist<T> private data member.)

```
template<class T> class Set {
public:
    // returns TRUE if picture list is empty
    Boolean isempty() const;

    // return current length of set
    int length() const;

    // set membership function; returns TRUE if x in set
    // else FALSE
    Boolean isin( T x) const;

    // add adds x to set
    // postcondition: isin( x)
    void add( T x);

    // del deletes x from set
    // precondition: isin( x)
    // postcondition: !isin( x)
    void del( int n);

    // set iteration facilities

    // prepare set for iteration
    void rewind();

    // get next element of set. returns a value exactly once.
    T get() const;

    // returns TRUE after last set element has been
    // gotten with get
    Boolean isdone();
private:
```

```
    Simplist<T> l;
};
```

Here is a code fragment that makes use of the iteration facilities (member functions) in the public interface of Set<T> to display a set of different kinds of shapes:

```
Set<Shape *> set;
...
set.rewind();
while( !set.isdone() )
set.get()->display();
```

## 8.8  Type Decomposition

Type decomposition, to review, is the sketching out of an implementation for a type. It consists of selecting a data structure to represent the state of objects of the type (modulo class derivation), and of (pseudo-)coding the operations.

I would like to work through a small piece of the type decomposition of the Picture type. Through its multiple derivation from Shape and List, Picture inherits a tremendous amount of implementation, both data structure as well as the implementation of member functions, particularly those in the public interface of Simplist<T>. However, we must override the inherited implementations of the Shape member functions in the public interface of Picture to consider Picture's list structure. We have put the cart before the horse; we must first extend the *requirements* for these member functions so that they consider Picture's list structure and then implement them.

For a concrete example, let's take Shape::display() and extend it to Picture::display(). Informally, the requirements on Shape::display() specify that the object receiving this message display itself in the appropriate manner and in the right place on the display device. Because Shape is an abstract base class, it is reasonable to demand that this requirement be met by all classes—such as Picture—derived from it. A way to extend this requirement to Picture that considers its list structure is through the

*Pass-the-Buck Principle*

That is, what it means to display a picture is to display each shape within it. Under the assumption that Shape::display() is declared **virtual** in the base class Shape, here is the code for Picture::display() that satisfies the requirements.

```
class Picture : public Shape, public Simplist<Shape *> {
public:
        ...
        void display()
        {
                Simplist<Shape *> p;
                for(p = *this;!p.isempty(); p = p.tail())
                        p.head()->display();
        }
};
```

The **virtual** declaration ensures that the message expression p.head()->display() is dynamically bound. That is, the display() function invoked is the one corresponding to the derived type of the object that p.head() points to.

## 8.9   Summary

We have applied an object-oriented design framework to a popular application, a graphics editor. In the process, we have identified additional design heuristics.

- Everything is an object—even the editor itself.

- Objects know their type at runtime—a restatement of dynamic binding.

- Pass the buck—a message to a container object is passed along to the objects within it.

We also discovered a very useful parameterized family of multiple inheritance diagrams, the triangle diagram, which describes a container (the **Buffer** type as being both a kind of heterogeneous list of **Thing** objects, as well as being a kind of `Thing` object itself. A wonderful consequence of the dual inheritance is that a `Buffer` object may contain sub-`Buffer` objects. The heart of the graphics editor is the triangle diagram with `Thing = Shape`.

Below is summarized the major types of which the graphics editor is constructed.

- `Window` and types derived from it

- `Shape` and types derived from it

- `Picture`—internal representation of picture under edit, a collection of shapes

- `File`—persistent store for pictures

- Picture `Editor`—parses command stream into actions against picture objects, windows

Below is a picture that summarizes the inheritance relationship between `Picture` and its parent types `Shape` and `Simplist<Shape *>`.

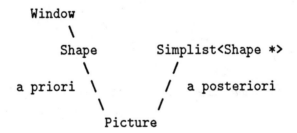

`Picture` is derived a priori from `Shape` and is derived a posteriori from `Simplist<Shape *>`. This particular derivation allows a `Picture` object to contain sub-`Pictures`, because, after all, a `Picture` is a kind of a `Shape`, and the address of any object of any type derived from `Shape` may be inserted into a `Simplist`. Thus a `Picture` is in fact a multiway tree.

# Bibliography

[GOLD]   Adelle Goldberg, *The Smalltalk-80 Programming Language*, 1984, Addison-Wesley.

[MEY]   Bertrand Meyer, *Object-Oriented Software Construction*, 1988, Prentice Hall. (Addresses object-oriented design, including parametric types.)

# Chapter 9

# Text Editor: Requirements

## 9.1 Introduction

In chapter 7 we presented a simple framework for object-oriented design. We now embark on a journey in that we apply the design framework to the problem of constructing a simple text editor. Along the way we will develop some types which, not only are useful in building the editor, but are also useful tools in general, and so can serve as members of a general-purpose object library.

Something to keep in mind as we travel together: Most languages, including C++, require that we represent our solution to a problem as a main program. And this we will do. However, our goal, paradoxically, is not to design and build programs, but rather to identify and construct useful types of objects, out of which we can construct infinite numbers of programs. In some sense akin to mathematics, we are constructing a solution not to one problem but rather to a family of related problems, for example, the problem of text editors. It is precisely this approach to problem solving, I believe, that permits an object-oriented design (design as a noun, the result of the design process) to be easily modified, enhanced, and reused. This approach is reflected in the brevity of the main programs that we build; typically they instantiate an object or two, and then invoke a couple of member functions. This is very much the same position that Bertrand Meyer [MEY] takes and supports in the Eiffel language. Indeed, in Eiffel, there is no such thing as a main program; one simply selects a first object to send a message to. The action associated with that message goes ahead and creates other objects

223

and sends messages to them ad infinitum ... worlds without end.

## 9.2 Design Framework

A brief summary of the design framework is in order. The framework manages a process that maps a requirements document to an implementable design document.

The heart of object-oriented design is the identification of the types in the program and the relationships between them. To identify a type is to specify its behavior (public interface). To identify relationships means bringing to light the relationships (inheritance and parametric types) in the behavior of the types. One can then implement the behavior in many ways. Here is the pseudocode for the design process.

```
initial decomposition(on requirements document);
while( stopping condition has not been met ) {
        abstraction;
        type relationships;
        type decomposition;
}

return design specification;
```

To begin the design process, we need a behavioral description of the object we want to build, namely, the text editor.

## 9.3 Requirements: Description of Editor

The ced editor allows the user to create new text files or edit existing ones. The editor views the file as just a sequence of characters (thus the c in ced) with no other structure, such as a sequence of lines. Because newline is just an ordinary character, we will be able to recover the traditional line structure of a file easily by using ordinary edit operations. The editor's simple view of a file (it also happens to be the view of the UNIX operating system), it is hoped will make for a simple design and ease of implementation. In addition, the editor maintains the notion of current point in the file. The point is regarded as being between two characters. Again, this notion of current point is pretty close to the concept of current offset in UNIX files.

At this point, we have to make a requirements decision about the user interface to the editor. For the sake of simplicity, let's assume that the editor has a traditional command line interface like edlin on MS/DOS systems or ed on UNIX systems. That is, the input command stream looks like a sequence of lines. Each line consists of an optional integer prefix followed by a character. The table below associates commands with the characters that invoke them.

```
Note:      Bracketed arguments are optional.

[n] g      Move point to just before nth character
           (zero based).  Default value for n is 0.

[n] p      Print n characters starting at the first character
           after point, followed by a newline.  n defaults
           to 1.  Increment point by n.

    i      Insert arbitrary number of characters before point.
           Terminate insertion with . on a line by itself.

[n] d      Delete n characters starting at the first character
           after point.  n defaults to 1.

[n] y      Paste whatever was last deleted n times just before
           point.  n defaults to 1.

w [file]   Write out the internal representation of the
           file (the buffer) to the named file.  The primary
           default for file is the filename command line
           argument to \verb|ced|.  If \verb|ced| was invoked without a
           filename, it selects the last file written to.

    q      Exit the editor.

    ?      Print out useful information, like filename,
           point, and size of file.
```

Normally the editor scans for commands from standard input. However, for flexibility, the editor should be able to get its command stream from a file or possibly some other source, like a string or a window.

When the editor is invoked with an argument at the command line interface

```
prompt> ced filename
```

if the file exists, `ced` opens it for editing or creates an empty file of that name. In either case, point is just before the first character in the file. If the editor is called without an argument

```
prompt> ced
```

the editor manages an editing session. It is up to the user to write out explicitly the contents to a named file.

A typical edit session might look like

```
36g
i
hello there
.
g
50p
w
q
```

## 9.4   Initial Decomposition

Our task now is to identify the high-level types from the requirements, out of which we will construct the editor. Well, certainly File is one of these types, and it is used in two ways: as the file to be created or modified, and as the command stream—typically standard input from the terminal.

In our description of the editor write command, we briefly mentioned the internal representation of the file under edit, traditionally known as the buffer. Is the Buffer type synonymous with the File type? In truth, we can easily answer this question once we have described (abstraction step) the public interface of both File and Buffer. Namely, if the public interfaces (really, the manual pages) of two types are the same, then the types are one and the same. At the risk of getting a bit ahead of ourselves, let's see if we can answer this question right now. Let's assume that a File object essentially has the semantics of a standard I/O FILE object (as supported by the standard runtime library of the ANSI C compiler [KR]). Files and Buffers may very well share the offset or point concept. Conversely, whatever a Buffer is, it must support the editor commands listed in the requirement section, in particular insertion and deletion. Well, there are no native insertion and deletion operators on Files. Although the operation that puts a character into a file (putc( int, FILE *)) can be considered as an insertion when appending at the end of the file, it certainly does not insert if the file offset is anywhere in the middle of the file; rather, it overwrites the character at the offset, which is not the behavior that we are looking for. The conclusion is that a Buffer is not a File, and so we must design and implement the Buffer abstraction. Now it may very well turn out that we can implement Buffer in terms of File, as some implementations of the full-screen editor vi do. But that is merely (yes, merely!) a matter of implementation, and is not to be confused with the behavior or semantics of the Buffer.

What about the editor itself? Is it a type? Even though it may feel unnatural at first, we ought to give the Editor type a try, for the sake of reaping all of the benefits listed above. So our design policy is clear, albeit extreme: Everything in the application is an object of one type or another. Well, then, what is the behavior of an editor object? From the requirements it would appear that an editor object interprets the command stream and performs actions both on a buffer and the user interface, which for now is just standard output. That is, the editor coordinates three objects: the input (command) stream, a buffer, and an output stream (a view of the buffer).

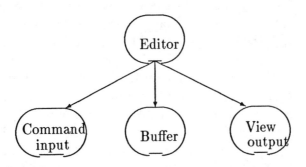

For simplicity of design, why don't we assume that an editor object manages precisely one buffer. And that a buffer corresponds to at most one file. Why do I say at most and not precisely one? Because the edit program **ced** can be invoked with no arguments. Presumably, in such a case, the program contains an editor object that is managing a buffer, which currently does not correspond to any file. Later, we will see how to build an edit program easily, based on the Editor type, which manages multiple buffers and files, something in the spirit of emacs.

To summarize, we have identified three types of objects from the requirements:

```
{ Editor, Buffer, File }
```

We must now perform the design process on each of the types in our working list above. What remains is to select the first one to work on.

## 9.5   File: Abstraction Step

Because File is the most familiar type in our working list of types, we pick it first to work on. Having said this, why even bother representing File as a class when all C++ compilers already support the standard I/O FILE structure? Several reasons follow:

1. *Consistency:* We want objects of all types—other than built-in types of the language—in our application to be represented by classes. This provides a uniform feel to developers and maintainers. Indeed the

uniform feel that we are after is that of object orientation. That is, we want to use the message expression

```
object.memberfunction()
```

as the sole means of communicating with an object. Directly using a standard I/O function like `putc('a', fp)` on a FILE pointer (`fp`) would violate this desideratum.

2. *Insulation :* We can regard our File type as an application-specific type layered on top of whatever I/O support there is in the environment. This helps to make the editor more portable. When the editor is ported to a new operating system, only the implementation of File need change. Any other code in the editor that uses File changes not one iota. In fact we can be even smarter. Because FILE is a guaranteed part of the runtime support library of any C++ compiler on any operating system, we can just implement or layer File on top of FILE. Furthermore, there need not be much of any runtime penalty for this layering, because we can declare all of the member functions of File to be inline!

Now let's work on the public interface of File. The minimal interface consists of the following four classical operations:

- `open`—connect the program to the named file or create it

- `close`—sever the connection between the program and the file

- `iseof`—returns true if at end of file, otherwise false

- `get`—get a character and advance the file offset

- `put`—put a character and advance the file offset

How can we map this interface into C++? We can elegantly get rid of explicit open and close member functions by use of a constructor and a destructor, respectively. The advantage of this approach is that an instantiated File object must always be initialized, and is guaranteed to be initialized properly. Furthermore, mapping close to the destructor guarantees that

when the File object dies (goes out of scope) in the program, the associated
file in the file system is automatically closed, without the client programmer
having to explicitly close it. Here is the public interface of File as a C++
class.

```
class File {
public:
    File( char *name = "", char *mode = "r");
    ~File();
    Boolean iseof();
    int get();
    void put( int c);
private:
    // data members
};
```

The constructor takes two arguments, and both are provided with defaults.
Here are the intended semantics. The declaration

```
    File f;
```

invokes the default constructor `File( "", "r" )`, which connects the object
f to standard input, for reading.

```
    File f( filename);
```

invokes File( filename, "r") and so opens filename for reading.

```
    File f( filename, mode);
```

opens filename with some mode (with the same semantics as fopen()). So,
for example,

```
    File f( "foo", "w" );
```

opens the file foo for writing.

Before we wax too lyrical about the joys of using constructors in place of an open function, we need to face a design problem. Namely, just after the constructor runs, how do we know that the file is really open? For if the open failed for any reason (the file doesn't exist, we don't have the correct permissions), it would be nonsensical to invoke any member function against the object.

One solution is to forget the constructor approach and just endow File with an explicit open function of the following form

```
typedef int Boolean;     // boolean type
Boolean File::open( char *filename, char *mode);
```

It could report success or failure of the operation in a manner similar to the C/C++ library functions fopen() and open() do—by returning a boolean value (the value is regarded as boolean by convention).

However, for those of you who want to stick with the constructor approach, here is another solution to the problem. Endow File with a member function

```
// returns TRUE if open succeeded in constructor
Boolean File::isok();
```

whose sole purpose in life is to report on the status of the open performed in the constructor. Perhaps we don't really need a separate isok() function; perhaps we can assign this job to iseof(). But this is bad design for two reasons: one, checking for end of file is conceptually a completely separate matter from checking to see if the open succeeded. And, second, how are we to interpret the return value of iseof() on a newly created file for writing? So we will play it safe and have two predicate functions.

The File type was originally developed to support a lexical scanner object. To make it easier to implement the scanner, we included the following additional member functions in File's public interface:

```
class File {
public:
    ...
    void unget(int c);
    int peek();
```

```
        . . .
   };
```

unget() pushes the character c back onto an input stream. It is the next character to be gotten by get(). peek() returns the value of the next character without removing it from the input stream.

As we have alluded, we can piggyback or layer the implementation of File on top of standard I/O FILE. Here is one easy implementation.

## 9.6   File: Implementation

```
class File {
public:
    File( char *name = "", char *mode = "r")
    {
        if( *name )
            fp = fopen( name, mode);
        else if( *mode == 'r' )
            fp = stdin;
        else
            fp = stdout;
        state = (int)fp;
    }

    ~File()          { if( fp) fclose( fp); }

    Boolean isok()   { return state; }

    Boolean iseof()  { return feof( fp); }

    int get()        { return getc( fp); }

    void unget(int c) { (void)ungetc( c, fp); }

    int peek()       { int c = get(); unget(c); return c; }

    void put( int c) { putc( c, fp); }
```

```
private:
    FILE *fp;
    int state;
};
```

The only difficult point about this implementation was figuring out that we needed a state data member for recording the status of the open. As you notice, all the member functions, with the exception of the constructor, are one-liners.

## 9.7 Summary

What we have done in this chapter is to begin to apply an object-oriented design framework to the problem of constructing a text editor. Starting from a description of the editor's behavior, we have identified three types of objects: Editor, Buffer, and File. We discussed how File might be used by other types and let that guide us in the identification of its public interface. We then wrote a portable implementation of File layered on top of the standard I/O FILE abstraction.

In the next chapter, we will continue on our journey, focusing our attention on the Buffer abstraction. In the course of designing Buffer, we will become acquainted with two useful parametric container types—Sloop[T] and Yacht[T]—that will make the implementation of Buffer pretty simple.

# Bibliography

[KR]   Brian Kernighan and Dennis Ritchie, *The C Programming Language*, second edition, 1988, Prentice Hall.

[MEY]  Bertrand Meyer, *Object-Oriented Program Construction*, 1988, Prentice Hall. (Addresses object-oriented design, including parametric types.)

# Chapter 10

# Buffers, Sloops, and Yachts

## 10.1 Introduction

In the previous chapter, we ended our object-oriented design of a text editor with an implementation of the `File` type. In this chapter, we continue the design process by selecting the `Buffer` type—identified in the initial decomposition—to work on.

Recall that an editor object interprets the command stream and performs actions both on a buffer and the user interface, which for now is just standard output. That is, the editor coordinates three objects: the input (command) stream, a buffer, and an output stream (a view of the buffer). Let's assume for simplicity that both the input and output streams are `Files` (e.g., standard input and output, respectively). Then once `Buffer` is designed and implemented, we should be able to layer the implementation of the `Editor` type on top of `File` and `Buffer`. Beyond mentioning layering, it is hard to predict how difficult it might be to design the `Editor`; depending on how fancy an editor we want, we may have to come up with all kinds of helping types that occur in the implementation of the editor. But, who knows, it all might be easier than we think!

We need to talk about the order in which we select types from our working list to work on. Remember, at this stage of the game, we have not yet sketched out the public interface of `Buffer` nor of `Editor`. Let's say that we had selected `Editor`, rather than `Buffer`, as the next type to design (after `File`). Having more or less determined that an `Editor` object contains a `Buffer` data member (layering), the implementation of `Editor` member functions would lead us toward presupposing the existence of certain member functions in the public interface of `Buffer`. Thus the advantage of working on `Editor` first is that `Buffer`'s public interface can be tailored to `Editor`'s implementational needs. Conversely, if `Buffer` already existed, its public interface would heavily influence the coding of the member functions of `Editor`. Nonetheless, the advantage of working on `Buffer` first is that we are more likely to design it in a more general way, making it a useful tool for implementing lots of different objects, not only editors. So, for the sake of generality, we work on `Buffer` first.

## 10.2  Buffer—High-Level Design and Public Interface

The `Editor` uses the `Buffer` as its internal representation of the file under edit. Because the editor views the file as a sequence of characters, we can (in terms of our design) pass the buck and require that a `Buffer` object is a sequence of characters. Using the same design principle (pass the buck) we also require that the `Buffer` maintain the notion of current point between two characters. A `Buffer` may optionally be connected with a file in the file system. To support this option, we need some means (i.e., member functions in the public interface) of initializing the `Buffer` from a `File` and some means of writing the `Buffer` out to a file.

A study of the command set supported by the editor (see requirements section in chapter 9) gives additional insight into what member functions should be in the public interface. The go operation permits the user to move the point to any place in the buffer—kind of like `lseek()` on files. Thus the `Buffer` needs a `seek()` or `go()` function. To support the `Editor` print operation, it suffices to be able to nondestructively get characters from the buffer in the same way that `getc()` gets a character from a standard I/O FILE. Namely, the `Buffer` `get()` function returns the character after point and advances the point. The `Editor` print operation can then simply print the character to standard output.

The `Editor` insert and delete operations imply the ability to insert and delete, respectively, a character into the `Buffer` in the vicinity of the point. The word vicinity is deliberately vague. Should the `Buffer` support one or two insert functions: insert-before-point() and insert-after-point()? Similarly, should the Buffer support two delete functions: delete-before-point() and delete-after-point()? We do not yet have enough information to make this decision. Of course, we could play it safe and opt for generality by throwing in all four functions!

The Editor paste operation is interesting because it requires cooperation with the last delete operation. If the Buffer type were implemented, we could implement this delete-and-paste feature by having the delete operation insert the deleted characters into an unnamed Buffer—just another data member of the Editor. The next paste operation could simply copy the characters from this anonymous buffer and insert them into the main buffer. So already we have gotten double the bang for our buck out of the Buffer abstraction. Here is a loose summary of the public interface of Buffer, as we understand it so far.

```
read( char *filename) - read (insert) the named file into
     the buffer after the point.

write( char *filename) - write the buffer out,
       from point to end of buffer to the named file.

go( int n) - move point to before nth character.

int where() - return offset of point relative to
     the beginning of the buffer.

int get() - return character after point and
     increments point.

puta( int c) - insert character c after point.

putb( int c) - insert character c before point.

dela() - delete character after point.

delb() - delete character before point.
```

We may discover that we need additional member functions later on in the design process.

## 10.3   Buffer—Type Relationships

Now let's apply the type-relationship step of the design framework to the
`Buffer` type. We would like to derive `Buffer` from a simpler type. That
type in turn may be derived from yet a simpler type. The design principle is
to let each type in the derivation chain be the bearer of one simple idea; the
type can inherit the rest of its properties from its ancestors. Well, then, can
we decompose our understanding (the public interface) of `Buffer` into two
or three ideas, and then recompose these ideas into an inheritance chain?

Imagine that `Buffer` is publicly derived from `Yacht` (let's have some fun
with class names).  Further, let's posit that `Yachts` know nothing about
`Files`. This assumption will significantly simplify the design of `Yacht`. Well
then, `Buffer` extends `Yacht` precisely in that it knows how to initialize itself
(read) from a `File` and write itself out to a file. So already we can say

```
class Buffer : public Yacht {
public:
    Boolean read( char *filename);
    Boolean write( char *filename);
private:
    // 0 or more data members
};
```

We may as well let `read()` and `write()` return a boolean value indicating
success or failure of the requested operation. Reasoning inductively, if `Yacht`
is already implemented (correctly!), it shouldn't take too much work to
implement `Buffer`.  All we have to do is possibly select some additional
private data members, and implement `read()` and `write()`.

The beauty of this decomposition (factorization) by inheritance is that `Yacht`
must be the bearer of the rest of `Buffer`'s public interface!

```
Class Yacht {
public:
    Boolean go( int n);
    int where() const;
    int get();
    Boolean puta( int c);
    Boolean putb( int c);
```

```
    int dela();
    int delb();
private:
    // 0 or more data members
};
```

We have added return types for `puta()`, `putb()`, `dela()`, `delb()`. The
delete operations return the value just deleted. The puts return TRUE if
the insertion succeeded, otherwise FALSE.


# 10.4   Yacht<T>—Parametric Type

Let's think a bit about what a `Yacht` is. A `Yacht` is an ordered homogeneous container (a sequence or list) of characters, with a notion of current
point. Is there anything sacrosanct about what the `Yacht` contains, namely
characters?  For I could just as easily imagine a Yacht-of-float in which
we insert or delete floating point numbers rather than integers. That is,
the public interface of Yacht-of-float looks just like the public interface of
`Yacht`, except all of Yacht-of-float's member functions are parameterized by
float rather than integer.  I think we have stumbled across a parametric
type—Yacht<T>—where our `Yacht` of characters is `Yacht<char>`. Here is
Yacht<T> as a parametric type in Bjarne Stroustrup's proposed notation
[STR2].

```
    template<class T> class Yacht {
public:
    Boolean go( int n);
    int where() const;
    T get();
    Boolean puta( T x);
    Boolean putb( T x);
    T dela();
    T delb();
private:
    // 0 or more data members
    };
```

Suppose Yacht<T> is derived from some (necessarily parametric) parent type—say Sloop<T>. What properties (member functions) should Sloop<T> bear, and what should Yacht<T> bear? Here we recall to the reader (see page 183) a minimality principle to help guide the design process.

*Definition:*  The public interface of a type is *minimal* if no member function can be implemented in terms of the public interface. Conversely, if a type has a member function that can be written in terms of the other member functions, then the public interface of the type is not minimal.

## 10.5   Sloop<T>—Abstraction Step

Suppose Sloop<T> is an ordered sequence of T values with a notion of current point, and suppose further that its public interface is minimal. We want Sloop<T> to bear the insert and delete properties. There is no way (that I know of) to prove that the inserts and deletes cannot be implemented in terms of each other. Perhaps proof could come from the theory of formal specification of types. Of course, the converse is a lot easier. All you need is one implementation connecting two member functions to demonstrate that a public interface is not minimal. Nonetheless, my instincts impel me to throw puta(), putb(), dela(), delb() into the public interface of Sloop<T>. We recall another definition from the design chapter (chapter 7) as a principle to guide the design further.

*Definition:*  The public interface of a type is *orthogonal* if there is no (well, minimal) overlap in the behavior (manual page specification) of any pair of member functions.

For Sloop<T>, we could decide that orthogonality requires the decoupling of point motion, to the extent possible, from the rest of the member functions. Such a design decision immediately rules out the Yacht get() function from being a member of the public interface of Sloop<T>, because it advances the point. In any event, let's provide Sloop<T> with two simple point motion operations

```
void next() - advance the point by one element.
void prev() - move the point backward by one element.
```

We can now position ourselves at any point in a Sloop. However, we still need some way of peeking at the element in the vicinity of the point without removing it. In symmetry with the puts and the deletes let's give ourselves two peek functions

```
T geta() - return the value after the point.
T getb() - return the value before the point.
```

# 10.6    Preconditions and Exception Handling

The functional prototype of geta() and getb()—specifically the type of the return value—raises a problem. Namely, what happens on Sloop boundary conditions:

- The Sloop is empty.

- The point is at the beginning (just before the first element).

- The point is at the end (just after the last element).

For example, if the Sloop is empty, what should geta() return? Because there is nothing in the Sloop, we want geta() to signal an exception (an error). The problem is that any T value that geta() returns could—and should—be interpreted as a legal value of an element in the Sloop. The same problem arises if we apply geta() when the point is at the end, or if we apply getb() when the point is at the beginning.

Well, we could dummy-proof the gets (and for that matter the dels) so that they detect the exception and set a global error variable that the client programmer explicitly checks after each invocation of a get or del. If the error variable is set, the program is supposed to ignore the (spurious) return value of the invoked member function. This is similar to how UNIX system calls handle errors. This solution is unsatisfactory for several reasons. First, global variables are something to be avoided in general because they are usually artifacts of a type implementation. Well, we can answer that objection by making the error variable a private static data member within class Sloop. Next, should we clear the error variable after successful calls? If we don't, somebody is going to be misled about error conditions. But, more fundamentally, this mechanism is too coarse grained; it establishes a single clearing house for errors from all the member functions of Sloop. What we want is an error mechanism per member function.

The Eiffel programming language [MEY] has such an exception detection and handling mechanism. C++ 3.0 also has such a mechanism, although it is not integrated into the syntax for user defined types. With a little work, we can implement an exception mechanism for C++ classes by hand.

*Definition:* A precondition for a member function is a predicate (boolean expression) concerning the state of the object before the member function is invoked against it. If the precondition is true, the member function can be safely invoked. If the precondition is false, all bets are off, nothing can be said about the invocation. It could result in a core dump or worse.

The exception handling approach we take will require cooperation (really, a contract) between the designer of the type and its users. The designer specifies in the type manual page the precondition for each member function. The precondition could very well be the constant expression TRUE. That is, the associated member function can be invoked unconditionally. Further, the type designer undertakes to provide her or his clients with explicit member functions for checking the various preconditions (apropos, this approach simplifies the design and implementation of member functions by eliminating the need for dummy-proofing code). The client, if she or he is smart, will always check the precondition before invoking its associated member function. If the condition is true, perform the operation. If it is false, do some kind of error recovery.

We can get away with providing Sloop with just two predicate functions.

```
Boolean isbegin() - point is just before first element.
Boolean isend()   - point is just after last element.
```

We know that the Sloop is empty if (and only if)

```
isbegin() && isend() == TRUE
```

We summarize below the public interface of Sloop together with the associated preconditions:

```
template <class T> class Sloop {
public:
    Boolean isbegin() const; // precondition:  unconditional
    Boolean isend() const;   // precondition   unconditional
```

```
        void next();            //                  !isend()
        void prev();            //                  !isbegin()
        T geta() const;         //                  !isend()
        T getb() const;         //                  !isbegin()
        Boolean puta( T x);     //                  unconditional
        Boolean putb( T x);     //                  unconditional
        T dela();               //                  !isend()
        T delb();               //                  !isbegin()
};
```

## 10.7  Sloop<T>—Implementation

The idea behind this implementation is that a Sloop consists of two linked lists of nodes. You've seen the parametric type Node<T> before on page 18. A node consists of a pointer to a next Node and a data member of type T for holding the value. The concept of current point is captured implicitly by being between the end of the "before" list and the beginning of the "after" list. Point motion is handled by transferring Node addresses between the two lists.

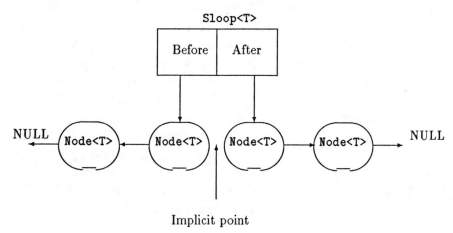

Implicit point

In the implementation below we handle parametry by parametrizing the source file with a typedef binding the symbol T to whatever type of thing we want the Sloop to contain. This is called the template file technique

[SHO]. We will refrain from commenting on the pointer gymnastics involved
in the implementation as it is the usual stuff. For convenience we reproduce
the implementation of the parametric Node type.

```
typedef int T;    // parametrize the file by T

typedef int Boolean;

class Node {
public:
    Node(T x) : Next(0), val(x) {}
    Node *next() const          { return Next; }
    T value() const             { return val; }
    void link( Node *p)         { Next = p; }
private:
    Node *Next;
    T val;
};

class Sloop {
public:
    Sloop()                 { before = after = 0; }
    Boolean isbegin() const { return (before == 0); }
    Boolean isend() const   { return (after == 0); }
    void next()             { move( &after, &before); }
    void prev()             { move( &before, &after); }
    T geta() const          { return after->value(); }
    T getb() const          { return before->value(); }
    Boolean puta( T x)      { return put( x, &after); }
    Boolean putb( T x)      { return put( x, &before); }
    T dela()                { return del( &after); }
    T delb()                { return del( &before); }
private:
    Node *before,
         *after;

    // these private functions are candidates for static
    // in C++ 2.0
```

```
// move moves a node from the head of the
// pre list to the head of the post list.
// pre is before point, post is after point
static void move( Node **pre, Node **post)
{
    if( (*pre) ) {
        Node *t = (*pre);
        (*pre) = (*pre)->next();
        t->link((*post));
        (*post) = t;
    }
}

static Boolean put( T x, Node **p)
{
    Node *t;
    if( t = new Node(x)) {
        t->link( *p);
        *p = t;
    }
    return (t != 0 );
}

static T del( Node **p)
{
    Node *t = (*p);
    (*p) = (*p)->next();
    T r;
    r = t->value();
    delete t;
    return r;
}
};
```

Notice that we have factored out the common behavior of paired before and after operations into private member functions. For example, next() and prev() are written in terms of move(). Because the functions move(), put() and del() do not modify or observe the state of the object against which they are invoked, they are excellent candidates for being declared static within class Sloop. Static member functions are a new feature of C++ 2.0. Like any other class member, they may partake of any of the three visibilities: private, protected, public.

## 10.8   Yacht<T>—Implementation

Here is an implementation of Yacht publicly derived from Sloop. Our guiding principle is layering: implement each member function of Yacht in terms of the public interface of Sloop. The most noteworthy thing about this implementation is that it requires no additional data members, which makes the design simpler in a certain regard. The consequence is perceived at runtime. Certain properties of the Yacht, its length, for example, are computed on the fly, which certainly takes more time than returning the value of a data member containing the current length. We have simply taken an extreme position along the speed-space spectrum of trade-offs. You can do it differently. We have also thrown in several additional member functions in implementing the editor.

```
// remember:  typedef char T ...
class Yacht : public Sloop {
public:
    // return current offset of point
    int where() const
    {
        int r = lengthb();
        go( r);
        return r;
    }


    // go moves point to desired offset.  If go fails,
    // it leaves point at end of yacht
    Boolean go( int n)
    {
        begin();
        for( ; !isend() && (n >= 0); next() )
            n--;
        return !n;
    }
```

```
    // get() returns value after point and advances the point
    // precondition:   !isend()
    T get()
    {
        T r;
        r = geta();
        next();
        return r;
    }

    // position point at beginning
    void begin()  { while( !isbegin() ) prev(); }

    // position point at end
    void end()    { while( !isend() ) next(); }

    // return number of elements in Yacht
    int length() const
    {
        int r = lengthb();
        for( int n = 0; !isend(); next() )
            n++;
        go( r);
        return n;
    }

    // print Yacht, from point to end, to standard I/O FILE
    void print( FILE *fp = stdout) const
    {
        while( !isend() ) {
            fprintf( fp, "%d\n", geta() );
            next();
        }
    }
private:
    // lengthb - moves  point to beginning and returns
    // previous offset of point
    int lengthb()
```

```
    {
        for( int n = 0; !isbegin(); prev() )
            n++;
        return n;
    }
};
```

## 10.9  Buffer—Implementation

Finally (here's what you have been waiting for so patiently), here is an implementation of Buffer publicly derived from Yacht (really Yacht<char>).

```
// a buffer is a kind of yacht of characters, which can
// optionally be associated with a File
class Buffer : public Yacht<char> {
public:
    Buffer() : () {}  // constructor for buffers not
                      // connected to a file

    Buffer( char *filename) : ()
    {
        if( filename == 0 )
            ;
        else if( read( filename) )
            ;
        else
            error( "could not open %s\n", filename);

        begin();
    }

    Boolean read( char *filename)
    {
        int r = 1;
        if( filename ) {
            File f( filename);
            if( f.isok() ) {
                for( ; !f.iseof(); next() )
```

```
                        putb( f.get() );
            } else r = 0;
        }
        return r;
    }

    Boolean write( char *filename)
    {
        int r = 1;
        if( filename ) {
            File f( filename, "w");
            if( f.isok() ) {
                for( ; !isend(); next() )
                    f.put( geta() );
            } else r = 0;
        }
        return r;
    }
private:
    void error( char *msg, char *arg) { printf( msg, arg); }
};
```

## 10.10  Summary

We have designed `Buffer` as the leaf of an inheritance chain

```
    class Buffer : public Yacht<char] { ... };
    template<class T> class Yacht : public Sloop<T> { ... }
```

where each type in the chain extends the properties of its parent by one simple idea

```
    Sloop<T>    ordered list of T values with current point
    Yacht<T>    luxury Sloop<T> with random access to values
    Buffer      A Yacht<char> with file I/O
```

We learned and applied several design principles

- Pass the buck and layering

- Minimality of public interface

- Orthogonality of public interface

In the next chapter we return to the `Editor` type, discuss its design, and suggest an implementation that relies heavily on the magic of dynamic binding (virtual functions).

# Bibliography

[MEY] Bertrand Meyer, *Object-Oriented Program Construction*, 1988, Prentice Hall. (Addresses object-oriented design, including parametric types.)

[SHO] Jonathan Shopiro, personal communication, November 1988.

[STR2] Bjarne Stroustrup, "Parameterized Types for C++," *Usenix Proceedings: C++ Conference*, Denver, CO, 1988.

# Chapter 11

# Extension of Text Editor

## 11.1  Introduction

In the last chapter, we designed and implemented the `Buffer`, which, together with `File`, are two of the main helping types we need to construct the `Editor`. In this chapter, we complete the construction of the `Editor` type. I use the word "complete" advisedly, because there are always future enhancements to think about, and there are certainly going to be bugs to fix!

## 11.2  Editor—High-Level Architecture

Let's summarize what we know about the `Editor` object so far. An `Editor` is in one-to-one correspondence with a `Buffer` object and coordinates changes against the `Buffer` with changes against the user's view of it. This view corresponds to a `File` object, which, for now, represents the terminal as an output device (standard output). The `Editor` has the job of parsing the command (input) stream into actions against itself. An action against the `Editor` object results in changes in the state of its constituent data members, which include, most likely, a `Buffer`, an input `File`, and an output `File`. Without much trouble, we can map this verbal description of the editor into C++.

```
class Editor {    // incomplete class declaration
```

255

```
public:
    void eval();  // parses the command stream
private:
    Buffer b;
    File input;
    File output;
};
```

We know what the operations are from a perusal of our requirements document in chapter 9. Refreshing our memory, here they are.

Note:    Bracketed arguments are optional.

[n] g    Move point to just before nth character
         (zero based).  Default value for n is 0.

[n] p    Print n characters starting at the first character
         after point, followed by a newline.  n defaults to 1.
         Increment point by n.

i    Insert arbitrary number of characters before point.
     Terminate insertion with . on a line by itself.

[n] d    Delete n characters starting at the first character
         after point.  n defaults to 1.

[n] y    Paste whatever was last deleted n times just before
         point.  n defaults to 1.

w [file] Write out the internal representation of the
         file (the buffer) to the named file.  The primary
         default for file is the filename command line
         argument to ced.  If ced was invoked without a
         filename, it selects the last file written to.

q    Exit the editor.

?    Print out useful information, like filename,
     point, and size of file.

Now, how shall we represent the actions or operations on the Editor? Here the object model itself provides the answer.

*Definition of object:* An object is a repository of state that responds to a fixed set of messages. The response may involve changing the state of the object, associating a return value with the message and sending messages to other objects.

In C++ terms, the answer is to represent each edit operation as a member function of class Editor. For now, let's assume that the return type of each of these member functions is void. This is reasonable because, certainly, each such member function changes the state of the Editor object, and besides, I can't think of any other return type! We don't have enough information to determine the argument type(s) of these member functions, so for now, let's make the simplest assumption: no arguments. In C++, the Editor class now looks like this.

```
class Editor {
public:
    void eval();     // parses the command stream
    void go();       // move point
    void print();    // print characters
    void insert();   // insert characters into buffer
    void del();      // delete characters from buffer
    void paste();    // paste last deletion after point
    void write();    // write buffer out to file
    void quit();     // quit the editor
    void info();     // display filename, point offset
                     // and file size
private:
    Buffer b;
    File input;
    File output;
};
```

## 11.3  Parser

The editor requirements state that, to invoke an operation, the user types an optional integer followed by a single character that represents the command. The easiest way, by far, of mapping a character to a function (member function or otherwise) is an array of pointers to functions, wherein the character plays the role of index. At most, the dimension of the array—call it action[]—is 128, which corresponds to the ASCII character set. And we know the type of the array, because each of its slots contains the address of a member function of Editor, which takes no arguments and returns void.

```
void (Editor::*action[128])();
```

For example, when the user types "g" to move the point, what essentially happens is

```
Editor e;
...
(e.*action['g'])();
```

By making the action[] array a private and static data member of class Editor, we render it invisible to Editor clients and shared by all Editor objects. Furthermore we can initial the array at compile time outside the class template like so.

```
Class Editor {
...
private:
    static void (Editor::*action[128])();
...
};

void (Editor::*action[128])() = {
    ...
    &Editor::go,     // corresponds to ASCII 'g'
    ...
};
```

We have built up enough machinery to sketch out the parsing function

```
typedef int Boolean;
const Boolean forever = 1;
```

```
void Edit::eval()  // parsing function
{
    while( forever) {
        // get character c from input stream
        int c = input.get();
        (this->*action[c])();
    }
}
```

The basic idea is to loop forever, getting command characters from the input stream. Each character is mapped to an edit operation via the **action[]** array. Because the loop never terminates, we need to describe how an edit session is terminated. Well, eventually the user types "q" which invokes

```
void Editor::quit()
```

via the **action[]** table. It suffices for **quit()** to call **exit(0)**, and the edit program terminates.

Another issue to handle is: What if the user types a character that does not correspond to any command, for example, "z"? A simple solution is to map—via **action[]**—all such characters to a single function that indicates an error, say,

```
void Editor::eerror()
{
    output.put( "?\n" );
}
```

where **put( char \*)** is an overloaded member function of **File** which knows how to write C strings to a **File**, just like the library function **fputs()**. **File** already has a **put(int c)** member function that knows how to write a single character. Apropos, this **put(char \*)** is an example of a useful addition to the public interface of a type, which is not discovered until well after the bulk of the design work has already been completed for that type. So, let's add **put( char \*)** to the public interface of **File** with the charming implementation

```
void File::put( char *p)
{
    for( ; *p; p++)
        put( *p);  // File::put( int)
}
```

Yet another issue is what to do with characters (e.g., white space: blank, newline and tab) from the input stream that are harmless. Following the previous solution, we map all such characters via the action[] to an Editor member function that does nothing and does it well

```
void Editor::donothing() {}
```

It is not clear yet whether eval() can handle the optional integer modifier to a command. We can either pretend that it can, or we can simplify the problem by temporarily eliminating the optional integers from the command stream. It is hoped that the simplification will give us enough insight into the problem so that we can recover the integer modifiers in the next design go-around.

## 11.4   Simple Main Program

Let's go for the jackpot and write a main program for our editor. It should look something like this.

```
// invoked as ced at the command line
main( int argc, char *argv[])
{
    Editor ed;
    ...
    ed.eval();
}
```

Namely, instantiate an Editor object and fire off an edit session with eval(). There is one more thing we have to do to complete the main program. And that is to associate optionally a file with the edit session. We could implement this feature with two Editor constructors. The first

```
Editor::Editor()
```

corresponds to the case

```
prompt> ced
```

where the program is invoked with no command-line arguments. This constructor doesn't have to do very much: just provide default values for the **Editor**'s data members. The second constructor

```
Editor::Editor( char *)
```

corresponds to the case

```
prompt> ced filename
```

where the edit program is invoked with a filename. The second constructor must handle several possibilities:

- The named file exists. Read it into the buffer.

- The file does not exist.

In both eventualities, the constructor squirrels away the name so that the **Editor** write operation has a default file name to write the buffer out to. We can squirrel away the name in an **Editor** data member

```
char *Editor::filename;
```

We can combine these two constructors into one

```
Editor::Editor( char *)
```

by employing the convention that the null string, "", corresponds to the absence of a file name command line argument. Returning to the main program, we can now write

```
main( int argc, char *argv[])
{
    Editor ed( argc > 1 ? argv[1] : "" );

    ed.eval();
}
```

which, you have to admit, is an awfully short main program! All we have
to do now is implement the constructor:

```
Editor::Editor( char *fname)
    : b( fname), input(), output( "", "w")
{
    // play it safe, make a copy of the file name
    filename = new char[strlen( fname) + 1];
    strcpy( filename, fname);
}
```

Here we have made use of an elegant and delightful feature of C++: the facility for constructing constructors out of constructors. That is, we initialize
the Editor object by invoking the constructor of each of its data members.
In the expression

```
    ...     : b( fname), input(), output( "", "w")
```

Buffer b initializes itself from the file name fname. No problem results if
fname is the null string; the buffer simply positions itself at the beginning.
The input File object connects itself to standard input, and the output File
object connects itself to standard output. Refer to the previous chapters for
the details of class Buffer and class File. The actual body of the Editor
constructor is thus small; it just copies the filename to the data member
filename. In fact, if we had an honest String class, we could get rid of the
body of the Editor constructor altogether by declaring the filename data
member as

```
    String filename;
```

and invoking the constructor

```
String::String( char *p);
```

in the constructor list

```
... : b( fname), input(), output( "", "w"), filename( fname)
```

which yields the following elegant form for the **Editor**'s constructor

```
Editor::Editor( char *fname)
    : b( fname), input(), output( "", "w"),
      filename( fname) {}
```

But we're not going to do it here. I leave the design of a String class to you, my readers.

## 11.5 Editor Commands—First Phase

What remains is to implement the edit operations—**go()**, **print()**, **insert()**, **del()**, **paste()**, **write()**, **quit()**, **info()**. We are going to talk through a couple of these operations to give the flavor of how it's done. We're not going to document the entire implementation because it will be subsumed under the second Phase implementation. Let's make the assumption that the parser **Edit::eval()** only has to handle single-command characters, with no numeric modifiers.

What this means for the **go()** function is that it advances the point in the buffer by one. The function should emit a warning if asked to beyond the end of the buffer. We can implement **go()** by passing the buck to the buffer

```
void Editor::go()
{
    if( b.isend() )
        eerror();
    else
        b.next();
}
```

The delete operator has to deal with the end-of-buffer boundary condition

```
void Editor::del()
{
    if( b.isend() )
        eerror();
    else
        b.dela();
}
```

## 11.6   Editor Commands—Second Phase

Let's come back to the original specification of the editor. Namely, each command may have an optional integer prefix that qualifies it. Furthermore, we place on ourselves the restriction to keep as much as possible of the code that we have developed up to now. We preserve the code of eval() unchanged. In fact we want to preserve the names of the Editor action functions (go(), insert(), ...) and to leave their addresses untouched in the very same slots in the action[] table. What is left to change is the implementation of the action functions.

What tool of object-oriented programming could come to our rescue to provide an elegant and reusable solution? Let's say we're trying to reimplement the Editor go() function. Well it has to handle (for now) two cases: with a numeric prefix and without one. In the case without a numeric prefix, the go() function must provide the default, 1.

Perhaps we need a switch statement with two cases. But then we need to figure out a type tag to switch on. As we have mentioned in chapter 3 on page 92, the wrong way to solve the problem is with a C-style switch-case statement, because it is a difficult structure to maintain and enhance. But it was worth proposing this solution because it points us in the direction of a better solution, namely, dynamic binding. In general, whatever can be done with a switch case statement in C can be done far better with dynamic binding in C++. Somehow we want the code of Editor::go() to pass the buck and to send a "go" message to a pointer to an object

```
p->go( ...);
```

where the pointer is formally of type Base (yet to be determined)

```
Base *p;
```

but at runtime, "p" points to either an object of type Base or to an object of type publicly derived from Base, say, D1 or D2; so the message expression invokes the **go()** function corresponding to the type of object that "p" points to. Each type in the inheritance hierarchy has its own implementation of **go()**, and **go()** is declared virtual in Base. In our case, Base can represent the default numeric prefix, and the derived type D1 can represent the explicit numeric prefix.

## 11.7   Class Register

It's time to give real names to the types in the hierarchy that we have discovered. Base we call **Register**, and D1 we call **Iregister** (I for integer). Why these names? Because I think of the hierarchy as a tree of registers out of which to construct an editing machine. A register may contain a value (an integer or a character) and responds to messages that involve editing.

Let's work through the functional prototype of **go()** in class Register. By the rules of C++, because this function is virtual and we want dynamic binding, all the **go()** functions in classes derived from Register (like Iregister) must have the identical prototype. Let's say the return type is **void**. What part(s) of the **Editor** object does **Register::go()** manipulate? At most, we could pass to **go()** the entire **Editor** object.

```
virtual void Register::go( Editor &e);
```

The problem here is that **go()** has no way to access directly the **Buffer** or the input and output **Files**, because they are private data members of the **Editor**. So, we must pass the individual **Editor** data members that are needed. Given our simple user interface, it suffices to pass the **Buffer** and the output **File**. So by the rule of parsimony (less is more) we select the prototype

```
virtual void Register::go( Buffer &b, File &f);
```

Note that the **Buffer** argument to **go()** is a reference, which makes perfect sense because we indeed want to change the state of the **Buffer**. The decisions we have made now make it trivial to implement **Editor::go()**

```
void Editor::go() { rp->go( b, output); }
```

where **rp** is a pointer formally of type Register, which, at runtime, may be pointing either to a Register or Iregister object. Because **rp** had better be visible to Editor::go(), and we don't like global variables, a simple solution is to add the following data members to the **Editor**

```
class Editor {
    ...
private:
    ...
    Register *rp;
    Register reg;
    Iregister ireg;
};
```

This way rp can simply point to data members within its own **Editor** object

```
    ...
rp = &reg;
    ...
rp = &ireg;
    ...
```

We can strengthen the typing and express the fact that **rp** is only going to point to data members of **Editor** of a particular type by declaring **rp**

```
Register Editor::*rp;
```

within class **Editor**. The declaration implies that rp is restricted to pointing to Editor data members of type derived from Register.

Now you can see why I think of the **Editor** as a little computer constructed out of these nice registers! We can reuse our work from Phase 1 to provide an implementation for Register::go()

```
virtual void Register::go( Buffer &b, File &output)
{
```

```
        if( b.isend() )
            output.put( "?\n" );
        else
            b.next();
    }
```

Notice that this implementation makes absolutely no assumptions about the data members of class Register!

We have seen that the existence of an `Editor` operation, like `Editor::go()`, implies the existence of a virtual member function of the same name in class `Register` (`Register::go()`). This is an application of the pass-the-buck principle. Well, what's sauce for the goose is sauce for the gander! That is, for each `Editor` operation, we may as well conclude that there is a virtual member function in class `Register` of the same name. Furthermore, this virtual function is overridden in class `Iregister`. This observation determines the public interface of class `Register` and `Iregister`, although there remains some work to determine the precise functional prototypes of the member functions. The whole situation seems to be intuitively pushing us in the direction of saying that class `Register` establishes an a priori interface. Meaning, types derived from `Register` inherit the semantics (manual page specification) of `Register`, while being at liberty to override the inherited implementation (of the member functions). Here we list the public interface of `Register` to date.

```
    class Register {
    public: // argument types to be determined
        virtual void go( ...);
        virtual void print( ...);
        virtual void insert( ...);
        virtual void del( ...);
        virtual void put( ...);
    };
```

# 11.8   Editor Implementation

We have cut down the job of building the `Editor` into little doable bite-size pieces: a member function in the public interface of some type derived from

**Register.** The architecture of the `Editor` is extensible: We can build features into the `Editor` gradually over a period, by adding new types derived from `Register`. The implementation of the `Editor` follows the pass-the-buck principle: each Edit operation sends a message of the same name to the `Register` pointer.

```
void Editor::operation() { rp->operation( ...); }
```

Now this is a little bit of a lie, because some operations (like `quit()`) have such simple implementations (currently) that there is no need to deal with registers. Here is our implementation of the `Editor`. In it, we show our choices for the functional prototypes of the member functions of `Register`:

```
const int forever = 1;
class Editor {
public:
    Editor( char *fname) :
        b( fname), input(fname), output( "", "w")
    {
        filename = new char[strlen( fname) + 1];
        strcpy( filename, fname);

        rp = &reg;
    }

    void eval()
    {
        while( forever)
            (this->*action[input.get()])();
    }

    void go()     { rp->go( b, output); }

    void print()  { rp->print( b, output); }

    void insert() { rp->insert( b, input); }

    void del()    { rp->del( b, kbuf, output); }
```

```
    void put()     { rp->put( b, kbuf); }

    void quit()    { exit(0); }

    void eerror() { output.put( "?\n"); } // error function

    void donothing()    {}
private:
    Buffer b;
    File input;
    File output;

    Register Editor::*rp;
    Register reg;
    Iregister ireg;
    Buffer kbuf;  // kill buffer
};
```

We have added a kill buffer so that `Editor::put()` can yank back what `Editor::del()` has deleted.

## 11.9 Meditation on Further Decomposition

Staring at the data members of class `Editor`, one notices that they seem to fall into two orthogonal groups.

- An editing machine—rp, reg, ireg, kbuf, action[] (class Editable?)

- An editable object whose state is modified by the editing machine—b, input, output (class Editmachine?)

Is this a reasonable decomposition? I wonder how we can exploit the identification of these two new types (Editable and Editmachine) for the purposes of code reuse, maintainability, and enhancement? We seem to have decoupled the parsing engine (Editmachine) from the object against which action is taken (Editable) as the result of the parse of a command. This simplifies the argument list of the member functions in the public interface of Register (and its derived types). Namely, they could all take a reference to an

Editable object. One benefit of the decomposition is that one Editmachine object could edit multiple Editable objects. So an edit session is a relation consisting of an Editmachine with an Editable object. Maybe we need a Session type. We leave the development of this idea to the reader.

## 11.10   Register Implementation

All we need for a working editor is an implementation of the base class Register. Without further ado, here is one.

```
class Register {
public:
    // move point forward one character
    virtual void go( Buffer &b, File &output)
    {
        if( b.isend() )
            output.put( "?\n" );
        else
            b.next();
    }

    // print character after point and move point forward
    virtual void print( Buffer &b, File &output)
    {
        if( b.isend() )
            output.put( "?\n" );
        else
            output.put( b.geta());
        go();    // Register::go()
    }

    // insert after point
    virtual void insert( Buffer &b, File &input)
    {
        int c;
        int prev = '\n';
        while( !input.iseof() ) {
            c = input.get();
```

```
                if( (prev == '\n') && (c == '.') )
                    if( input.peek() == '\n' ) {
                        input.get();
                        break;
                    }
                b.putb( c);
                prev = c;
            }
        }


    virtual void del( Buffer &b, Buffer &kbuf, File &output)
    {
        if( b.isend() )
            output.put( "?\n" );
        else {
            // need to capture deletion into kill buf
            // empty out the kbuf ...
            for( kbuf.begin(); !kbuf.isend(); kbuf.next())
                kbuf.dela();
            kbuf.putb( b.dela());
        }
    }

    virtual void put( Buffer &b, Buffer &kbuf)
    {
        b.putb( kbuf.geta());
    }


    // no need for data members. defaults are implicit!
};
```

## 11.11  Iregister Implementation

We need to clarify how the Editor manages the register pointer rp. Perhaps its management has something to do with how the Editor parses the input stream.

Recall that the input command stream looks like a sequence of lines. Each line consists of an optional integer prefix followed by a character. The character is mapped via the action[] array to an Editor member function, which, in turn, may send a message to the object pointed to by rp.

Here's a way of handling the optional integer prefix. Via the Editor action[] array map the digit characters (ASCII '0' through '9') to a common Editor member function

```
void isinteger( int c)
```

The above function takes a character argument that tells it what character invoked it (e.g., 1 as opposed to 2). However, in order for Editor::eval() to vector to this function through the action[] table, we must mildly change the functional prototype to match

```
void (Editor::*action[128])( int character);
```

Of course, this requires that we modify the functional prototypes of all the Editor operations whose addresses appear in the action[] table, for example,

```
void Editor::quit( int c)    { exit(0); }
```

whether or not they really need to know by which character they were invoked. At worst, we incur a slight runtime cost of pushing the invoking character onto the runtime stack.

Back to isinteger(). This function scans for a sequence of ASCII digits. As soon as it encounters a nondigit, it ungets that character to the input stream, and converts the digit sequence into an internal integer. Fine, but how does this relate to Iregister? Easy. Let's posit that an Iregister object has an integer data member (val) that can be set or inspected via member functions load() and store(), respectively:

```
class Iregister : public Register {
public:
    Iregister()         { val = 0; }
    void load( int x)    { val = x; }
    int store()          { return val; }
```

```
     // other member functions
private:
     int val;
};
```

Isinteger() can set the Iregister (ireg) data member of an Editor object

```
ireg.load( atoi(buf));
```

where buf is a character array containing the digit sequence, and where atoi() is a standard library function (for both C and C++), which converts null-terminated strings into integers (if possible). Just before it returns, isinteger() sets the Editor's rp pointer with the address of the Editor's Iregister data member

```
rp = &ireg;
```

But now everything is set up just right, for the next character that Editor::eval() sees corresponds (it is hoped) to an edit command. All that command does is to send a message (go, insert) to rp

```
rp->message(...);
```

which is dynamically bound. However, each Editor command must take care to reset rp

```
rp = &reg;
```

before it returns to prepare properly for the next command line. For we never know whether the next command will be prefixed with an integer or not. All that remains is to implement the messages sent to rp (go, print, insert, del, put), which we present subsequently.

```
class Iregister : public Register {
public:
     Iregister()          { val = 0; }
     void load( int x)    { val = x; }
```

```
    int store()          { return val; }

    void go( Buffer &b, File &output)
    {
        if( !b.go( store()))
            output.put( "?\n" );
    }

    // print
    void print( Buffer &b, File &output)
    {
        for( int n = store(); !b.isend() && n; n-- )
            output.put( b.geta() ), b.next();
        output.put( '\n');
    }

    // Inherit parent class insert(), ignore prefix

    void del( Buffer &b, Buffer &kbuf, File &output)
    {
        // flush previous contents of kill buffer
        for( kbuf.begin(); !kbuf.isend(); kbuf.next() )
            kbuf.dela();

        for( int n = store(); !b.isend() && n; n-- )
            kbuf.putb( b.dela());
        if( n)
            printf( "? %d characters left undeleted\n", n);
    }

    // reuse kill buffer by geta'ing and not deleting from it
    void put( Buffer &b, Buffer &kbuf)
    {
        for( kbuf.begin(); !kbuf.isend(); kbuf.next())
            b.putb( kbuf.geta());
    }
private:
    int val;
};
```

We would like to comment on some of the highlights of this implementation of class Iregister. First, Iregister inherits the implementation of `insert()` from its parent class Register. Second, when we delete and put a bunch of characters, they remain in the kill buffer so that they can be put again some place else. This is a result of using `Buffer geta()` instead of `dela()` to "get" characters from the kill buffer.

As noted, the design of class Iregister caused some modifications to be made to class `Editor`. We document our latest version of the `Editor` in the last section of this chapter.

## 11.12   Summary

We have accomplished what we set out to: the object-oriented design and implementation of a simple text editor with a command-line user interface. In the process, we discovered several types

```
Editor, Buffer, File, Yacht<T>, Sloop<T>
```

## 11.13   class Editor—Implementation

Here is the complete implementation of class Editor:

```
const int forever = 1;
class Editor {
public:
    Editor( char *fname) :
        b( fname), input(fname), output( "", "w")
    {
        strcpy( filename, fname);

        rp = &reg;
    }

    void eval()
    {
        while( forever) {
```

```
        int c = input.get();
        (this->*action[c])( c);
    }
}

void go( int c)     { rp->go( b, output); rp = &reg; }

void print( int c) { rp->print( b, output); rp = &reg; }

void insert( int c) { rp->insert( b, input); rp = &reg; }

void del( int c) { rp->del( b, kbuf, output); rp = &reg; }

void put( int c)    { rp->put( b, kbuf); rp = &reg; }

void info( int c)
{
    char buf[128];
    int point = b.lengthb();
    b. go( point);
    output.put( filename);
    sprintf( buf, ":  point %d, length %d\n",
        point, b.length());
    output.put( buf);
}

void write( int c)
{
    output.put( "file? ");
    char buf[128];
    char *p = buf;

    // candidate member function of File:
    // getline( char *buf)
    while( (c = input.get()) != '\n' )
        *p++ = c;
    *p = 0;
    if( !*p)
        p = filename;
```

```
        File f( p, "w" );
        if( f.isok() )
            for( ; !b.isend(); b.next() )
                f.put( b.geta() );
        else
            output.put( "cannot open file\n" );
    }

    void quit( int c)    { exit(0); }

    void isinteger( int c)
    {
        char buf[64];
        char *p = buf;

        for( *p = c; !input.iseof(); p++) {
            c = input.get();
            if( isdigit(c) )
                *p = c;
            else {
                input.unget( c);
                break;
            }
        }

        *p = 0;   // null termination of string
        ireg.load( atoi( buf));
        rp = &ireg;
    }

    // error function
    void eerror( int c) { output.put( "?\n"); }

    void donothing( int c)    {}
private:
    Buffer b;
    File input;
    File output;
```

```
    char filename[128];

    Register Editor::*rp;
    Register reg;
    Iregister ireg;
    Buffer kbuf;   // kill buffer
    static void (Editor::*action[128])( int character);
};

// here we initialize the action[] array
// most entries are &Editor::eerror.  To save space, we show the
// non eerror entries

void (Editor::*action[128])( int character) = {
    &Editor::eerror,   // '\0'
    ...
    &Editor::donothing,   // tab
    &Editor::donothing,   // newline
    ...
    &Editor::donothing,   // 0x20   blank
    ...
    &Editor::isinteger,   // 0x30 '0'
    &Editor::isinteger,   // '1'
    &Editor::isinteger,   // '2'
    &Editor::isinteger,   // '3'
    &Editor::isinteger,   // '4'
    &Editor::isinteger,   // '5'
    &Editor::isinteger,   // '6'
    &Editor::isinteger,   // '7'
    &Editor::isinteger,   // '8'
    &Editor::isinteger,   // '9'
    ...
    &Editor::info,     // '?'
    ...
    &Editor::del,     // 'd'
    &Editor::eerror,
    &Editor::eerror,
    &Editor::go,     // 'g'
    &Editor::eerror,
```

```
    &Editor::insert,  // 'i'
    ...
    &Editor::print,   // 0x70 'p'
    &Editor::quit,    // 'q'
    ...
    &Editor::write,   // 'w'
    &Editor::eerror,
    &Editor::put,     // 'y'
    ...
    &Editor::eerror   // 0x80
};
```

# Appendix A

# Data Abstraction and Hierarchy

Barbara Liskov
MIT Laboratory for Computer Science
Cambridge, Ma. 02139

## Abstract

Data abstraction is a valuable method for organizing programs to make them easier to modify and maintain. Inheritance allows one implementation of a data abstraction to be related to another hierarchically. This paper investigates the usefulness of hierarchy in program development, and concludes that although data abstraction is the more important idea, hierarchy does extend its usefulness in some situations.

This research was supported by the NEC Professorship of Software Science and Engineering.

## 1. Introduction

An important goal in design is to identify a program structure that simplifies both program maintenance and program modifications made to support changing requirements. Data abstractions are a good way of achieving this goal. They allow us to abstract from the way data structures are implemented to the behavior they provide that other programs can rely on. They permit the representation of data to be changed locally without affecting programs that use the data. They are particularly important because they hide complicated things (data structures) that are likely to change in the future. They also simplify the structure of programs that use them because they present a higher level interface. For example, they reduce the number of arguments to procedures because abstract objects are communicated instead of their representations.

Object-oriented programming is primarily a data abstraction technique, and much of its power derives from this. However, it elaborates this technique with the notion of "inheritance." Inheritance can be used in a number of ways, some of which enhance the power of data abstraction. In these cases, inheritance provides a useful addition to data abstraction.

This paper discusses the relationship between data abstraction and object-oriented programming. We begin in Section 2 by defining data abstraction and its role in the program development process. Then in Section 3 we discuss inheritance and identify two ways that it is used, for implementation hierarchy and for type hierarchy. Of the two methods, type hierarchy really adds something to data abstraction, so in Section 4 we discuss uses of type hierarchy in program design and development. Next we discuss some issues that arise in implementing type hierarchy. We conclude with a summary of our results.

## 2. Data Abstraction

The purpose of abstraction in programming is to separate behavior from implementation. The first programming abstraction mechanism was the procedure. A procedure performs some task or function; other parts of the program call the procedure to accomplish the task. To use the procedure, a programmer cares only about what it does and not how it is implemented. Any implementation that provides the needed function will do, provided it implements the function correctly and is efficient enough.

Procedures are a useful abstraction mechanism, but in the early seventies some researchers realized that they were not enough [15, 16, 7] and proposed a new way of organizing programs around the "connections" between modules. The concept of *data abstraction* or *abstract data type* arose from these ideas [5, 12].

Data abstractions provide the same benefits as procedures, but for data. Recall that the main idea is to separate what an abstraction is from how it is implemented so that implementations of the same abstraction can be substituted freely. The implementation of a data object is concerned with how that object is represented in the memory of a computer; this information is called the *representation,* or *rep* for short. To allow changing implementations without affecting users, we need a way of changing the representation without having to change all using programs. This is achieved by encapsulating the rep with a set of operations that manipulate it and by restricting using programs so that they cannot manipulate the rep directly, but instead must call the operations. Then, to implement or reimplement the data abstraction, it is necessary to define the rep and implement the operations in terms of it, but using code is not affected by a change.

Thus a data abstraction is a set of objects that can be manipulated directly only by a set of operations. An example of a data abstraction is the integers: the objects are 1, 2, 3, and so on and there are operations to add two integers, to test them for equality, and so on. Programs using integers manipulate them by their operations, and are shielded from implementation details such as whether the representation is 2's complement. Another example is character strings, with objects such as "a" and "xyz," and operations to select characters from strings and to concatenate strings. A final example is sets of integers, with objects such as { } (the empty set) and {3, 7}, and operations to insert an element in a set, and to test whether an integer is in a set. Note that integers and strings are built-in data types in most programming languages, while sets and other application-oriented data abstractions such as stacks and symbol tables are not. Linguistic mechanisms that permit user-defined abstract data types to be implemented are discussed in Section 2.2.

A data or procedure abstraction is defined by a *specification* and implemented by a program *module* coded in some programming language. The specification describes what the abstraction does, but omits any information about how it is implemented. By omitting such detail, we permit many different implementations. An implementation is correct if it provides the behavior defined by the specification. Correctness can be proved mathematically if the specification is written in a language with precise semantics; otherwise we establish correctness by informal reasoning or by the somewhat unsatisfactory technique of testing. Correct implementations differ from one another in how they work, i.e., what algorithms they use, and therefore they may have different performance. Any correct implementation is acceptable to the caller provided it meets the caller's performance requirements. Note that correct implementations need not be identical to one another; the whole point is to allow implementations to differ, while ensuring that they remain the same where this is important. The specification describes what is important.

For abstraction to work, implementations must be *encapsulated.* If an implementation is encapsulated, then no other module can depend on its implementation details. Encapsulation guarantees that modules can be implemented and reimplemented independently; it is related to the principle of "information hiding" advocated by Parnas [15].

### 2.1. Locality

Abstraction when supported by specifications and encapsulation provides *locality* within a program. Locality allows a program to be implemented, understood, or modified one module at a time:

1. The implementer of an abstraction knows what is needed because this is described in the specification. Therefore, he or she need not interact with programmers of other modules (or at least the interactions can be very limited).

2. Similarly, the implementer of a using module knows what to expect from an abstraction, namely the behavior described by the specification.

3. Only local reasoning is needed to determine what a program does and whether it does the right thing. The program is studied one module at a time. In each case we are concerned with whether the module does what it is supposed to do, that is, does it meet its specification. However, we can limit our attention to just that module and ignore both modules that use it, and modules that it uses. Using modules can be ignored because they depend only on the specification of this module, not on its code. Used modules are ignored by reasoning about what they do using their specifications instead of their code. There is a tremendous saving of effort in this way because specifications are much smaller than implementations. For example, if we had to look at the code of a called abstraction, we would be concerned not only with its code, but also with the code of any modules it uses, and so on.

4. Finally, program modification can be done module by module. If a particular abstraction needs to be reimplemented to provide better performance or correct an error or provide extended facilities, the old implementing module can be replaced by a new one without affecting other modules.

Locality provides a firm basis for fast prototyping. Typically there is a tradeoff between the performance of an algorithm and the speed with which it is designed and implemented. The initial implementation can be a simple one that performs poorly. Later it can be replaced by another implementation with better performance. Provided both implementations are correct, the calling program's correctness will be unaffected by the change.

Locality also supports program evolution. Abstractions can be used to encapsulate potential modifications. For example, suppose we want a program to run on different machines. We can accomplish this by inventing abstractions that hide the differences between machines so that to move the program to a different machine only those abstractions need be reimplemented. A good design principle is to think about expected modifications and organize the design by using abstractions that encapsulate the changes.

The benefits of locality are particularly important for data abstractions. Data structures are often complicated and therefore the simpler abstract view provided by the specification allows the rest of the program to be simpler. Also, changes to storage structures are likely as programs evolve; the effects of such changes can be minimized by encapsulating them inside data abstractions.

## 2.2. Linguistic Support for Data Abstraction

Data abstractions are supported by linguistic mechanisms in several languages. The earliest such language was Simula 67 [3]. Two major variations, those in CLU and Smalltalk, are discussed below.

CLU [8, 11] provides a mechanism called a *cluster* for implementing an abstract type. A template for a cluster is shown in Figure 2-1. The header identifies the data type being implemented and also lists the operations of the type; it serves to identify what procedure definitions inside the cluster can be called from the outside. The "rep = " line defines how objects of the type are represented; in the example, we are implementing sets as linked lists. The rest of the cluster consists of procedures; there must be a procedure for each operation, and in addition, there may be some procedures that can be used only inside the cluster.

int_set = **cluster is** create, insert, is_in, size, ...

    **rep** = int_list

    create = **proc** ... **end** create

    insert = **proc** ... **end** insert

    ...

**end** int_set

**Figure 2-1:** Template of a CLU Cluster.

In Smalltalk [4], data abstractions are implemented by *classes*. Classes can be arranged hierarchically, but we ignore this for now. A class implements a data abstraction similarly to a cluster. Instead of the "rep =" line, the rep is described by a sequence of variable declarations; these are the *instance variables*.[1] The remainder of the class consists of *methods*, which are procedure definitions. There is a method for each operation of the data type implemented by the class. (There cannot be any internal methods in Smalltalk classes because it is not possible to preclude outside use of a method.) Methods are called by "sending messages," which has the same effect as calling operations in CLU.

---

[1] We ignore the class variables here since they are not important for the distinctions we are trying to make. CLU has an analogous mechanism; a cluster can have some "own" variables [9].

Both CLU and Smalltalk enforce encapsulation but CLU uses compile-time type checking, while Smalltalk uses runtime checking. Compile-time checking is better because it allows a class of errors to be caught before the program runs, and it permits more efficient code to be generated by a compiler. (Compile-time checking can limit expressive power unless the programming language has a powerful type system; this issue is discussed further in Section 5.) Other object-oriented languages, e.g., [1, 13], do not enforce encapsulation at all. It is true that in the absence of language support encapsulation can be guaranteed by manual procedures such as code reading, but these techniques are error-prone, and although the situation may be somewhat manageable for a newly-implemented program, it will degrade rapidly as modifications are made. Automatic checking, at either runtime or compile-time, can be relied on with confidence and without the need to read any code at all.

Another difference between CLU and Smalltalk is found in the semantics of data objects. In Smalltalk, the operations are part of the object and can access the instance variables that make up the object's rep since these variables are part of the object too. In CLU, operations do not belong to the object but instead belong to a type. This gives them special privileges with respect to their type's objects that no other parts of the program have, namely, they can see the reps of these objects. (This view was first described by Morris [14].) The CLU view works better for operations that manipulate several objects of the type simultaneously because an operation can see the reps of several objects at once. Examples of such operations are adding two integers or forming the union of two sets. The Smalltalk view does not support such operations as well, since an operation can be inside of only one object. On the other hand, the Smalltalk view works better when we want to have several implementations of the same type running within the same program. In CLU an operation can see the rep of any object of its type, and therefore must be coded to cope with multiple representations explicitly. Smalltalk avoids this problem since an operation can see the rep of only one object.

## 3. Inheritance and Hierarchy

This section discusses inheritance and how it supports hierarchy. We begin by talking about what it means to construct a program using inheritance. Then we discuss two major uses of inheritance, implementation hierarchy and type hierarchy; see [18] for a similar discussion. Only one of these, type hierarchy, adds something new to data abstraction.

### 3.1. Inheritance

In a language with inheritance, a data abstraction can be implemented in several pieces that are related to one another. Although various languages provide different mechanisms for putting the pieces together, they are all similar. Thus we can illustrate them by examining a single mechanism, the subclass mechanism in Smalltalk.

In Smalltalk a class can be declared to be a *subclass* of another class[2], which is its *superclass*. The first thing that needs to be understood about the mechanism is what code results from such a definition. This question is important for understanding what a subclass does. For example, if we were to reason about its correctness, we would need to look at this code.

From the point of view of the resulting code, saying that one class is a subclass of another is simply a shorthand notation for building programs. The exact program that is constructed depends on the rules of the language, e.g., such things as when methods of the subclass override methods of the superclass. The exact details of these rules are not important for our discussion (although they clearly are important if the language is to be sensible and useful). The point is that the result is equivalent to directly implementing a class containing the instance variables and methods that result from applying the rules.

For example, suppose class T has operations $o_1$ and $o_2$ and instance variable $v_1$ and class S, which is declared to be a subclass of T, has operations $o_1$ and $o_3$ and instance variable $v_2$. Then the result in Smalltalk is effectively a class with two instance variables, $v_1$ and $v_2$, and three operations, $o_1$, $o_2$, $o_3$, where the code of $o_2$ is supplied by T, and the code of the other two operations is supplied by S. It is this combined code that must be understood, or modified if S is reimplemented, unless S is restricted as discussed further below.

One problem with almost all inheritance mechanisms is that they compromise data abstraction to an extent. In languages with inheritance, a data abstraction implementation (i.e., a class) has two kinds of users. There are the "outsiders" who simply use the objects by calling the operations. But in addition there are the "insiders." These are the subclasses, which are typically permitted to violate encapsulation. There are three ways that encapsulation can be violated [18]: the subclass might access an instance variable of its superclass, call a private operation of its superclass, or refer directly to superclasses of its superclass. (This last violation is not possible in Smalltalk.)

When encapsulation is not violated, we can reason about operations of the superclass using their specifications and we can ignore the rep of the superclass. When encapsulation is violated, we lose the benefits of locality. We must consider the combined code of the sub- and superclass in reasoning about the subclass, and if the superclass needs to be reimplemented, we may need to reimplement its subclasses too. For example, this would be necessary if an instance variable of the superclass changed, or if a subclass refers directly to a superclass of its superclass T and then T is reimplemented to no longer have this superclass.

Violating encapsulation can be useful in bringing up a prototype quickly since it allows code to be

---

[2]We ignore multiple inheritance to simplify the discussion.

produced by extension and modification of existing code. It is unrealistic, however, to expect that modifications to the implementation of the superclass can be propagated automatically to the subclass. Propagation is useful only if the resulting code works, which means that all expectations of the subclass about the superclass must be satisfied by the new implementation. These expectations can be captured by providing another specification for the superclass; this is a different specification from that for outsiders, since it contains additional constraints. Using this additional specification, a programmer can determine whether a proposed change to the superclass can usefully propagate to the subclass. Note that the more specific the additional specification is about details of the previous superclass implementation, the less likely that a new superclass implementation will meet it. Also, the situation will be unmanageable if each subclass relies on a different specification of the superclass. One possible approach is to define a single specification for use by all subclasses that contains more detail than the specification for outsiders but still abstracts from many implementation details. Some work in this direction is described in [17].

### 3.2. Implementation Hierarchy

The first way that inheritance is used is simply as a technique for implementing data types that are similar to other existing types. For example, suppose we want to implement integer sets, with operations (among others) to tell whether an element is a member of the set and to determine the current size of the set. Suppose further that a list data type has already been implemented, and that it provides a *member* operation and a *size* operation, as well as a convenient way of representing the set. Then we could implement set as a subclass of list; we might have the list hold the set elements without duplication, i.e., if an element were added to the set twice, it would be appear in the list only once. Then we would not need to provide implementations for *member* and *size*, but we would need to implement other operations such as one that inserts a new element into the set. Also, we should suppress certain other operations, such as *car*, to make them unavailable since they are not meaningful for sets. (This can be done in Smalltalk by providing implementations in the subclass for the suppressed operations; such an implementation would signal an exception if called.)

Another way of doing the same thing is to use one (abstract) type as the rep of another. For example, we might implement sets by using list as the rep. In this case, we would need to implement the *size* and *member* operations; each of these would simply call the corresponding operation on lists. Writing down implementations for these two operations, even though the code is very simple, is more work than not writing anything for them. On the other hand, we need not do anything to take away undesirable operations such as *car*.

Since implementation hierarchy does not allow us to do anything that we could not already do with data abstraction, we will not consider it further. It does permit us to violate encapsulation, with both the benefits and problems that ensue. However, this ability could also exist in the rep approach if desired.

### 3.3. Type Hierarchy

A type hierarchy is composed of subtypes and supertypes. The intuitive idea of a *subtype* is one whose objects provide all the behavior of objects of another type (the *supertype*) plus something extra. What is wanted here is something like the following substitution property [6]: If for each object $o_1$ of type S there is an object $o_2$ of type T such that for all programs P defined in terms of T, the behavior of P is unchanged when $o_1$ is substituted for $o_2$, then S is a subtype of T. (See also [2, 17] for other work in this area.)

We are using the words "subtype" and "supertype" here to emphasize that now we are talking about a semantic distinction. By contrast, "subclass" and "superclass" are simply linguistic concepts in programming languages that allow programs to be built in a particular way. They can be used to implement subtypes, but also, as mentioned above, in other ways.

We begin with some examples of types that are not subtypes of one another. First, a set is not a subtype of a list nor is the reverse true. If the same element is added to a set twice, the result is the same as if it had been added only once and the element is counted only once in computing the size of the set. However, if the same element is added twice to a list, it occurs in the list twice. Thus a program expecting a list might not work if passed a set; similarly a program expecting a set might not work if passed a list. Another example of non-subtypes are stacks and queues. Stacks are LIFO; when an element is removed from a stack, the last item added (pushed) is removed. By contrast, queues are FIFO. A using program is likely to notice the difference between these two types.

The above examples ignored a simple difference between the pairs of types, namely related operations. A subtype must have all the operations[3] of its supertype since otherwise the using program could not use an operation it depends on. However, simply having operations of the right names and signatures is not enough. (A operation's *signature* defines the numbers and types of its input and output arguments.) The operations must also do the same things. For example, stacks and queues might have operations of the same names, e.g., *add_el* to push or enqueue and *rem_el* to pop or dequeue, but they still are not subtypes of one another because the meanings of the operations are different for them.

Now we give some examples of subtype hierarchies. The first is indexed collections, which have operations to access elements by index; e.g., there would be a *fetch* operation to fetch the $i^{th}$ element of the collection. All subtypes have these operations too, but, in addition, each would provide extra operations. Examples of subtypes are arrays, sequences, and indexed sets; e.g., sequences can be concatenated, and arrays can be modified by storing new objects in the elements.

---

[3] It needs the instance methods but not the class methods.

The second example is abstract devices, which unify a number of different kinds of input and output devices. Particular devices might provide extra operations. In this case, abstract device operations would be those that all devices support, e.g., the end-of-file test, while subtype operations would be device specific. For example, a printer would have modification operations such as *put_char* but not reading operations such as *get_char*. Another possibility is that abstract devices would have all possible operations, e.g., both *put_char* and *get_char*, and thus all subtypes would have the same set of operations. In this case, operations that not all real devices can do must be specified in a general way that allows exceptions to be signalled. For example, *get_char* would signal an exception when called on a printer.

An inheritance mechanism can be used to implement a subtype hierarchy. There would be a class to implement the supertype and another class to implement each subtype. The class implementing a subtype would declare the supertype's class as its superclass.

## 4. Benefits of Type Hierarchy

Data abstraction is a powerful tool in its own right. Type hierarchy is a useful adjunct to data abstraction. This section discusses how subtypes can be used in the development of the design for a program. (A detailed discussion of design based on data abstraction can be found in [11].) It also discusses their use in organizing a program library.

### 4.1. Incremental Design

Data abstractions are usually developed incrementally as a design progresses. In early stages of a design, we only know some of a data abstraction's operations and a part of its behavior. Such a stage of design is depicted in Figure 4-1a. The design is depicted by a graph that illustrates how a program is subdivided into modules. There are two kinds of nodes; a node with a single bar on top represents a procedure abstraction, and a node with a double bar on top represents a data abstraction. An arrow pointing from one node to another means that the abstraction of the first node will be implemented using the abstraction of the second node. Thus the figure shows two procedures, P and Q, and one data abstraction, T. P will be implemented using Q (i.e., its code calls Q) and T (i.e., its code uses objects of type T). (Recursion is indicated by cycles in the graph. Thus if we expected the implementation of P to call P, there would be an arrow from P to P.)

This figure represents an early stage of design, in which the designer has thought about how to implement P and has invented Q and T. At this point, some operations of T have been identified, and the designer has decided that an object of type T will be used to communicate between P and Q.

The next stage of design is to investigate how to implement Q. (It would not make sense to look at T's

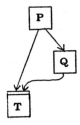

**Figure 4-1:** The Start of a Design.

implementation at this point, because we do not know all its operations yet.) In studying Q we are likely to define additional operations for T. This can be viewed as refining T to a subtype S as is shown in Figure 4-2. Here a double arrow points from a supertype to a subtype; double arrows can only connect data abstractions (and there can be no cycles involving only double arrows).

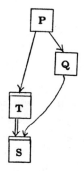

**Figure 4-2:** Later in the Design.

The kind of refinement illustrated in the figures may happen several times; e.g., S in turn may have a subtype R and so on. Also, a single type may have several subtypes, representing the needs of different subparts of the program.

Keeping track of these distinctions as subtypes is better than treating the group of types as a single type, for several reasons. First it can limit the effect of design errors. For example, suppose further investigation indicates a problem with S's interface. When a problem of this sort occurs, it is necessary to look at every abstraction that uses the changed abstraction. For the figure, this means we must look at Q. However, provided T's interface is unaffected, we need not look at P. If S and T had been treated as one type, then P would have had to be examined too.

Another advantage of distinguishing the types is that it may help in organizing the design rationale. The design rationale describes the decisions made at particular points in the design, and discusses why they were made and what alternatives exist. By maintaining the hierarchy to represent the decisions as they are made over time, we can avoid confusion and be more precise. If an error is discovered later, we can identify precisely at what point in the design it occurred.

Finally, the distinction may help during implementation, for example, if S, but not T, needs to be reimplemented. However, it may be that the hierarchy is not maintained in the implementation. Frequently, the end of the design is just a single type, the last subtype invented, because implementing a single module is more convenient than having separate modules for the supertype and subtypes. Even so, however, the distinction remains useful after implementation, because the effects of specification changes can still be localized, even if implementation changes cannot. For example, a change to the specification of S but not T means that we need to reimplement Q but not P. However, if S and T are implemented as a single module, we must reimplement both of them, instead of just reimplementing S.

### 4.2. Related Types

The second use of subtypes is for related types. The designer may recognize that a program will use several data abstractions that are similar but different. The differences represent variants of the same general idea, where the subtypes may all have the same set of operations, or some of them may extend the supertype. An example is the generalized abstract device mentioned earlier. To accommodate related types in design, the designer introduces the supertype at the time the whole set of types is conceived, and then introduces the subtypes as they are needed later in design.

Related types arise in two different ways. Sometimes the relationship is defined in advance, before any types are invented; this is the situation discussed above. Alternatively, the relationship may not be recognized until several related types already exist. This happens because of the desire to define a module that works on each of the related types but depends on only some small common part of them. For example, the module might be a sort routine that relies on its argument "collection" to allow it to fetch elements, and relies on the element type itself to provide a " $<$ " operation.

When the relationship is defined in advance, hierarchy is a good way to describe it, and we probably do want to use inheritance as an implementation mechanism. This permits us to implement just once (in the supertype) whatever can be done in a subtype-independent way. The module for a subtype is concerned only with the specific behavior of that subtype, and is independent of modules implementing other subtypes. Having separate modules for the super- and subtypes gives better modularity than using a single module to implement them all. Also, if a new subtype is added later, none of the existing code need be changed.

When the relationship is recognized after the types have been defined, hierarchy may not be the right way to organize the program. This issue is discussed in Section 5.1.

### 4.3. Organizing a Type Library

There is one other way in which hierarchy is useful, and this is to aid in the organization of a type library. It has long been recognized that programming is more effective if it can be done in a context that encourages the reuse of program modules implemented by others. However, for such a context to be usable, it must be possible to navigate it easily to determine whether the desired modules exists. Hierarchy is useful as a way of organizing a program library to make searching easier, especially when combined with the kind of browsing tools present, e.g., in the Smalltalk environment.

Hierarchy allows similar types to be grouped together. Thus, if a user want a particular kind of "collection" abstraction, there is a good chance that the desired one, if it exists at all, can be found with the other collections. The hierarchy in use is a either a subtype hierarchy, or almost a subtype hierarchy (i.e., a subtype differs from an extension of the supertype in a fairly minor way). The point is that types are grouped based on their behavior rather than how they are used to implement one another.

The search for collection types, or numeric types, or whatever, is aided by two things: The first is considering the entire library as growing from a single root or roots, and providing a browsing tool that allows the user to move around in the hierarchy. The second is a wise choice of names for the major categories, so that a user can recognize that "collection" is the part of the hierarchy of interest.

Using hierarchy as a way of organizing a library is a good idea, but need not be coupled with a subclass mechanism in a programming language. Instead, an interactive system that supports construction and browsing of the library could organize the library in this way.

## 5. Type Hierarchy and Inheritance

Not all uses of type hierarchy require language support. No support is needed for the program library; instead all that is needed is to use the notion of type hierarchy as an organizing principle. Support is also usually not needed for hierarchy introduced as a refinement technique. As mentioned earlier, the most likely outcome of this design technique is a single type at the end (the last subtype introduced), which is most conveniently implemented as a unit. Therefore any language that supports data abstraction is adequate here, although inheritance can be useful for introducing additional operations discovered later.

Special language support may be needed for related types, however. This support is discussed in Section 5.1. Section 5.2 discusses the relationship of inheritance to multiple implementations of a type.

**5.1. Polymorphism**

A *polymorphic* procedure or data abstraction is one that works for many different types. For example, consider a procedure that does sorting. In many languages, such a procedure would be implemented to work on an array of integers; later, if we needed to sort an array of strings, another procedure would be needed. This is unfortunate. The idea of sorting is independent of the particular type of element in the array, provided that it is possible to compare the elements to determine which ones are smaller than which other ones. We ought to be able to implement one sort procedure that works for all such types. Such a procedure would be polymorphic.

Whenever there are related types in a program there is likely to be polymorphism. This is certainly the case when the relationship is indicated by the need for a polymorphic module. Even when the relationship is identified in advance, however, polymorphism is likely. In such a case the supertype is often *virtual*: it has no objects of its own, but is simply a placeholder in the hierarchy for the family of related types. In this case, any module that uses the supertype is polymorphic. On the other hand, if the supertype has objects of its own, some modules might use just it and none of its subtypes.

Using hierarchy to support polymorphism means that a polymorphic module is conceived of as using a supertype, and every type that is intended to be used by that module is made a subtype of the supertype. When supertypes are introduced before subtypes, hierarchy is a good way to capture the relationships. The supertype is added to the type universe when it is invented, and subtypes are added below it later.

If the types exist before the relationship, hierarchy does not work as well. In this case, introducing the supertype complicates the type universe: a new type (the supertype) must be added, all types used by the polymorphic module must be made its subordinates, and classes implementing the subtypes must be changed to reflect the hierarchy (and recompiled in a system that does compilation). For example, we would have to add a new type, "sortable," to the universe and make every element type be a subtype of it. Note that each such supertype must be considered whenever a new type is invented: each new type must be made a subtype of the supertype if there is any chance that we may want to use its objects in the polymorphic module. Furthermore, the supertype may be useless as far as code sharing is concerned, since there may be nothing that can be implemented in it.

An alternative approach is to simply allow the polymorphic module to use any type that supplies the needed operations. In this case no attempt is made to relate the types. Instead, an object belonging to any of the related types can be passed as an argument to the polymorphic module. Thus we get the same effect, but without the need to complicate the type universe. We will refer to this approach as the *grouping* approach.

The two approaches differ in what is required to reason about program correctness. In either case we require the argument objects to have operations with the right signature and behavior. Signature requirements can be checked by type-checking, which can happen at runtime or compile time. Runtime checking requires no special mechanism; objects are simply passed to the polymorphic module, and type errors will be found if a needed operation is not present. Compile-time checking requires an adequate type system. If the hierarchy approach is used, then the language must combine compile-time type checking with inheritance; an example of such a language is discussed in [17]. If the grouping approach is used, then we need a way to express constraints on operations at compile-time. For example, both CLU and Ada [19] can do this. In CLU, the header of a *sort* procedure might be

sort = **proc** [T: type] (a: array[T])
    **where** T **has** lt: **proctype** (T, T) **returns** (bool)

This header constrains parameter T to be a type with an operation named *lt* with the indicated signature; the specification of *sort* would explain that *lt* must be a "less than" test. An example of a call of *sort* is

sort[int](x)

In compiling such a call, the compiler checks that the type of *x* is array[int] and furthermore that int has an operation named *lt* with the required signature. We could even define a more polymorphic sorting routine in CLU that would work for all collections that are "array-like," i.e., whose elements can be fetched and stored by index.

The behavior requirements must be checked by some form of program verification. The required behavior must be part of the specification, and the specification goes in different places in the two methods. With hierarchy, the specification belongs to the supertype; with related types, it is part of the specification of the polymorphic module. Behavior checking also happens at different times. With hierarchy, checking happens whenever a programmer makes a type a subtype of the supertype; with grouping, it happens whenever a programmer writes code that uses the polymorphic module.

Both grouping and hierarchy have limitations. More flexibility in the use of the polymorphic module is desirable. For example, if *sort* is called with an operation that does a "greater than" test, this will lead to a different sorting of the array, but that different sorting may be just what is wanted. In addition, there may be conflicts between the types intended for use in the polymorphic module:

1. Not all types provide the required operation.

2. Types use different names for the operation.

3. Some type uses the name of the required operation for some other operation; e.g., the name *lt* is used in type T to identify the "length" operation.

One way of achieving more generality is to simply pass the needed operations as procedure arguments, e.g., *sort* actually takes two arguments, the array, and the routine used to determine ordering.[4] This method is general, but can be inconvenient. Methods that avoid the inconvenience in conjunction with the grouping approach exist in Argus [10] and Ada.

In summary, when related types are discovered early in design, hierarchy is a good way to express the relationship. Otherwise, either the grouping approach (with suitable language support) or procedures as arguments may be better.

### 5.2. Multiple Implementations

It is often useful to have multiple implementations of the same type. For example, for some matrices we use a sparse representation and for others a nonsparse representation. Furthermore, it is sometimes desirable to use objects of the same type but different representations within the same program.

Object-oriented languages appear to allow users to simulate multiple implementations with inheritance. Each implementation would be a subclass of another class that implements the type. This latter class would probably be virtual; for example, there would be a virtual class implementing matrices, and subclasses implementing sparse and nonsparse matrices.

Using inheritance in this way allows us to have several implementations of the same type in use within the same program, but it interferes with type hierarchy. For example, suppose we invent a subtype of matrices called *extended-matrices*. We would like to implement extended-matrices with a class that inherits from matrices rather than from a particular implementation of matrices, since this would allow us to combine it with either matrix implementation. This is not possible, however. Instead, the extended-matrix class must explicitly state in its program text that it is a subclass of sparse or nonsparse matrices.

The problem arises because inheritance is being used for two different things: to implement a type and to indicate that one type is a subtype of another. These uses should be kept separate. Then we could have what we really want: two types (matrix and extended-matrix), one a subtype of the other, each having several implementations, and the ability to combine the implementations of the subtype with those of the supertype in various ways.

---

[4]Of course, this solution would not work well in Smalltalk because procedures cannot conveniently be defined as individual entities nor treated as objects.

# 6. Conclusions

Abstraction, and especially data abstraction, is an important technique for developing programs that are reasonably easy to maintain and to modify as requirements change. Data abstractions are particularly important because they hide complicated things (data structures) that are likely to change in the future. They permit the representation of data to be changed locally without affecting programs that use the data.

Inheritance is an implementation mechanism that allows one type to be related to another hierarchically. It is used in two ways: to implement a type by derivation from the implementation of another type, and to define subtypes. We argued that the first use is uninteresting because we can achieve the same result by using one type as the rep of the other. Subtypes, on the other hand, do add a new ability. Three uses for subtypes were identified. During incremental design they provide a way to limit the impact of design changes and to organize the design documentation. They also provide a way to group related types, especially in the case where the supertype is invented before any subtypes. When the relationship is discovered after several types have already been defined, other methods, such as grouping or procedure arguments, are probably better than hierarchy. Finally, hierarchy is a convenient and sensible way of organizing a library of types. The hierarchy is either a subtype hierarchy, or almost one; the subtypes may not match our strict definition, but are similar to the supertype in some intuitive sense.

Inheritance can be used to implement a subtype hierarchy. It is needed primarily in the case of related types when the supertype is invented first, because here it is convenient to implement common features just once in the superclass, and then implement the extensions separately for each subtype.

We conclude that although data abstraction is more important, type hierarchy does extend its usefulness. Furthermore, inheritance is sometimes needed to express type hierarchy and is therefore a useful mechanism to provide in a programming language.

## Acknowledgments

Many people made comments and suggestions that improved the content of this paper. The author gratefully acknowledges this help, and especially the efforts of Toby Bloom and Gary Leavens.

## References

1. Bobrow, D., et al. "CommonLoops: Merging Lisp and Object-Oriented Programming". *Proc. of the ACM Conference on Object-Oriented Programming Systems, Languages and Applications, SIGPLAN Notices 21*, 11 (November 1986).

**2.** Bruce, K., and Wegner, P. "An Algebraic Model of Subtypes in Object-Oriented Languages (Draft)". *SIGPLAN Notices 21*, 10 (October 1986).

**3.** Dahl, O.-J., and Hoare, C. A. R. Hierarchical Program Structures. In *Structured Programming*, Academic Press, 1972.

**4.** Goldberg, A., and Robson, D. *Smalltalk-80: The Language and its Implementation*. Addison-Wesley, Reading, Ma., 1983.

**5.** Hoare, C. A. R. "Proof of correctness of data representations". *Acta Informatica 4* (1972), 271-281.

**6.** Leavens, G. *Subtyping and Generic Invocation: Semantics and Language Design*. Ph.D. Th., Massachusetts Institute of Technology, Department of Electrical Engineering and Computer Science, forthcoming.

**7.** Liskov, B. A Design Methodology for Reliable Software Systems. In *Tutorial on Software Design Techniques*, P. Freeman and A. Wasserman, Eds., IEEE, 1977. Also published in the Proc. of the Fall Joint Computer Conference, 1972.

**8.** Liskov, B., Snyder, A., Atkinson, R. R., and Schaffert, J. C. "Abstraction mechanisms in CLU". *Comm. of the ACM 20*, 8 (August 1977), 564-576.

**9.** Liskov, B., et al.. *CLU Reference Manual*. Springer-Verlag, 1984.

**10.** Liskov, B., et al. *Argus Reference Manual*. Technical Report MIT/LCS/TR-400, M.I.T. Laboratory for Computer Science, Cambridge, Ma., 1987.

**11.** Liskov, B., and Guttag, J.. *Abstraction and Specification in Program Development*. MIT Press and McGraw Hill, 1986.

**12.** Liskov, B., and Zilles, S. "Programming with abstract data types". *Proc. of ACM SIGPLAN Conference on Very High Level Languages, SIGPLAN Notices 9* (1974).

**13.** Moon, D. "Object-Oriented Programming with Flavors". *Proc. of the ACM Conference on Object-Oriented Programming Systems, Languages, and Applications, SIGPLAN Notices 21*, 11 (November 1986).

**14.** Morris, J. H. "Protection in Programming Languages". *Comm. of the ACM 16*, 1 (January 1973).

**15.** Parnas, D. Information Distribution Aspects of Design Methodology. In *Proceedings of IFIP Congress*, North Holland Publishing Co., 1971.

**16.** Parnas, D. "On the Criteria to be Used in Decomposing Systems into Modules". *Comm. of the ACM 15*, 12 (December 1972).

**17.** Schaffert, C., et al. "An Introduction to Trellis/Owl". *Proc. of the ACM Conference on Object-Oriented Programming Systems, Languages, and Applications, SIGPLAN Notices 21*, 11 (November 1986).

**18.** Snyder, A. "Encapsulation and Inheritance in Object-Oriented Programming Languages". *Proc. of the ACM Conference on Object-Oriented Programming Systems, Languages, and Applications, SIGPLAN Notices 21*, 11 (November 1986).

**19.** U. S. Department of Defense. *Reference manual for the Ada programming language*. 1983. ANSI standard Ada.

# Index

## A

A *posteriori* inheritance, 189
Abstract base class, 107, 108
Abstraction, 177-86
  data, 1-4
  definition of, 179
  procedural, 2-4
ANSI C, notation for functions pointers
  in, 158-59
A *priori* inheritance, 187-89

## B

**bar( )**, 69
**baseof( )**, 67-69
Base type, 54-55
Behavioral inheritance, 54-56, 60
  applying to **Stack** and **Queue**, 77-78
  as a substitution principle, 61
  class derivation and, 63-65
  programming guidelines, 67-69
**Buffer**, 227-28, 233, 238-41
  implementation, 250-51
  public interface of, 239-40

type relationships, 240-41
  *See also* **Sloop; Yacht**
Built-in types, 113-15
  categories of, 113
  vs. user-defined parametrized types,
  120

## C

C++:
  classes, non-behavioral relationships
    between, 168
  concurrency extensions to language,
    179
  **constant**, 172
  constructors, 35-37
  container types in, 193-94
  destructor class member function,
    36-37
  heap storage de-allocator (**delete**), 37
  implementation inheritance and,
    57-59
  inlining support, 18
  mapping data abstraction in, 15-18
  multiple inheritance in, pitfalls of, 190

parametrization, 112
pointers to member functions, 97-100, 155-65
substitution principle, 59-60
synchronous exception handling and, 46-47
type system of, 119-20
Chaining conditioning, 23
Child type, 54-55
Class derivation:
   behavioral inheritance and, 63-65
   example of, 58-59
   protected visibility and, 79-84
Classes, 119-20
   definition of, 15
   non-behavioral relationships between, 168
Class instance objects:
   inspecting/modifying state of, 16
Class members, visibilities of, 15-16
Common Lisp, parent classes, 190
**constant**, 172
Constructors, 35-37
Container types, 125-27, 190-91
   heterogeneous containers, 191-94
   homogeneous containers, 191
   parametric, 190-91

separation of interface from implementation, 19-24
state sanity and, 16
Data member, pointer to, 157
Debugging, macros, 129
Deferred binding, 88
**delete** (heap storage de-allocator), 37
Denver syndrome, 70-75
Derivation, 120
Derived type, 54-55
Design:
   definition of, 169
   graphics editor case study, 205-21
   text editor case study, 223-33
   *See also* Object-oriented design
Destructor class member function, 36-37
Dummy proofing, 43-47
Dynamic binding:
   abstract base types and pure virtual member functions, 106-7
   definition of, 87-90
   pointers to functions, solution with, 97-100
   restrictions on, 87-88
   switch-case, 95-96
   unions, 92-95
   uses of, 91-92

## D

Data abstraction, 1-12
   benefits of, 47
   change of implementation and, 19-24
   classical, 17
   definition of, 15
   initialization/clean up, 33-37
   layering and dummy proofing, 42-47
   list iterators/friend functions, 37-41
   list type, 30-33
   mapping in C++, 15-18
   specification and correctness, 24-30
Data hiding:
   advantages of, 16
   definition of, 14-15
   member function invocation and, 18

## E

**Editor**, 255-57
   commands, 263-65
      first phase, 263-64
      second phase, 264-65
   data members, orthogonal groups of, 269
   implementation, 267-69
eiffel language:
   designing heterogeneous container types in, 209
   exception detection and handling mechanism, 243-44
   **List[Shape]** in, 209
      system concept in, 179
External design spec, 169, 172-75

## F

Factorization, 199
Faking parametrized types, 128-38
   inheritance, 135-37
   macros, 129-42
   template file, 133-34
**File** type:
   abstraction step, 228-32
   implementation, 232-33
**foo( )**, 69
Fortran, type system, 120
Framework, design, 168, 177-78, 224-25
Friend functions, 37-41
   situations requiring, 38

## G

Grammatical analysis, requirements
   document and, 169
Graphics editor:
   case study, 205-21
   **Editor** type, 212-14
   interaction model, 215-16
   operations supported, 206
   **Picture** type, 208-12
      multiply deriving, 211
   public interface of **Set<T>**, 210-11,
      216-18
   requirements, 206-7
   **Shape** type, 207-8
   type decomposition, 218-19
   user interface, 206-7

## H

Has-a-component, 167, 194-96
Heap storage de-allocator (**delete**), 37
Heterogeneous containers, 191-94
Heuristics, 60, 169
Hoare triple, 25
Homogeneous containers, 191

## I

Implementation:
   **Buffer**, 250-51

**Editor**, 267-69
**File**, 232-33
**Iregister**, 271-75
**Register**, 270-71
**Sloop**, 245-48
**Yacht**, 248-50
Implementational relationships, 168
Implementation inheritance, 57-59
Inheritance, 92, 135-37, 186-90
   a *posteriori* inheritance, 189
   a *priori* inheritance, 187-89
   behavioral, 54-56, 60, 63-65, 67-69,
      77-78
   categories of, 53
   Denver syndrome, 70-75
   implementation, 57-59
   multiple inheritance in C++, pitfalls
      of, 190
   private class derivation, 75-79
   protected visibility, 79-84
   substitution principle, 59-63
Initial decomposition, 178-79
   text editor, 226-28
**inspector**, 172
Instantiation, 7-8
Internal design spec, 169, 175-76
**Iregister**, 265
   implementation, 271-75
*isakindof* relationship, 55

## L

Layering, 42-43
Lisp:
   mapping operations, 159
   polymorphism, 161-64
List iterators, 37-41
List type, 30-33

## M

Macros, 129-42
   debugging, 129
   macro class definitions:
      advantages/disadvantages of
         use, 131-32
      porting to other machines, 132

Main program, text editor, 260-63
Member visibility, *See* Visibilities of
  class members
Messages, objects and, 4, 9, 10-14
Modular programming, 149-51
Modules, 38
Multiple inheritance, 195
  in C++, pitfalls of, 190

**N**

Node, 18-24

**O**

Object-oriented design, 167-203
  definition, 169, 257
  framework, 168, 177-78
  interaction model, 171-72
  performance, 198-99
  process, 176-98
    abstraction, 177-86
    initial decomposition, 178-79
    stopping condition, 197-98
    type decomposition, 196-97
    type relationships, 186-96
  requirements, 169-71
  specification, 168-69
    external design spec, 169, 172-75
    internal design spec, 169, 175-76
  terminology of, 1-2
Object-oriented messaging, properties
  of, 10
Object-oriented programming, tools,
  170
Objects:
  definition of, 4-5, 7, 9
  instantiating, 7-8
  interaction between, 10-14
  interaction model, 5-6
  invoking an operation against, 17-18
  performance of, 198-99
  public interface of, 4
  relationship between concepts of
    type and, 6
Object-state sanity, necessary

conditions for, 16-17, 33-37
Object-type, 9-10
Over-ride, 57, 59, 67

**P**

Parametric container types, 190-91
Parametric stack type:
  sample manual page for, 172-75
    bugs, 175
    description, 173
    diagnotics, 175
    files, 175
    name, 172
    public interface, 174-75
    synopsis, 172-73
Parametric types, 190-94
  domain of class, 191
Parametrization:
  benefit of, 111-12
  container types, 125-27
  definition of, 111
  faking parametrized types, 128-38
  sorting, 127-28
  **Stack**, 121-22
  **Table**, 122-25
  type system:
    **Array**, 116-17
    built-in types, 113-15
    built-in vs. user-defined
      parametrized types, 120
    of C++, 119-20
    definition of, 113
    of Fortran, 120
    **Function**, 118-19
    justification, 112-13
    **Pointer**, 117
    **Product**, 115-16
    **Union**, 118
  *See also* Faking parametrized types
Parametrized type, definition of, 111
Parent type, 54-55
Parser, text editor, 257-60
Performance of an object, 198-99
**Picture** type, 208-12
  multiply deriving, 211

Pointers to member functions, 97-100,
    155-65
  **class Frog**, 156-57
      pointer to data member, 157
  **class Pond**, 159-61
  **mapcar**, 159
  polymorphism, 161-64
  syntax for, 157
Pointer to data member, 157
Pointer variables, instantiating, 7-8
Post-condition of a member function,
    22-23
Precondition of a member function,
    22-23, 244-45
Private class derivation, 75-79
  multiple classes and, 78
Private member functions, 15-16
Procedural abstraction, 2-4
  benefits of, 4
  classical example of, 3-4
Properties, 24
Protected visibility, class derivation
    and, 79-84
Pseudo-code, 175-76, 197
  for design process, 224
Public interface of a type, 224
  **Buffer**, 239
  **Editor** type, 212
  global criteria for goodness, 182-86
      completeness, 183
      convenience, 184
      correctness, 183
      minimality, 183-84
      orthogonality, 194
      performance, 184-85
  identifying, 179-82
  orthogonal, 242
  requirements and, 210
  Set<T>, 210-11, 216-18
Public member functions, 15-16

**R**

**Register**, 265-67
  implementation, 270-71
Representation invariant, 16-17

Requirements:
  graphics editor, 206-7
  object-oriented design, 169-71
  performance and, 199
  text editor, 224-26
Requirements document, 169-71,
    178-79

**S**

**Set<T>**, public interface of, 210-11,
    216-18
**Shape** type, 207-8
**Sloop**, 242-48
  implementation, 245-48
  preconditions/exception handling,
      243-45
  *See also* **Buffer; Yacht**
Smalltalk:
  designing heterogeneous container
      types in, 209
  inheritance in, 193
Software community, changes in, 91-92
Static binding, 88-90
Static class members, 146-48
Stopping condition, 197-98
Substitution principle, inheritance,
    59-63
Switch-case statement, 95-96
Synchronous exception handling, 46-47
System, definition of, 177

**T**

Template file technique, 133-34, 245
Text editor:
  **Buffer**, 227-28, 233, 238-41
  case study, 223-33
  design framework, 224-25
  **Editor**, 255-57
      commands, 263-65
      implementation, 267-69
  **File** type:
      abstraction step, 228-32
      implementation, 232-33
      initial decomposition, 226-28

**Iregister**, 265
    implementation, 271-76
main program, 260-63
parser, 257-60
**Register**, 265-67
    implementation, 270-71
    requirements, 224-26
Type, 6-7
  definition, 6, 9
  as object, 141-53
    faking in C++ 1.2, 148-49
    modular programming, 149-51
    static class members, 146-48
Type behavior, 60
Type decomposition, 177-78, 196-97,
  218-19
Type hierarchy, 59
Type manual page, 172-75
  performance and, 198
Type-object, 9-10
Type relationships, 177-78, 186-96
  has-a-component, 167, 194-96
  inheritance, 186-90
  parametric types, 190-94

**U**

Unions, 92-95
User interface, graphics editor, 206-7

**V**

Variable declaration, instantiating
  objects by, 7-8
**virtual** class member functions, 100-101
Visibilities of class members, 15-16,
  195-96
  protected visibility, 79-84

**W**

Wheeler, Tom, 195
**Window** base class, 188-89, 208

**Y**

**Yacht**, 241-42
  implementation, 248-50
  *See also* **Buffer; Sloop**